C+H

THE ST. PIERRE AND MIQUELON
AFFAIRE OF 1941

Admiral Muselier, December 25, 1941

THE
ST. PIERRE
AND
MIQUELON
AFFAIRE
OF 1941

A Study in Diplomacy in the
North Atlantic Quadrangle

DOUGLAS G. ANGLIN

Vice-Chancellor
University of Zambia

UNIVERSITY OF TORONTO PRESS

To Mary

PREFACE

ON CHRISTMAS MORNING, 1941, news that the Free French had liberated St. Pierre and Miquelon from Vichy rule flashed around the globe, providing a welcome relief to the dismal succession of Allied disasters elsewhere in the world. Now, nearly a quarter of a century later, it is at last possible to piece together the strange story of the developments that led up to the seizure and the consequences which flowed from it, and to assess their significance for the course of the war.

Although the St. Pierre and Miquelon *affaire* certainly had its comic opera aspect, it was more than an amusing diversion in the midst of a grim struggle. The underlying cause of the storm it created was the divergent attitudes of Britain and the United States towards Marshal Pétain and General de Gaulle. The incident also focused attention on fundamental factors in the foreign policies of the four countries involved. These became of even greater importance after the war. Although the Vichy regime quickly faded into history, relations between the United States, the United Kingdom, France, and Canada became extremely close. The formation of the North Atlantic alliance emphasized this fact. Moreover, the return of Charles de Gaulle to power in France restored to international politics the same personal element which gave the events of more than two decades ago their special flavour. A study of the St. Pierre and Miquelon *affaire* of 1941 is, therefore, more than a curious footnote to history. It is an enquiry of continuing relevance to international relations within the North Atlantic quadrangle.

This book has grown out of a paper originally prepared in 1958. Since then, much fresh information has come to light. The picture is now, I trust, substantially complete and reasonably accurate, although the facts related will continue to be subject to varying interpretations. For the opportunity of recording this version of the story, the author is grateful to the numerous actors in the drama who wrote of their experiences or discussed them with him. Biographical details on many of them will be found in the list of Dramatis Personae appended to the book.

It is not possible to acknowledge adequately all my accumulated debts here. However, I do want to express a special word of appreciation to the Governor and brave people of St. Pierre and Miquelon for their willing co-operation and for the many personal kindnesses extended to me and my family. I cherish the hope that, even though they may not always agree with what I have said, they will feel that I have attempted to write about them sympathetically and objectively. I hope, too, that they will understand the reasons why it seems wiser not to thank any of them individually by name. The fact that they remain anonymous in no way lessens my gratitude to them.

The Select Bibliography and the Notes at the end of the volume indicate the extent to which I have been able to rely on published memoirs, private papers, and official documents. For permission to consult the invaluable Jay Pierrepont Moffat Papers, I have Mrs. Albert Levitt and the Harvard University Library to thank. Among the persons with whom I have had helpful conversations or correspondences are: Dean Acheson, Miss Gladys Arnold, George Britt, Jean Callède, Preston R. Cook, Stetson Conn, Sister Clare Elizabeth, the late Maj.-Gen. W. H. P. Elkins, Henri Gauthier, James A. Gibson, Emile Guillot, Raymond Gushue, the late Emile-Charles Hamel, Jean-Charles Harvey, Oscar LaRivière, F. A. J. Laws, Mme. LeBret and the late Jean LeBret, François LeBuf, Hugh L. Keenleyside, Bruce A. Macdonald, D. Millar Marshall, Sir Desmond Morton, Rear-Admiral L. W. Murray, the late Admiral Emile Muselier, Frank Paturel, L. B. Pearson, J. Hubert Penson, Rear-Admiral J. Pepin Lehalleur, C. G. Power, Mme. Maurice Quédrue, Samuel Reber, Howard C. Rice, Harold J. Riley, George Ronald, George F. G. Stanley, the late Thomas Stone, Louis de Villefosse, and officers of the Canadian Department of External Affairs, the Directorate of Historical Services of Canadian Forces Headquarters, the Department of State, and the United States Embassy in Ottawa. I hasten to add that I alone accept any responsibility for the opinions contained in this book. The maps and drawings are the handiwork of Mrs. Eloise Johnson.

My final word of appreciation is to the Canada Council for assistance in visiting St. Pierre and Miquelon in the summer of 1961, the Canadian Institute of International Affairs for a grant-in-aid of publication, and to the Publications Fund of the University of Toronto Press.

Douglas G. Anglin

Carleton University
August, 1965

CONTENTS

INTRODUCTION

ONE COLD DECEMBER DAY in 1941, shortly after Pearl Harbor, a Free French submarine and three small corvettes slipped out of Halifax harbour, ostensibly to engage in manoeuvres. Two days later, the day before Christmas, they suddenly appeared off St. Pierre and Miquelon and liberated it from Vichy control.

Normally one would have expected such a trivial event as the bloodless seizure of a mere speck in the North Atlantic to evoke no more than a ripple of interest and a hearty cheer, especially as the war had entered upon one of its grand climactics with the fate of nations, and indeed whole continents, in the balance. Such was not to be the case. Overnight the incident assumed world prominence out of all proportion to its intrinsic significance. The British were embarrassed, the Americans enraged, and the Canadians distressed at the resulting unseemly display of Anglo-American disharmony. In Ottawa and Washington, Christmas dinners were left to spoil as statesmen hurriedly conferred. In the White House, Roosevelt and Churchill were forced to set aside pressing problems of world strategy to deal with the matter. At one time, there was even talk of despatching a battleship to dislodge the Free French. Admiral Darlan in Vichy feigned injury, while Admiral Muselier, who led the expedition, eventually resigned from the Free French National Committee in protest. In the United States, an angry public debate boiled up over the whole question of the State Department's Vichy policy. Cordell Hull felt humiliated, persecuted, and betrayed by almost everyone: de Gaulle, Churchill, Roosevelt, even the Canadians. At one time, he contemplated resigning as Secretary of State, though on second thoughts he went sulking off to Florida for a rest cure instead.

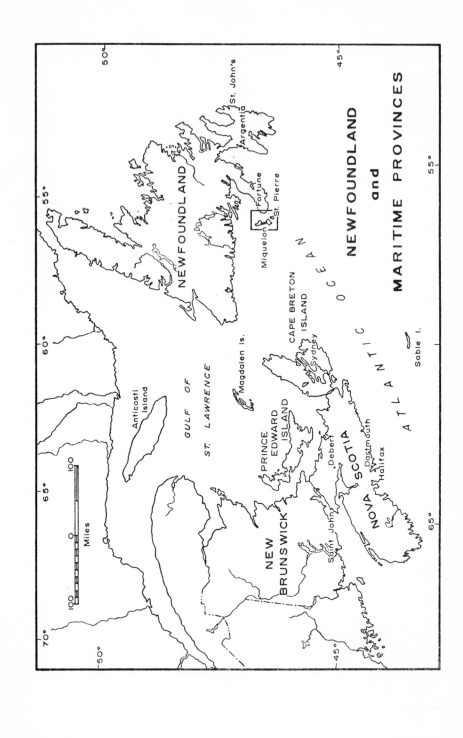

NEWFOUNDLAND and MARITIME PROVINCES

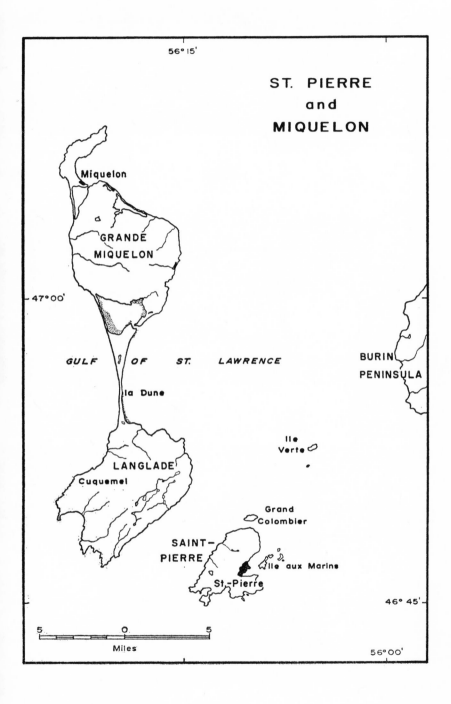

ST. PIERRE
and
MIQUELON

56° 15'

Miquelon

GRANDE
MIQUELON

47° 00'

GULF OF ST. LAWRENCE

la Dune

BURIN
PENINSULA

Ile
Verte

LANGLADE

Cuquemel

Grand
Colombier

SAINT-
PIERRE

Ile aux Marins

St.-Pierre

46° 45'

5   O   5

Miles

56° 00'

Throughout the affair, Mackenzie King buzzed about trying his best to cool tempers and soothe the injured pride of all concerned. The whole episode left a legacy of bitterness, suspicion, and misunderstanding which continued to bedevil relations among the Allies in the North Atlantic until the end of the war, and may even provide a clue to present tensions within the troubled Western Alliance.

THE ST. PIERRE AND MIQUELON
AFFAIRE OF 1941

1

REMNANTS OF EMPIRE

St. Pierre and Miquelon is France's oldest and smallest colony, and one of the least well-known, even in France.* Its continued survival in the face of the vicissitudes of war, a harsh physical environment, a series of devastating fires, and economic adversity is a tribute to French energy and perseverance.

The territory lies some twelve miles off the south coast of New-foundland near the entrance to the Gulf of St. Lawrence. It consists of three main islands: St. Pierre, Grande Miquelon, and Langlade or Petite Miquelon, the latter two connected since 1781 or so by a sinister sandbar known as the Dune. In addition, there are half a dozen smaller islands in the group as well as a number of nearby rocks with picturesque names such as Ile au Massacre, Ile aux Pigeons, and Enfant Perdu. The total area of the territory is only ninety-three square miles, the tricky currents, treacherous reefs, and crippling fogs around the islands have earned for them a grim reputation as the "Cemetery of the Sea," the graveyard of over six hundred ships. One old story related by St. Pierrais alleges that the Miquelonnais hung lamps on the horns of cows with the deliberate intention of misleading ships at sea and pillaging them when they became ship-wrecked.

Although certain Americanizing trends have become apparent in St. Pierre and Miquelon in recent years, visitors are still struck by the "utter Frenchness" of nearly everything in the colony. As one

*Metropolitan Frenchmen have sometimes forgotten that the territory is their only white colony. When the first contingent of St. Pierrais recruits landed in France in 1914, they were sent to a camp with African troops for acclimatization. Also, on the occasion of one Colonial Exposition, the Governor was invited to send a group of natives to Paris to demonstrate "native dress and customs, dances, musical instruments, nose rings, etc."[1]

Canadian observer has commented: "It is a bit of old France adrift in the Western Atlantic—far more truly French in its architecture, its customs, its accent, its social life and traditions than the Province of Quebec."[2] The population has remained almost exclusively French, despite a considerable amount of intermarriage over the years with Newfoundland girls who have emigrated to the islands. The language, too, is remarkably pure. There are a number of local expressions, mainly reflecting maritime influences, but surprisingly few corrupt anglicizations considering that the islands are practically surrounded by English-speaking territories. (This situation may change now that the colony is within range of Canadian television.) The great bulk of the population of around five thousand is crowded into the quaint, old-worldish town of St. Pierre.* This is the colony's only real port and historically its principal asset. While life still centres around the sea, only a small percentage of the people now derive their meagre livelihood directly from it. The majority are engaged in administration and commerce. Fur-farming and the tourist trade have also developed considerably since the war.

The archipelago is noted for its high, craggy coastline, its skimpy vegetation, its blizzards of powdery snow, and the damp, chilling fog, that envelopes the islands for much of the year. Actually, the terrain is not as rugged nor the climate as inhospitable as is commonly supposed. Like Nova Scotia and Newfoundland, the islands are geological extensions of the Appalachian range worn flat by glacial erosion. The highest "mountain" is, in fact, a mere 850 feet above sea level. There are rich deposits of iron and copper, but not in sufficient quantity to invite commercial exploitation. The island of St. Pierre is particularly desolate, but Miquelon is more fertile and Langlade with its rushing streams is partially wooded. Temperatures range from a high of 80 degrees or so in summer to zero in winter. The harbour of St. Pierre is rarely frozen over.

It is not certain who the first Europeans to discover the islands were, possibly the Vikings who roamed the region in the eleventh century. John Cabot gave the name Trinity Islands to them in 1497,[3] while Joas Alvares Fagundes, who visited these barren rocks on St.

*In 1963, the estimated population was 4,990—4,362 on St. Pierre and 628 on Miquelon. Except in summer, virtually no one now lives outside the two towns. In November, 1941, the estimated population was 4,425.

Ursula's Day, 1520, called them the Eleven Thousand Virigins.
Jacques Cartier is commonly credited with naming the islands after
the patron saint of fishermen, although they were already known
as St. Pierre well before he arrived on the scene. Cartier reported,
during his visit in June, 1536, that he had encountered "several
ships both from France and from Brittany" in the harbour; and it
is clear that Breton and Norman fishermen had frequented the place
since at least 1504 and possibly for a hundred years before that. The
first permanent French settlement was not established until 1604. A
century later, there were still fewer than two hundred wretched souls,
almost all of Breton origin, eking a miserable existence out of these
rocky shores.

Throughout the eighteenth century, St. Pierre and Miquelon
constituted a minor pawn in the global struggle raging between
England and France. During one sixteen-year period, the settlement
at St. Pierre was attacked nine times. Eventually, under the terms
of the peace treaty of 1713, France ceded the colony to England in
return for fishing rights along the Newfoundland shore and, for
the next fifty years, the islands were annexed to Newfoundland.
The French population was repatriated to France and English settlers
took their place. Then, in 1763, following the Seven Years' War and
fierce diplomatic bargaining, St. Pierre and Miquelon was restored
to France in compensation for the loss of Canada and Cape Breton.
This concession represented more than a consolation prize; in the
eighteenth century, the Newfoundland fisheries were regarded as
a greater economic asset than the furs of new France. For this reason,
the English were most reluctant to surrender the islands. They also
feared, with considerable justification, that the territory might menace
the security of their nearby possessions and serve as a centre of
disaffection and smuggling for the conquered French population
on the mainland. Accordingly, as the price for the retention of this
last precarious foothold in North America, Great Britain insisted that
France should agree "not to fortify the said Islands; to erect no buildings upon them, but merely for the convenience of the fishery; and
to keep upon them a guard of fifty men only for the police." The
Royal Navy was also accorded rights of surveillance—which were fully
exercised—to ensure compliance with the strict letter of the treaty.

Although the Treaty of Paris had intended that the colony should serve merely as a shelter for fishermen, it quickly acquired settlers. Some 1700 or 1800 Acadians, who had been expelled from their homes in Nova Scotia nearly a decade earlier for refusing to take the oath of allegiance, descended on St. Pierre. This created an acute crisis as the embarrassed French authorities were unable to cope with such numbers with the meagre resources available on the islands. The refugees for their part were dismayed to discover how unbearably harsh life in the islands would be in contrast with what they had experienced in the fertile Annapolis valley. Besides, they preferred farming to fishing. Eventually, Louis XV tired of subsidizing the surplus population and reduced the ration. As a result, during the next several years, approximately a thousand Acadians were deported to France or returned at their own request to Nova Scotia to take the oath.

Despite the hardships of the first critical years, peace did bring a measure of prosperity to the islands. Fishing flourished and the population increased. In reporting to Paris the death of the colony's only midwife, one distraught Governor stated in 1770 that: "The population of this place increases daily, as the women are accustomed to giving birth to twins. The loss of this lady and the fertility of the women make it necesary for me to insist on the point that her replacement, Monseigneur, is a necessary evil."[4] This was in fact the real beginning of French settlement in St. Pierre, even if firm control was not finally established for another fifty years.

The next interruption in French rule came in 1778 when France went to the aid of the rebellious American colonies, much against the wishes of the inhabitants of St. Pierre and Miquelon who had derived considerable commercial profit by remaining neutral. The Governor of Newfoundland promptly seized the almost defenceless settlement, razed it to the ground and repatriated the population once more to France. Five years later, at the conclusion of the war, the colony was again restored to France, this time "in full right," without the humiliating military restrictions England imposed twenty years earlier. Instead, each country solemnly assured the other of its determination to prevent St. Pierre and Miquelon from becoming "an object of jealousy between the two nations." At first, France was tempted to establish a permanent military base with substantial forces stationed on the islands, but she thought better of it and reduced her garrison to a mere sixty men.

The French Revolution was greeted in St. Pierre and Miquelon with sympathy, if not complete comprehension. There were no clearcut class distinctions in the islands as everyone was preoccupied with the same everlasting struggle for survival. On the other hand, the latent discontent generated by the terrible living conditions predisposed the colonists to assume that any change would be an improvement.

The first reforms were welcomed with remarkable unanimity. The tricolour replaced the Bourbon lilies, a tree of liberty was planted, and a General Assembly was set up presided over by the governor. Its meetings were announced from the pulpit by the Apostolic Prefect and even held in the sanctuary of the church. In time, however, a sharper division of opinion emerged. Certain of the clergy refused to ascribe to the oath to the republican constitution and instead led their flocks into exile. As a result, some 250 Acadians in Miquelon established a colony in the Magdalen Islands in the Gulf of St. Lawrence, while 115 St. Pierrais migrated to Cape Breton. Moreover, as early as 1790, a Jacobin party had appeared which organized a *Club des Amis de la Constitution*, appointed a "deputy" to the National Assembly in Paris, and indulged in inflammatory speeches and provocative acts. For a time, St. Pierre was rent with riots, as a result of which one woman was killed. A local Committee of Public Safety then voted to deport nine agitators but, when they arrived in France, the National Assembly championed their cause and allowed them to return. The turbulence came to an abrupt end, however, with the outbreak of war with Great Britain. In May, 1793, an English fleet, sailing out of Halifax, landed a force on the west coast of St. Pierre, captured the colony without firing a shot and evacuated the population of 1502—"violent democrats to a man"— to Nova Scotia and, then, in 1796, to France.* For many of the Acadians, or Cadiens as they were known locally, this was the fifth major upheaval they had undergone. That same year, a French naval

*The British general reported that, "the greatest part of the Inhabitants are Canadians and Acadians, and are in general an inoffensive industrious people. Nevertheless, the demon of Equality and Liberty had reached this remote and barren spot, and some Excesses had been committed."[5]

squadron retaliated against the English fishermen who had settled in St. Pierre, by destroying the town.

Although this time the English intended to remove this bone in their throat once and for all by annexing St. Pierre and Miquelon permanently, the French were now more determined than ever to regain control. This they did in 1802. But no sooner had French sovereignty been re-established than the war was resumed and the islands fell into British hands for the fourth time. During the negotiations of the peace treaty in 1814, Britain offered France Mauritius as compensation for the loss of St. Pierre and Miquelon, but this was refused and, once again, the islands were handed back to France. The cession was confirmed by the Treaty of Paris the following year, and made effective in 1816 with the return of one hundred and fifty families who had been expelled from their homes nearly a quarter of a century before.

St. Pierre and Miquelon has remained French ever since, though there have been occasions when it appeared that France's control might be challenged. During the Crimean War, there was a somewhat fanciful fear of a Russian raider escaping into the Atlantic through the Northwest Passage. Accordingly, a detachment of infantry was rushed to the islands and a battery of coastal guns hastily mounted at Point aux Canons and on Ile aux Marins to protect the entrance to St. Pierre harbour.[6] Needless to say, the threat never materialized and the guns rusted in their mountings. Half a dozen of them still "guard" the harbour entrance. (Unfortunately, there is no plaque to enlighten the enquiring tourist interested in knowing their historical significance.) Some years later, at the conclusion of the Franco-Prussian War, there was talk in Germany of annexing the colony, but again nothing came of it. In 1898, at the time of the Anglo-French confrontation over Fashoda in the Sudan, the commander of the British garrison at Halifax actually drew up plans to seize the islands within twenty-four hours of the outbreak of war. At one stage, it was even proposed that the Canadian militia be used as reinforcements or relief troops. However, the crisis blew over and St. Pierre was saved.[7]

Earlier that year, during the Spanish-American War, Admiral Camara's cruiser squadron was ordered to attack American shipping between the latitudes of Bermuda and Halifax. According to one account, the squadron was to call in at St. Pierre for coal on the way. However, before the operation could be executed, Camara received fresh instructions to sail east to the Philippines.[8] If St. Pierre and Miquelon had in fact served as a base for raids off the New England seaboard, there would undoubtedly have been demands in the United States for annexation of the islands; and this would have had repercusions in Canada. Five years later, rumours that Senator Henry Cabot Lodge was advocating American ownership created a mild flurry in Canada and provoked considerable public discussion of a proposal to forestall American action by purchasing the islands first.* During the negotiation of the Anglo-French Convention of 1904, France once again managed to hang on to St. Pierre and Miquelon, even though she was compelled to give up her longstanding rights to dry fish along the "French shore" of Newfoundland. If the Newfoundland Government had had its way, the British would have taken over the islands and eliminated the French from the area completely.[9]

The dogged determination with which successive French regimes have clung to this last surviving remnant of France's once vast dominions in North America has in recent times been largely a matter of sentiment. But up until the late nineteenth century, it reflected the very real economic and especially military significance of the islands. The Grand Banks fishery based on St. Pierre was undeniably profitable, but even more important it served as a nursery for seamen. However, with the passing of the sailing ship, the fate of the islands was sealed. Large steam trawlers could go directly to the Banks from France without the necessity of touching at St. Pierre. The enforcement of the Newfoundland Bait Act of 1887 and, even more, the application of the French Tariff Assimilation Law of 1892 further contributed to the ruination of the economy of the islands. Within twenty years, they lost two-thirds of their trade and over one-third

*The idea of annexation to the United States enjoyed a brief period of popularity in the islands. In November, 1908, nearly a thousand people marched through the streets of St. Pierre to the Administrator's residence carrying the American flag. "It is remarkable," the American consul reported to Washington, "how outspoken people are in the advocacy of union with the United States. . . . I am frequently approached by people who want to talk to me about uniting St. Pierre with the United States. I try to be polite but never express an opinion myself, and do nothing to encourage such interviews." Between 1936 and 1940, there was considerable pressure in the United States, mainly from Congress, to annex St. Pierre and Miquelon in part payment of the French war debt.[10]

of their population—mainly to Quebec Province, to Boston and New York, and to France. Only the reversion to tariff autonomy in 1911 and the providential adoption of prohibition in the United States in 1920 permitted these relics of an earlier economic and political system to survive at all.

St. Pierre and Miquelon has been notorious as a smuggler's haven since the collapse of the French empire in 1763, and indeed still is. (Today, aircraft as well as high-speed launches and innocent-looking fishing craft are used in the trade). Nevertheless, it was not until the 1920's that smuggling became the prinicpal preoccupation of the people. For fifteen giddy years—known as the *Temps du Whisky* or the *Temps de la Fraude*— the islands enjoyed an unprecedented boom as fantastic quantities of French wine, Jamaican rum, and Canadian rye were funnelled through them to undisclosed destinations.* In the meantime, the fishermen neglected their nets and forgot their fish in the scramble for easy money and adventure. As a result, when the bubble burst and the American racketeers departed, the people were left worse off than they had been before. With the end of the noble experiment in 1933 and French efforts two years later to suppress the smuggling trade—a move which presumably reflected the growing concern in Paris with the threat of Hitler—the islands were suddenly plunged from the peak of comparative prosperity to the depths of a depression. Thus, the outbreak of the Second World War found St. Pierre and Miquelon with over half the population on relief and almost as poverty stricken as the adjoining coast of Newfoundland.

Economic retrenchment precipitated political reorganization. Although St. Pierre and Miquelon had experienced a brief period of radical democracy during the Revolution, it was not until the founding of the Third Republic that representative institutions were formally introduced. In 1872, both St. Pierre and Miquelon became municipalities with their own elected mayors and councils. At the same time, a *Conseil d'Administration* was established, though until 1923 it generally had a minority of elected members. In 1936, following tax riots at the time of repeal and two missions of investigation by the Inspector-General of Colonies, the colony was officially designated a Territory and a new constitution promulgated, simplifying the administrative structure of the islands. The municipal councils were

*This was the setting for Damon Runyan's short story, "The Lily of St. Pierre."

abolished, the courts downgraded, and many of the civil servants repatriated to France. The *Conseil d'Administration* was also suppressed, but this decision raised such a storm of protest that the council was quickly revived with a slightly more representative membership. It now consisted of the Administrator as president, three ex-officio officials, and seven elected members, five from St. Pierre and one each from Miquelon and Ile aux Marins.

The constitutional changes introduced after the Second World War were even more sweeping and involved a significant increase in local self-government. A fully-elected territorial council of fourteen members—the *Conseil général*—was created, the mayors and municipal councils were restored, and direct representation in the French Parliament was granted for the first time. Under the Third Republic, the colony had elected a delegate to the *Conseil supérieur des Colonies* set up in 1883, but this was purely an advisory body and in any case met infrequently. Now, the territory has its own senator, chosen by an electoral college composed principally of the local general councillors, and a deputy elected on the basis of universal suffrage. Henri Claireaux, a prominent local figure and Christian Democrat, has served as St. Pierre and Miquelon's senator from the beginning, while four deputies, only one of them a St. Pierrais, have represented the islands in the National Assembly:

Henri Debidour (1945–46). A Paris surgeon who had served with the Free French in St. Pierre and Miquelon during the war.

Dominique Laurelli (1946–51, 1959–62). A Corsican lawyer and customs official from 1927 to 1936 at St. Pierre, where he married a St. Pierraise. A perennial candidate, he had been defeated in the elections of 1945, June 1946, 1951, 1956 and 1962. He supports de Gaulle's *Union pour la Nouvelle République*.

Alain Savary (1951–58). The Free French Administrator in the islands, 1941–43, and a leading socialist.

Albert Briand (1962–   ). Local businessman and publisher of the weekly *L'Echo des îles Saint-Pierre et Miquelon*. Although both he and his brother-in-law, Senator Claireaux, had been *Vichyard* leaders, had been arrested by the Free French in January 1944 for their opposition to conscription, and remain anti-de Gaulle, they are now political opponents. Briand was elected on a non-party ticket.

Despite the shifts and splits in post-war French politics, the appeal of General de Gaulle continues strong among the people of St. Pierre and Miquelon. In each of his referenda in recent years, his majority in the islands has been even more impressive than in metropolitan France, as is evident from Table I. In the first of these referenda, in September, 1958, President de Gaulle offered all French colonies complete political (and financial) independence. Faced with this choice, the electorate of St. Pierre and Miquelon not only expressed itself overwhelmingly in favour of retaining the ties with France but, through its General Council, voted unanimously to remain an Overseas Territory.

TABLE I

	Sept. 28, 1958	Jan. 8, 1961	Apr. 8, 1962	Oct. 28,1962
"YES"	2,325 (98%)	2,308 (92%)	1,974 (92%)	2,108 (91%)
"NO"	46	83	170	198

The decline in support for de Gaulle in 1962, and the fact that over 20% of the electorate stayed away from the polls, can be explained by local circumstances at the time, notably the traditional opposition to conscription which had become an issue.

The idea of joining Canada is revived occasionally, usually by visiting journalists, only to be dismissed as inconceivable. The emotional bond with France, based on an historical connection extending back more than three hundred years, is too strong. Moreover, even the minority of St. Pierrais who are prepared to contemplate union with Canada doubt whether it would be economically advantageous. Current welfare benefits are extraordinarily generous. The French subvention to the territory amounts to $660 per capita and covers well over half its budget. Moreover, investment funds amounting to millions of dollars annually are poured into the tiny colony by the European Economic Community as well as by the French Government directly. These have financed, among other things, a new fish-processing plant and harbour improvements. No wonder the St. Pierrais is regarded in Paris as the world's "most expensive Frenchman."

Independence, even in association with France, has also been ruled out. There are a few optimists who think the islands might be able to survive by becoming the Monte Carlo of North America or by offering a flag of convenience to foreign shipping, but the majority repudiate such suggestions as unworthy, disloyal, or impractical. More surprising, perhaps, is the rejection of departmental status. The fear here is that the loss of local fiscal autonomy involved in full integration with Metropolitan France would lead to serious difficulties—as experience in the French Antilles has shown.[11]

Despite the colonial mentality often apparent among the people in the past, they have not always acquiesced in French policies without complaint—far from it, especially when it concerned conscription, taxes, or the church. In all three spheres, they have insisted on, and generally received, though usually only after a struggle, special privileges not accorded Frenchmen at home.

The status of the Roman Catholic Church is an example. Because of the fierce devotion of the islanders to their religion, the territory was exempted from the provisions of the law of 1905 separating church and state in France. As a result, the Napoleonic Concordat of 1802 continues in effect, and the Apostolic Prefect and his clergy remain employees of the state. The territorial administration also subsidizes church schools. When, in November, 1908, it refused to permit the opening of a "free school", an angry crowd smashed the windows of the government school and paraded an American flag through the streets of the town to symbolize its demand for freedom of belief. In the end, Paris capitulated.[12]

In time of need, St. Pierre and Miquelon has always given unstinting support to the mother country. During the First World War, four hundred islanders served overseas, over one hundred giving their lives for France, while in the Second World War, 550 enlisted, the vast majority of them volunteers, and 27 died. "No other French territory, I believe," Jacques Soustelle has claimed, "has suffered so great a loss or given so much of its blood in proportion to its population as these tiny bits of land."[13] At the same time, the colony has consistently resisted the imposition of any form of compulsory military service. The reasons for this are primarily historical and traditional. According to local tradition, the French Government solemnly promised those who resettled the colony in 1816 that neither they nor their descendants would ever be conscripted. Whether or not this claim is historically valid may never be finally established as many of the relevant documents have disappeared or been destroyed. However, the people of St. Pierre and Miquelon certainly believe it to be true. Moreover, such an arrangement would clearly have made good sense at the time. It could reasonably have been argued that the exacting task of maintaining a precarious French presence in the islands was in itself a form of national service, and at least as dangerous and demanding as anything required of a soldier. Besides, the colony needed every available able-bodied man if it was to survive. In the event of a military call-up, not only would the fisheries suffer, but the families left behind would face virtual starvation.

Nevertheless, despite these compelling arguments, conscription has been imposed on the islands on four occasions—in 1856, 1915, 1944, and 1961—and each time it has provoked loud protests. The very first request that Admiral Muselier received from his supporters on the morning of his arrival in St. Pierre in 1941 was for an assurance that there would be no conscription. However, all he was prepared to promise at the time was that there would be none "for the moment." When, two years later, a system of compulsory military service was instituted, considerable opposition developed, particularly among supporters of Marshal Pétain, resulting in the arrest of several prominent citizens, including the territory's present Senator and Deputy. The reintroduction of conscription on July 31, 1961 again produced a public outcry. A mass meeting organized in St. Pierre approved a petition of protest which was then despatched to President de Gaulle. When, after three months, no reply had been received, members of the General Council, the Municipal Council, and the Chamber of Commerce registered their dissatisfaction in the traditional manner by resigning *en masse*. The depth of public feeling on this explosive issue was also reflected in the 1962 referendum in St. Pierre and Miquelon on de Gaulle's Algerian policy. Eventually a compromise was effected; the law formally remains in force, but is not applied in practice in recognition of the islands' voluntary sacrifices in two world wars.[14]

The ingrained opposition in the islands to taxes is more a national characteristic shared by all French than one peculiar to St. Pierre and Miquelon. Nevertheless, because of the poverty of the territory, its population is particularly sensitive to any worsening of its economic status. In 1954 for example, two-thirds of the general and municipal councillors resigned in protest against the reappointment of a governor who had levied a 25 per cent duty on imported French perfumes and liqueurs. In 1960, a $40,000 cut in French subsidy, following the introduction of the revalued franc, provoked a further sharp reaction among the islanders. Senator Claireaux and eleven other general councillors promptly threatened to resign, thereby forcing an election which they won impressively, taking all but one seat on the Council.*[15]

The most serious crisis in the postwar history of St. Pierre and Miquelon erupted in April, 1965, following a simmering dispute, ostensibly over minimum wage levels, but actually involving a bitter power struggle between two brothers-in-law, Senator Claireaux and Deputy Briand, for the political leadership of the colony. The situation appeared so serious that at the request of the frightened Governor, Paris rushed a force of 132 gardes mobiles, complete with jeeps, gas-masks and automatic weapons, to St. Pierre to head off bloody revolution. The puzzled population of the islands resented so deeply this unprecedented peacetime invasion—officially described as a routine reinforcement—that they staged an impressive three-day general strike to back up their demand for the withdrawal of the troops and the recall of the Governor.[16] Four months later, the members of the General Council, who had of course resigned, were swept back into office with a firm popular mandate to purge the administration of expatriates who, like the Governor, were allegedly "unqualified." Fortunately for the Governor, his term of office expired shortly afterwards, thus enabling him to retire with some semblance of dignity. However, the internal issues which touched off the explosion remain unresolved.† Thus, it can be seen that the spirit of the hardy inhabitants of St. Pierre and Miquelon is a flinty as the rocks on which they have built their homes. Their sturdy independence was also evident in their response to the tragic events of 1940.

*The reduction of the subvention and the imposition of conscription were due to the war in Algeria, which consequently was unpopular in St. Pierre and Miquelon. Even prior to the referendum of September, 1958, Senator Claireaux had urged the electorate to vote YES "in the hope that the election of General de Gaulle as President of the Republic would ensure the carrying out of a liberal policy in North Africa and Black Africa."[17]

2

RESISTANCE

The fall of France came as a tremendous psychological shock to the people of St. Pierre and Miquelon. It also had serious economic and political consequences; the colony was suddenly confronted with a cessation of supplies from France, on which it was almost completely dependent, as well as with the loss of its markets in Europe. The situation was further aggravated by the diversion to St. Pierre of the French fishing fleet on the Grand Banks, thus tripling the number of able-bodied men in the town overnight. The presence of some 1,385 lusty, bearded sailors impatiently waiting the signal to rejoin their families and collect their pay in France understandably created a number of problems, but none more pressing than the need to replenish the islands' rapidly dwindling stocks of food. In mid-July, the Administrator of the colony, Count Gilbert de Bournat, anxiously reported to Vichy that the food situation was "critical and worsening steadily." So scarce were supplies of meat that, for a month, butcher shops were permitted to open only on Thursdays and Saturdays.[1]

The only hope of salvation lay in turning to the United States and Canada for help. Both were well-disposed to assist. Yet the difficulties were formidable and delays inevitable. The problem was not merely one of procuring supplies, but of paying for them—in dollars. The solution sought was permission to tap blocked Vichy funds in New York and Montreal.* This was agreed to in principle following visits by de Bournat to Washington and Ottawa in the latter part of July. Under the procedure finally worked out, the United States Treasury, on the formal request of the Vichy Ambassador in Washington, trans-

* The Bank of Canada held $400 million in gold in Canada on behalf of the Bank of France, and $500 million in US dollars in its account in the Federal Reserve Bank in New York on behalf of "The State of France." Personal accounts in American and Canadian banks of residents of St. Pierre and Miquelon were also frozen immediately after the Armistice.

ferred $25,000 a month to the French American Banking Corporation for the use of the island administration. In Ottawa, the Vichy Minister presented Canadian authorities with a similar monthly request. The Canadian releases were, on the average, about twice as great as the American ones, though the amount varied from month to month with the current requirements of the territory.[2] In both cases, the money was deposited in an account in the Bank of Nova Scotia in Halifax. Canadian dollars acquired in this way could only be spent on approved imports from Canada, chiefly foodstuffs, lumber, and coal, and then only on condition that these were not stock-piled or re-exported. This was to ensure that St. Pierre and Miquelon was not used to circumvent the Allied economic blockade of Europe. The wisdom of this precaution was demonstrated later when de Bournat lifted the ban imposed at the beginning of the war on trade with the Axis powers.[3] These financial arrangements enabled the islands to survive the immediate economic crisis. They also had one other important result: they bolstered de Bournat's shaky position and almost certainly saved him from being deposed by the Gaullists.

The immediate effect of the news of the collapse of the French armies was to unite the people of St. Pierre and Miquelon in a remarkable expression of fervent loyalty to the mother country. They also responded warmly to the appeal of the unknown general whose voice came over the BBC on the evening of June 18 with the comforting assurance that "the cause of France is not lost." Overnight, opinion in the colony became almost solidly Free French. The next day, following a moving public demonstration of patriotism, representatives of all sections of the community drafted a telegram to the President of the Republic. Even the Administrator lent his support, though he insisted on watering down the wording and may have been responsible for the delay in its despatch until June 23, the day after the signing of the Armistice. The message read:

Population of St. Pierre and Miquelon unanimously ready for all sacrifices. Beseech you to continue the struggle against invader with assistance of all French colonies and the full fraternal collaboration of the British Empire. Long live immortal France!

> BOURNAT, Administrator
> MGR. POISSON, Apostolic Prefect
> GLOANEC, Senior Councillor
> DUPONT, President, Chamber of Commerce
> LEBUF, President, War Veterans Association.[4]

This initial unity was soon shattered. The turning point came on July 3, 1940 with the British attack on the French fleet at Mers-el-Kébir. Thereafter, the colony was split into two sharply antagonistic camps, each claiming with equal fervour that it alone was upholding the true honour of France.

On one side were the loyal supporters of Vichy: the Administrator and his attractive wife, the leading clergy, all but one of the officers of the warship *Ville d'Ys*, most senior civil servants and members of the professional class, and the more prosperous merchants.* In addition, there were those who looked to the islands' *notables* for guidance or felt it expedient to please their employers. Their numbers fluctuated, but never exceeded 35 to 40 per cent of the population.

The motives of even the most ardent *Vichyards*—as they were called in the islands—were often mixed. Most, no doubt, were broadly sympathetic with the ideological aims of the Pétain regime, but many also had personal reasons for maintaining their allegiance. Some hoped thereby to avoid conscription. Among officials generally, with certain honourable exceptions, the mere fact that Vichy remained the legal government of France was in itself good and sufficient grounds for continuing to support it. The Administrator's response to the new order was more positive. While at first he appeared sympathetic to de Gaulle, his attitude quickly changed in July, following the sharp deterioration in relations with Britain and his discussions with the Vichy Ambassador in Washington. With characteristic optimism de Bournat argued that, as long as the colony did nothing foolish, all would turn out well in the end. In the meantime, it was necessary to maintain ties with Vichy, as it alone would pay the subventions on which the economic survival of the territory depended. Later, with Canada and more especially the United States allegedly pursuing pro-Vichy policies, he warned that it would be equally suicidal to risk the loss of their goodwill. In any case, there was no salvation in rallying to Britain as she would soon have to capitulate. How far his fanatical loyalty to Vichy was a matter of conviction and not simply expediency, and the extent to which he was under the influence of his Alsatian German wife, who seemed to have pronounced anti-British and collaborationist tendencies, are still matters of contro-

---

*Among the most active *Vichyards* were: François Compagnon, René Delort, Dr. François Dunan, Edouard Floquet and François Leroux.

versy. However, one senior official in St. Pierre at the time states categorically that de Bournat openly expressed his admiration for Hitler and Mussolini and his sympathy for nazism and fascism.* The naval officers, too, though not all the trawler captains, were bitter towards the British. Although, under the initial shock of the Armistice terms, some of them considered continuing the fight alongside their ally, Mers-el-Kébir quickly changed that and provided them with a convenient pretext for swinging into line behind Admiral Darlan's policy of collaboration.

The wealthier citizens of St. Pierre, principally those who had profited by prohibition, had investments in French Government bonds and therefore a financial stake in the status quo. Besides, after August, they could afford to be pro-Vichy thanks to the liberality of the Canadian and American Governments in permitting them to convert their otherwise worthless francs into dollars at an artificial rate of exchange. Ottawa also allowed them to withdraw small amounts from their personal accounts in Canadian banks without having to secure special permission from the Foreign Exchange Control Board each time. Even Newfoundland helped the Vichy cause indirectly. In September, 1940, Eric Price, Chairman of the Newfoundland Board of Liquor Control, visited St. Pierre and spent about $50,000 buying up large quantities of liquor at bargain prices. The group which principally benefited were the merchants, who otherwise would have faced ruin.

The active or passive partisans of de Gaulle, as de Bournat himself noted, included "a large proportion of the local population, with nearly all the war veterans and most of the crews of the metropolitan ships."†5 They rejected the Armistice as dishonourable and, certainly insofar as St. Pierre and Miquelon was concerned, unnecessary. In their view, the defeat of France made it all the more imperative for her Empire to carry on the struggle until final victory was achieved.

The political unrest occasioned by St. Pierre and Miquelon's withdrawal from the war was accentuated by economic distress, enforced

---

*On January 28, 1940, de Bournat wrote to Radio Rome to congratulate it on its French broadcasts and to ask for further information on the Italian corporative state and autarchy.6

†Though in the end, virtually all these seamen were persuaded by their officers (who were in the main non-committal on the question of allegiance) to return to their families in France rather than support de Gaulle.

idleness, and irksome restrictions. So desperate did the situation become that the Administrator felt compelled, amongst other things, to restrict withdrawals from savings accounts "in order to prevent panic." At the same time, he endeavoured to keep local shops open "for propaganda purposes." Otherwise, he warned the Minister of Colonies on July 12, there would be an "immediate rally" to Great Britain and de Gaulle. The population was "getting nervous," he added, and "a strict observation of regulations would inevitably result in rebellion. In my opinion, everything must be attempted to prevent it."[7]

Matters came to a head in the autumn of 1940. Despite de Bournat's subsequent assertion that there was a "complete absence of any kind of discord" or "any disturbance of the public order" in the islands during his administration, a number of nasty incidents did occur.[8] On Sunday, September 8, an attempt to enforce the ten o'clock curfew on the sale of liquor triggered a rowdy demonstration in support of de Gaulle, or at least in opposition to the Administrator. Shortly after closing hour, the chief of police, Pierre Raymond, entered the *Café de France* where a crowd of French seamen and local residents had gathered, drinking and singing Gaullist songs. He demanded silence. Then, according to one account, he approached two sailors sitting at a table. "He picked up a glass and smelled it. Whereupon the second man at the table threw the contents of his own glass into the gendarme's face, crying 'Smell this, too!' Immediately thereafter the helpless policeman was picked up and thrown into the street. He literally flew through the air and landed flat on his face."

Undaunted by this humiliating experience, Raymond returned to the fray. Provoked by cries of "dirty cow," "German mercenary," "blackguard," "idler," and "coward," the 52-year-old gendarme courageously tackled his young adversaries who numbered over thirty and in the end emerged triumphant. Five of the rioters were arrested, convicted of resisting lawful authority and committing outrages against the police, and sentenced to modest fines or jail terms.

In more normal times, the administration's firm action might have been regarded as reasonable but, in the circumstances of September, 1940, it appeared to those involved to have been politically inspired. News of the incident swiftly spread through the town and precipitated an impromptu parade of forty to fifty French seamen reinforced by a number of St. Pierrais who marched on the prison, singing patriotic songs and shouting *"Vive de Gaulle."* De Bournat's reaction was to order all cafés to close two hours earlier in future. This aroused public resentment further, and contributed to strengthening the Gaullist movement—even though the incident arose out of a simple bar-room brawl and was in no way instigated by the local opposition. The Free French leadership was in fact somewhat embarrassed by the unsolicited support it received. Raymond was subsequently promoted by the Free French in January, 1942.[9]

The following Saturday, a meeting of war veterans took place at which a personal message in General de Gaulle's own handwriting was read. The association responded by endorsing by an overwhelming majority, an enthusiastic and forthright telegram of support for Free France, which was subsequently forwarded to de Gaulle in Africa. Of the 106 veterans present, 94 voted for the resolution, 6 opposed it, and 6 did not vote. The resolution pointed to the "dishonour and danger" of obedience to the government at Vichy which was "completely under German domination," and declared: "The War Veterans of St. Pierre, confident in the final victory of General de Gaulle and his army, which is fighting alongside the British army for the liberty of France and of the world, address to them the expression of their profound admiration and of their gratitude and hope that, by their arms, they will rapidly liberate the soil of France. Long live France! Long live the British Empire! Long live de Gaulle!"[10]

Next day, September 15, 1940, a second and angrier fracas ensued following the appearance overhead of two Royal Canadian Air Force reconnaissance planes, one of which swooped low over the town several times to photograph the *Ville d'Ys.** When the crew of the warship stripped an anti-aircraft gun for action with the apparent intention of firing at the aircraft, the Sunday crowd which had congregated as usual on the *Quai de la Roncière* (since renamed the *Quai du Général de Gaulle*) reacted violently. In addition to voicing vociferous support for the Free French, it hurled insults and even stones at the Vichy warship. In retaliation, her officers turned a firehose on the demonstrators and, when this failed to disperse them,

---

*One RCAF Digby stood off at some distance while the other, piloted by Squadron-Leader (now Air Vice-Marshall) H. M. Carscallen, flew in at about 200 feet.

threw a cordon of seamen armed with rifles and fixed bayonets around the quay. Raymond Gushue, Eric Price and F. A. J. Laws, the three Newfoundland Government officials whose arrival in St. Pierre two days earlier bearing de Gaulle's message had in part prompted the disturbance, were arrested, escorted to the *Hôtel Robert* and confined to their rooms under naval guard overnight. However, they were freed the next day, following an indignant protest by Archibald Bartlett, the British Vice-Consul. De Bournat then attempted to make amends by calling on them in person, and later holding a reception in their honour at the governor's residence. The Newfoundlanders responded by entertaining the Administrator and his staff in return.

The immediate aim of the War Veterans Association was to force a plebiscite on the issue of rallying to Free France. The outcome was never in doubt. According to Bartlett, 85 per cent of the population at this time was pro-British, 65 per cent pro-de Gaulle, and only 15 per cent pro-Vichy. Realizing this, the Administrator did everything possible to avoid an appeal to the people. Although he intimated at one stage that he might be prepared in principle to accept the authority of General de Gaulle if it were legally sanctioned by popular vote, in practice he consistently vetoed every attempt to hold a plebiscite. Moreover, when François LeBuf, the veterans' president, sought permission to post their resolution on the public notice board, de Bournat refused and remonstrated with him on the error of his ways.

De Bournat also sought to counter the Free French campaign by capitalizing on a mischievous leading article which appeared in a St. John's newspaper, the *Daily News*. This asserted that St. Pierre and Miquelon had been "a constant thorn in the flesh" to Newfoundland, since "the inhabitants were quite ready to encourage the undermining of our customs laws and they have provided a great deal of unfair competition in the fish trade because of the large subsidies paid both by France and the colonial administration. . . . If France, willingly or unwillingly, surrenders possession [the editorial concluded], there can be only one rightful claimant to ownership. That is Newfoundland."[11] The actual wording was provocative enough to reopen old wounds and inflame passions, but the cleverly distorted translation de Bournat circulated and the anti-British bias in the accompanying commentary compounded the damage.

A month later, on his return from a second mission to the mainland, de Bournat detected a further distinct deterioration in the political situation. This he attributed to the colony's isolation from the mother country and its saturation with British and Free French propaganda. On October 24, the veterans held another mass meeting at which they planned to demand a plebiscite.[12] If the administration refused, they intended to conduct one themselves. On learning of this, de Bournat, himself a veteran with a distinguished record in the First World War, decided to attend in person in the hope of heading off the threat. On his arrival at the *Salle des Fêtes*, he was greeted with a chorus shouting *"Vive de Gaulle"*. However, he ignored the hostile reception, made his way through the packed hall, and at the invitation of the President mounted the rostrum to address the assembly. He at once launched into a crude attack on the anonymous authors of a recent Gaullist leaflet: '*Que la lumière soit*'. *Adresse aux jeunes*. This identified de Bournat as the "enemy" and described him as "the assiduous and attentive listener of Radio Paris, D.N.B., and Radio Rome whose news reports he spreads treating them as truth."*[13] Taking a bundle of papers from his pocket, de Bournat declared: "These sheets, bearing the signature *Un groupe d'anciens combattants* have been circulating. I therefore ask the executive of the Association kindly to give me the names of those responsible." He added, rather curiously, that he was not present in any official capacity, but simply as an ordinary member. "Comrade de Bournat," he assured the meeting, "is not going to tell Administrator de Bournat what he has heard here."

The President, François LeBuf, interjected that he did not know who was involved and, moreover, he was not interested. At this, de Bournat exploded. "If the authors are not cowards," he exclaimed, "they should make themselves known." This outburst caused the Secretary, Henry Humbert, to jump to his feet. "I am no more cowardly than you," he replied. "I am one of the authors of these papers. . . . As for telling who the others are, I will never do that. In any case, I accept full responsibility." Although Humbert advised his collaborators not to reveal themselves, Louis Plantegenest, another member of the executive and Chief Clerk of the court, also spoke up. "I am not a coward either," he told the Administrator. "I do not want

---

*A subsequent tract was entitled *Appel au bon sens de Saint-Pierrais (No. 2)*. Another leaflet, *Nous, les jeunes*, expressed the opinion of "*un groupe de jeunes*."

Comrade Humbert to accept complete responsibility because I have shared in this propaganda work." De Bournat commented drily that he already knew Plantegenest was involved.

By this time, the meeting was in an uproar with cries of "Some of us have just been called cowards" and "Shame" filling the hall. Some members were so indignant that they rushed to the platform angrily shouting at de Bournat: "You have called our comrades cowards." This, he hotly denied, but his attempts to explain himself only brought forth further cries of "Yes, you did!" At another point in the proceedings, when de Bournat was warning his audience against listening to the BBC, he commented that "Radio-Paris has said. . . ." Before he completed his sentence, he was interrupted by a lone voice, singing a familiar ditty broadcast daily from London:

> Radio-Paris lies,
> Radio-Paris lies,
> Radio-Paris is German. . . .

This interjection brought the house down. Yet, despite the gales of laughter that shook the hall, the solitary figure at the front of the room remained unmoved. In the face of such a crushing humiliation, a man of greater sensitivity and less courage would have fled in disarray. De Bournat, however, managed to stand his ground and keep his composure.

Eventually, when the uproar subsided, de Bournat embarked on his speech. This was a two-hour harangue which ranged widely over a variety of subjects, but in essence consisted of three points. The first was that economic conditions in the islands would be worse rather than better under a Free French administration. He maintained that both the United States and Canada opposed an alteration in the status quo and implied that they might not continue their assistance in the event of a Free French takeover. Secondly, he ridiculed any suggestion of one or other neighbour seizing the islands. The Canadians, he alleged, *could* not intervene successfully because their navy was no match for the French West Indies fleet, and the Americans *would* not intervene as they were still neutral. He was particularly contemptuous of the state of American military preparedness. As on other occasions, he charged that their guns were wooden and their tanks made of paper. Finally, de Bournat contended that now was not the time to break with Vichy—a position he continued to uphold until he was deposed. Accordingly, he reaffirmed his determination personally to "oppose a plebiscite of any kind." He did, however, indicate that if at some unspecified future date the situation changed, he would be the first to rally the territory to de Gaulle. This was a clever argument since it seemed to suggest that the division of opinion was not on fundamentals but simply a matter of timing. At the same time, it involved no commitment on de Bournat's part. Even after the liberation, he argued with Admiral Muselier that the Free French had come too soon. "Perhaps later on" their arrival would have been "timely," but in December, 1941, it was still "too early" to know "what changes the war may ultimately bring about."[14]

The veterans listened to de Bournat's lengthy discourse in polite silence. But immediately it was over, the President, on the pretext of the lateness of the hour, adjourned the meeting until the following evening—when the Administrator would not be present.

LeBuf opened the reconvened meeting with a personal statement.

The first words of Comrade de Bournat last evening [he declared] were an affront to me and my committee, an affront I will not forget. In asking us to divulge the names of our comrades who had drawn up the propaganda sheets in favour of Free France, he tried to make policemen and spies out of us. . . . To think us capable of filling such a role, to treat us as spies in his pay is, for me, the most grievous insult anyone could level at us. Therefore, just as I am not going to wear my Légion d'honneur until France is liberated, likewise I will not in future attend any official function at which M. de Bournat is present.

The next speaker was Henry Humbert. He insisted that he and other members of the groupe d'anciens combattants had every right to circulate Free French leaflets.

Neither I nor anyone else contested Comrade de Bournat's right to come here and speak for more than two hours against any movement in favour of Free France. No one interrupted him. We all listened with patience. I am, therefore, very sure that no one will challenge my right to make propaganda outside meetings of the Association. And, besides, we are not yet under a dictatorial regime. We still have the right to express our opinions. I also have something else to say. I have been present at every general assembly of this Association since its formation nineteen years ago. Last evening was the first time Comrade de Bournat was present. It was also the first time I have heard one veteran call other veterans "cowards". . . . I would ask you not to forget that.

Later, another member—Emmanuel Cazier-Ruault—rose from the floor to remind the meeting of its declaration only six weeks earlier in favour of de Gaulle. In view of the decisive nature of that vote, he urged the entire membership of the Association to give those engaged in propaganda on behalf of Free France their full support. This appeal was enthusiastically endorsed by shouts of approval from all parts of the hall. There were no dissenting voices.

The real business of the evening was consideration of a proposal calling for a plebiscite to enable the people of the territory to decide between Free France and Vichy. This was completed in short order. A resolution was drafted, voted on by secret ballot, and carried by an impressive majority. Seventy-nine members supported a plebiscite, eleven were opposed, and five abstained.

Although de Bournat failed to forestall a demand for a plebiscite, he still believed—or at least led his superiors in Vichy to believe—that his dramatic intervention had had "an influence beyond all my hopes." His speech may have caused some waverers to pause, but it certainly did not have the "decisive" impact he claimed. In any case, the situation was dramatically changed when, a week later, the *Ville d'Ys* at long last sailed for Martinique. The withdrawal of the only Vichy forces in the islands was, as the Administrator noted sadly, "immediately interpreted as an abandoning of the colony by France." Once again "the atmosphere became charged," with shouts of *Vive de Gaulle* heard "almost everywhere." "Rare are those," de Bournat confided to Vichy, "who dare still support me openly."

On November 8, 1940, information reached the Administrator that the veterans were planning a coup d'état on Armistice Day. This was inaccurate. At various times, there had been vague talk of seizing control of the government, but no decision had been reached and certainly no date set.* Opinion within the Resistance on the wisdom of such action was divided, particularly as there was uncertainty

*One resistance leader recalls that "We came very close at one of [our later] meetings to overwhelming or laying seige to the local authority, but Governor de Bournat, warned in time by a police spy present at the meeting, took precautions and the police were able to disperse people as they came out before the main group was formed to march on the public buildings." Another Free Frenchman has commented: "A coup d'état might have been possible in St. Pierre, as most men owned several hunting guns. But, prior to the Armistice, St. Pierre was one large family where everyone knew everyone else and lived in peace. We did not wish to risk shedding French blood, which perhaps might have been necessary."

concerning the reaction of the United States and Canada. Nevertheless, de Bournat took the threat seriously, and reacted immediately. He begged people to suspend judgment on his regime until he had had an opportunity to explain the true facts of the situation to them. He also let it be known "by all possible means" that he would not give in without a struggle and that, in the event of trouble, he could count on assistance from Vichy warships, which he certainly could not. Yet no one dared call his bluff. Everyone remembered that, in the past, France had always dealt swiftly with any disturbance in the islands by rushing a naval vessel to St. Pierre to remove the agitators.

The Administrator's desperate moves may have taken some of the steam out of the Free French demonstration organized for November 11. Several hundred people assembled before the War Memorial, but in de Bournat's view they showed little enthusiasm. "Many are suspicious," he claimed, "and want to wait to see what my poster will contain." The situation might have been different if General de Gaulle's message, delivered later that day, had been received earlier. The war veterans suspected de Bournat of deliberately delaying its delivery until after their rally, though the governor hotly denied the charge.[15] "I thank you for your attachment," de Gaulle cabled from Brazzaville in reply to the resolution of support forwarded to him two months earlier. "The Free French forces are worthy of your confidence. Long live Free France! Long live our British Allies! Long live St. Pierre and Miquelon, the free!"

The following day, de Bournat countered with a lengthy proclamation of his own.* This was a clever piece of Vichy propaganda. It played on the sentiments and fears of the people, praised Pétain, denounced the purveyors of "false rumours," and defended the maintenance of the status quo. To modify the existing position of the colony, de Bournat asserted, "would result in raising doubts in people's minds, would cause embarrassment to our great neighbours and friends, would be a disservice to France and would place the Territory in a very difficult financial situation"—all of which was of doubtful validity. Nevertheless, it was remarkably effective. "The fight is won," the Administrator reported exuberantly to Vichy. "I may from this moment guarantee the loyalty of the colony."[16]

The publication of de Bournat's proclamation marked the end of

*See Appendix A.

the first phase in the internal struggle for power in St. Pierre and Miquelon. This is not to suggest that the Administrator's optimistic assessment of the situation can be accepted at face value; he was obviously exaggerating the extent of his triumph to impress his superiors with his skill in handling an explosive situation. Nor can he take all the credit for his success in surviving the immediate crisis. A more important factor in lessening tensions in the islands was the timely departure of the metropolitan fishing fleet. This greatly simplified the task of maintaining public order and eased the strain on the economy. Admittedly, conditions remained difficult. The fishing season in 1940 and again in 1941 was poor; the territory suffered from a chronic shortage of coal; and a severe epidemic of influenza swept the islands forcing the schools to close for a time. Nevertheless, the situation was no longer as desperate as it had been the previous summer.*

This caused the opposition to reassess its position. Up until this point, the Gaullists had assumed that the pressure of public opinion, assisted perhaps by a locally engineered putsch, would be sufficient to topple the regime. It was now apparent that de Bournat was determined to fight back with every weapon at his disposal† and that, with the financial and, so it seemed, political support of the United States and Canada, external assistance would be necessary. This was not forthcoming for another year. In the meantime, both sides concentrated on consolidating their positions.

De Bournat set about transforming St. Pierre and Miquelon into a little Vichy. He promoted the cult of the Marshal, appealed to the people to "participate with confidence in the task of national rehabilitation," and systematically extended to the territory the political philosophy and legislative enactments of the Vichy regime. *Travail, Famille, Patrie* superseded *Liberté, Egalité, Fraternité* as the motto of government. In these efforts, he was actively supported by Monseigneur Poisson, the "bishop" of St. Pierre, who echoed eloquently

---

*Vichy continued to meet the minimum costs of unemployment relief and other welfare benefits. In addition, some six hundred families benefited from donations of food, coal, and used clothing received in response to an appeal for aid issued by the French Consul in Boston towards the end of 1940.[17]

†De Bournat's cache of arms included two guns, two machine guns, ten automatic rifles, and one hundred and thirty rifles, most of them acquired from the French trawlers before their departure. All he lacked was a sufficient number of supporters who could be trusted with these weapons.[18]

Pétain's theme of regeneration through suffering. France, Poisson argued, had been defeated by her sins and was paying the inevitable penalty of her godlessness.[19]

This alliance between church and state became increasingly intimate. Even under the Third Republic, subsidies had been paid to the free (parochial) schools; but now compulsory religious instruction was introduced into the public schools. Commissions were also appointed to revise the school curriculum and to censor textbooks. At the same time, steps were taken to purge society of dangerous elements, particularly Jews, freemasons, foreigners, and communists. The fact that there were no Jews or freemasons and few foreigners on the islands, and that almost no one was even suspected of being a communist, was perhaps irrelevant. The operative motive was a determination to parrot Vichy.[20]

The War Veterans Association posed a more serious threat. De Bournat attempted to undermine it by creating a series of paramilitary organizations of his own. In June, 1941, he announced the formation of a *Union française des Combattants** and personally invited all veterans to join. Despite the forced dissolution, four months later, of their own association and the confiscation of their welfare funds amounting to $1,200, less than forty could be induced to accept membership, and many of these did so out of fear for their jobs. (Other estimates of the numbers involved range from 14 to 125.) Actually, no meeting of the *Union* was ever held. Nor was one really necessary, as all officers had been personally picked by the Administrator, who was also president of the organization.

At the same time, de Bournat sought to enlist young men as *Amis de la Légion* (or *Compagnons de France*), an organization modelled on Pétain's *Légion des Combattants volontaires française* and described by the American Ambassador in Vichy as "intended to become an effective Ku Klux Klan." If this move was intended to stem the steady exodus of youths fleeing the islands to enlist in the Free French forces, it failed in its purpose. Only twenty-one are said to have been recruited, sixteen of them government employees. One reason for the poor response was that, within two days of the adoption of the

*This was a branch of Pétain's *Légion française des Combattants*, subsequently (on August 31) converted into Vichy's single legal political party and renamed the *Légion française de Vétérans et des volontaires de la Révolution nationale* with a membership open to all.

decree formally establishing the *Amis de la Légion*, the Resistance published a "Notice to Fathers" which read in part:

The nazification of the country is being continued openly. A Hitler Youth organization is being built up. . . . Those who sign up will have to do whatever the Germanized France of Darlan requires of them for a thousand francs a month [$20]. Fathers, you are not reduced to selling your sons to the Germans for a thousand francs. You will not do it. You will remember that Jesus was sold for thirty pieces of silver.[21]

In addition to imitating the positive accomplishments of Pétain's National Revolution, de Bournat's rule also became more and more repressive. Every manifestation of Free French spirit was promptly denounced, proscribed, and where possible, suppressed. There were, of course, limits to what could be done without provoking open rebellion; dictatorship had to some extent to be tempered with diplomacy. Moreover, many of the measures tended to be more irritating than restrictive. The censorship, for example, handicapped opponents of the regime without crippling their activities. Copies of the militantly Free French Montreal weekly *Le Jour*, though officially banned, continued to find their way to the islands where they were eagerly passed from hand to hand and avidly read.* Equally ineffective were administration efforts to legislate against listening to foreign radio stations, including the BBC London and WRUL Boston, both of which broadcast regularly in French. Newfoundland programmes were also popular, though reports that efforts were made to jam them are untrue. Similarly, official attempts to encourage people to tune in to the daily diet of Vichy propaganda or worse served up by *Radio Saint-Pierre* and the *Voix de la France* were also largely unsuccessful. (De Bournat is alleged to have said that "there was no reason why London radio should be trusted more than the Rome or Berlin radio.") On one occasion, a thousand dollar reward was offered for information leading to the arrest of the author of an allegedly subversive song, *La nouvelle Marseillaise*.[22]

There were also reprisals against disloyal members of the public service, though their extent and severity are a matter of controversy. The Free French accusation that the Administrator had "instituted a regime of terror, threatening the partisans of Free France with repres-

---

*The *Petit Journal* too was sometimes confiscated, but the pro-Vichy *le Devoir* also of Montreal was always allowed in.

sive measures and dismissing numerous officials under no other pretext than that of their personal opinions" may have been exaggerated. But de Bournat's repudiation of these charges as "absolutely false and without any foundation" is nonsense. His actions at the time, and his reports to Vichy, tell a very different story. Admittedly, he realized it would be imprudent as well as impracticable to attempt to punish every official who had been misled by Free French propaganda. He did, however, single out particular individuals for reprimand, demotion, transfer, retirement, or outright dismissal. Others were intimidated by threats of disciplinary action. Since there were few other avenues of employment on the islands, this served as a pretty effective sanction. Finally, applicants for positions in the public service were carefully screened. When one young man applied for a job as fireman, de Bournat ordered the police (on July 9, 1941) to "please make enquiry, especially as to his morality, temperance, physical fitness and *attitude towards the government of the Marshal*." A week earlier, before awarding a scholarship, the Administrator had asked for a report on a student's "loyalty to the Marshal's government and the loyalty of his parents."[23]

In December, 1940, Emile Guillot, an outspoken Free French judge, was quietly posted to Martinique—though he defected to de Gaulle en route. On the 70th anniversary of the founding of the Third Republic (September 4), he had defied de Bournat publicly by flying the Tricolour from the kitchen window of his apartment above the Post Office overlooking the main square of the town. Even more daringly, he displayed the Cross of Lorraine in the same manner to commemorate Armistice Day and the entry of Free French forces into Libreville in the Gabon.[24] As head of the judiciary, Guillot was the second ranking official in the territory and Acting Administrator in the absence of de Bournat, as well as a member of the *Conseil d'Administration*, secretary of defence and chief censor. He was thus strategically placed to advise, encourage and protect the Resistance in many ways—which he did until the governor restricted his activities and eventually got rid of him.*

---

*Guillot was on the point of escaping to Newfoundland by dory at night when he was ordered to Fort-de-France, ostensibly on promotion. On arrival in Halifax, he was immediately sought out by the Canadian immigration authorities who offered him every assistance including political asylum. (On November 1, the Canadian Government had suggested his name to the Americans as a "possible alternative"

Although Guillot was the senior official opposed to the Vichy regime in the islands, he was by no means the only one against whom action was taken. Earlier, the islands' only veterinary had had his contract cancelled. The following April, de Bournat appointed an investigating commission composed of notorious *Vichyards* to inquire into "the attitude of certain local administrative officials or agents towards the policy of national regeneration" being pursued by Marshal Pétain. Among those dismissed as a result of its findings was Henry Humbert, the leader of the Resistance.[25] Later, Madame Henrietta Bonin, the headmistress of the girls' public school, was reprimanded and finally relieved of her duties; shortly afterwards, she left for the United States, returning only after the liberation of the islands. She had responded to de Gaulle's call to observe five minutes' silence at four o'clock on October 31, 1941, in memory of the more than one hundred innocent French hostages shot by the Germans in retaliation for the assassination of a few German soldiers.[26] Even a year later, long after the Free French liberation of the islands and de Bournat's return to France, Vichy was still merrily "firing" officials in St. Pierre!*[27]

The increasingly tyrannical nature of the de Bournat regime partly reflected the growing strength and confidence of the Resistance. The movement in St. Pierre and Miquelon was very different from its counterpart in France at a later date. In particular, it was less highly organized and did not indulge in any overt acts of violence. Nevertheless, it carried on a sustained campaign of defiance which kept the administration in a state of permanent uneasiness.

Although a large majority of the population was generally sympathetic to de Gaulle, the proportion of active *résistants* was comparatively small, numbering perhaps a hundred or so. They were

---

to de Bournat as Administrator.) However, Guillot preferred for personal reasons to go on to New York, which he did after a brief visit to Montreal to contact the Saint Pierrais community there. He joined Free France formally on January 6, 1941. Presumably de Bournat was fully aware that Guillot would defect, but was more concerned to have him out of St. Pierre than in Vichy hands. As chief censor of the colony, Guillot had been required to intercept all incoming and outgoing mail, including that of Archibald Bartlett, the British Vice-Consul.

*In October, 1942, three officials were dismissed: Auguste Goupillière, a postman, and Joseph Clochet and Léon Ruellan, both clerks. In January, 1942, Vichy had extended to St. Pierre and Miquelon emergency legislation imposing penalties for activities jeopardizing the security of the state.

informally organized into three strata which corresponded in part to different age groups. The core of the movement centred on the War Veterans Association, led by its courageous Secretary, Henry Humbert, the acknowledged *chef de la Résistance*. His closest collaborators were François LeBuf, President of the Association, and two young assistants, Armand Slaney and André Clément.* After the war all four were awarded the coveted *Médaille de la Résistance avec Rosette*, the last two posthumously.†28 Slaney and Clément represented a younger generation of daring leaders, most of whom were in their twenties.‡ They constituted perhaps the most active element in the Resistance and were responsible for its most dramatic exploits. Finally, there was a third group composed in the main of older persons, often parents or relatives of young *résistants*. They gave the movement strong moral and, where possible, material support and, after the liberation, formed a "Cross of Lorraine" Association which organized welfare service for the armed forces and published a weekly newspaper, *La Liberté*.§

The principal preoccupation of the Resistance was publicity. Scurrilous leaflets were secretly printed and distributed, and provocative posters plastered on walls in public places. One such notice, issued on February 9, 1941, called on the people to join in the votive mass for a British victory being celebrated by Cardinal Villeneuve in Montreal and in 1,500 parishes throughout Quebec that day.29 As usual, the posters were quickly torn down by the authorities and, in retaliation, some one would add a black swastika alongside de Bournat's signature on official notices. The most ambitious undertaking

---

*Others included: Joseph Clochet, Georges Daguerre, Auguste Goupillière, Joseph Grosvalet, M. Miadonnet, Henri Paturel, Louis Plantegenest, Gustave Roblot and Léon Ruellan. It is interesting to note, in view of the attitude later adopted by the United States, that Humbert's sister and Slaney were both employees of the American consulate in St. Pierre throughout this period.

†In addition, Auguste Goupillière earned the Legion of Honour and R. Autrui and Pierre Renou, the Military Medal partly for their Resistance activities. Joseph Renou, Fernand Ferron, and Auguste Sollier also received Resistance Medals although apparently for their service overseas in the military police, not in the St. Pierre underground. Sollier had in fact served as an auxiliary policeman under de Bournat.

‡Others included: Fernand Apestéguy, M. Beloir, Jean Boudreau, Georges Farvacque, M. Fouchard, H. Gautier, J. Hebditch, Pierre Renou, M. Roverch, and Joseph Vigneau.

§Among its members were: E. Admond, C. Barphayre, Mme. Henrietta Bonin, I. Boudreau, Pierre Olaïsola, F. and O. Olano, Joseph Renou (père) and Mlle. B. Slaney.

Resistance literature, St. Pierre and Miquelon, 1941

Les Journaux Canadiens sont de plus en plus censurés á **Saint-Pierre**

Canadiens! Ne laissez pas la gestapo nous nazifier! S'ils interdisent vos Journaux, refusez leur le ravitaillement.

Resistance literature, St. Pierre and Miquelon, 1941

was the publication of *L'Eclaireur*. Nearly a hundred issues of this underground news-sheet appeared prior to liberation. All of these propaganda outlets angrily denounced the *Vichyards* for collaborating with the enemy, harped on the economic plight of the people, clamoured unceasingly for a plebiscite—and effectively countered de Bournat's own rather pathetic *Bulletins documentaires d'information*.[30]

The bitter tone of much of the Resistance literature was indicative of the intensity of feeling dividing the rival camps. So firmly were political convictions held by partisans on both sides that it was not uncommon for longstanding friendships to dissolve under the strain and even for families to split. The small town character of St. Pierre also sharpened the clash of principles and accentuated the element of personal tragedy.

During 1941, the Resistance also organized public demonstrations of various kinds in support of de Gaulle, notably on New Year's Day when people stayed indoors between 3 and 4 o'clock in the afternoon, on Jeanne d'Arc Day (May 11) when they poured into the streets from 3 to 4 o'clock, on Bastille Day (July 14) and on Armistice Day. De Bournat, for his part, did his best to frustrate his opponents' plans and keep the situation under control. Celebration of the *fête nationale* was for instance postponed for a month. Nevertheless, about one hundred young men disregarded this decree and paraded defiantly in front of the governor's official residence. A number of those present were arrested for singing the *Marseillaise*, though most of them were quickly released.[31] The previous autumn, the date of the official ceremony commemorating armistice day had, as in France, been advanced to November 2 in deference to German feelings, but this procedure was not considered advisable in 1941. Instead, two competing services were held in front of the War Memorial—the official one at nine o'clock in the morning for a handful of *Vichyards* and the genuine one at eleven o'clock, sponsored by the recently dissolved War Veterans Association and attended by more than six hundred people, the largest gathering on record.[32]

Another means of proclaiming one's sympathy for de Gaulle was by flying the Free French Cross of Lorraine. Although de Bournat tried his best to ban "the wearing or exhibition in any manner of insignias, emblems and generally anything constituting a rallying symbol for any movement likely to disturb the peace," he failed to stamp out the practice. As early as the summer of 1940, Pierre Renou, an enterprising foreman at the government brickyard at Petit Barachois, Joseph Vigneau and Jacques Legassé laid out a thirty-foot Cross of Lorraine on the remote northwest slope of Cuquemel hill on Langlade where it was in full view of patrolling ships and planes, but difficult to see from the land. Eventually, after three months, the cross was discovered and Renou dismissed. Unable thereafter to obtain regular employment, he devoted his free time to resistance activities, organizing in July, 1941, a group of young men to assist him. Their most spectacular undertaking took place on the night of December 12, 1941, when they succeeded in tying a home-made Free French flag securely to the top of the 170-foot high radio mast, where it remained for nearly a week. At the same time, another Cross of Lorraine was boldly run up the flagpole outside de Bournat's residence.*[33]

Another incident occurred on May 27, 1941, when some workmen employed on a relief project "hissed" in characteristic French fashion at a policeman sent to haul down an illegal Free French flag. De Bournat reacted swiftly. "Such circumstances," he insisted, "cannot be tolerated, especially under present conditions. Please give the names of the workmen to the gendarmes and if at 5 p.m. tomorrow the culprits have not been found, all the workers will be dismissed for a week." Two unfortunates were in fact found and, in due course, sentenced to fines of fifty francs and six days in jail for this "outrage."[34]

Thirdly, the underground encouraged young men without family responsibilities to enlist in the Free French forces. In December, 1940, thirteen persons crossed to Newfoundland at night by dory, and others made the hazardous journey in later months.† They all carried identity cards, signed by Louis Plantegenest, the Chief Clerk of the court, testifying to their character and patriotism. This procedure proved necessary because two French seamen who escaped from the islands in the summer of 1940 were promptly arrested by the Newfoundland authorities, returned to St. Pierre, and jailed as deserters from their ships. They were released only because a sympathetic judge, Emile Guillot, in a celebrated decision, cleverly insisted on the

---

*Those involved were Pierre Renou, Joseph Vigneau, H. Gautier and J. Hebditch.
†Several sources quote exaggerated figures of 40 to 50, and one even says "about 150," but 20 seems more accurate.[35]

production of their police dossiers from occupied France before proceeding with the case. Although de Bournat has since suggested that he was "very happy whenever one of the young men of St. Pierre left" and never refused to issue a passport, this was certainly not the impression he created at the time. In fact, he promulgated a law specifically providing for the loss of nationality and the seizure of property of Frenchmen leaving the islands without permission. There were also instances of families of volunteers being persecuted or deprived of state support by, for instance, being struck off relief rolls, denied their rations of free coal, or refused educational assistance.[36]

The ultimate aim of the Resistance was to shed the yoke of Vichy oppression. After the events of the autumn of 1940, however, it became apparent that this could not be accomplished without outside support. Hence the flood of appeals to the Free French in London and Montreal, and to the British in St. John's to assist in the rescue. There was never any doubt in the minds of the people of St. Pierre and Miquelon that their prayers would be answered. Throughout the autumn of 1941, excitement mounted as the conviction grew that the day of liberation was approaching. When, therefore, early in December, the Voice of America announced Admiral Muselier's arrival in nearby Newfoundland, the news was greeted as a sure sign that deliverance was imminent. One Free Frenchman (Captain Flahaut) even cabled Muselier asking him to come to St. Pierre.[37]

Even so, the fear existed that intervention might come too late, that the presence of a Free French flotilla in the area might provoke de Bournat into some last desperate act of vengeance. The Resistance had already learned from a sympathetic gendarme, Sergeant-Major Roger Potier, of the existence of a government blacklist containing the names of some twenty-two leaders whom de Bournat intended to deport to Martinique for trial at the first available opportunity.* Among those marked down for banishment were the defiant veterans'

---

*It was believed locally that the cruiser *Emile Bertin* might turn up in St. Pierre at any moment. Actually, the aircraft carrier *Béarn* had planned to sail from Martinique, December 10, on a ten-day cruise in undisclosed waters to provide "recreation for the crew"—until Washington objected. Two days later, at American insistence, Vichy categorically forbade the movement of any French naval ships in the West Indies. The US Navy had orders to capture or sink any ship disregarding this ban.[38]

leaders, François LeBuf and Henry Humbert, as well as Archibald Bartlett who earlier had been forced to resign as British Vice-Consul.* Consequently, there was a certain urgency to the increasingly insistent pleas of the islanders for help.

*The existence of this blacklist was confirmed after the liberation of the islands. Others on the list included: A. Blancy, Maurice Briand, Emmanuel Casier-Ruault, André Clément, J. Clochet, Georges Daguerre, A. Desdouet, Albert Flahaut, Auguste Goupillière, Joseph Grosvalet, P. M. Lesenechal, Louis Plantegenest, Pierre Renou, Gustave Roblot, Léon Ruellan, and Armand Slaney. Several others had previously escaped to Newfoundland. According to one account, there were 120 names on the list.

3

INTERVENTION

From the first, General de Gaulle envisaged rallying St. Pierre and Miquelon to his cause as part of his plan to liberate all French colonies in the Americas. However, his hopes for an early and easy takeover were frustrated when, shortly after the Armistice, the armed fishery patrol ship *Ville d'Ys* made good its escape from St. John's, Newfoundland, and reached St. Pierre. De Gaulle's principal interest in the islands stemmed from his burning desire to bring as many French territories as possible back into the war on the Allied side and also to build up the prestige of his Free French movement. Following Mers-el-Kébir, he even contemplated retiring to St. Pierre, in the event of war between Britain and Vichy France, to carry on the struggle against Germany independently of his ally. As time progressed, he also felt a growing compulsion to liberate his countrymen overseas from an increasingly oppressive Vichy yoke. In the case of St. Pierre and Miquelon, there was the added consideration that both Newfoundland and Canada were suspected of having designs on it.[1]

There was no mistaking Newfoundland's acquisitive interest in St. Pierre and Miquelon. As early as June 27, 1940, Edward Emerson, Newfoundland's able Commissioner for Defence, then in Ottawa, boldly asserted his Government's claim to primacy in the islands. He sketched the broad outlines of a plan whereby Newfoundland would take over the general administration of the territory temporarily and govern it either directly, or indirectly through its French Administrator. Canada's role was envisaged as backing up Newfoundland's initiative with such financial and military assistance as was required. As a first step, Emerson proposed the despatch to the islands of a

joint mission composed of a senior Newfoundland administrative
official and a high-ranking Canadian naval or military officer to assess
conditions on the spot.

The British Government also showed an early and lively concern
with St. Pierre and Miquelon, though it was less disturbed over the
fate of the islands themselves than over the disposition of France's
Grand Banks fishing fleet, then seeking shelter and safety in St.
Pierre. Some thirty vessels in all were involved, including twelve
modern trawlers. Their return to France with their crews and cargoes
of fish would have constituted a substantial contribution to the
German war effort and a corresponding loss to the Allied cause. Even
if they remained in the Western Atlantic, it was always possible that
they might be used to report Allied shipping movements to the
German authorities. Accordingly, Raymond Gushue, a Newfoundland official then in New York, was ordered to St. Pierre in great
secrecy and haste to survey the situation. The reception he received
from the Administrator during his brief visit (June 29 to July 1) was
extremely hostile. As far as de Bournat was concerned, the war had
been lost and the sooner the British and Americans realized this, the
better. In his report to London, Gushue stressed the strategic importance of the trawlers, but advised against seizure of the islands.
Action by Newfoundland would be unwise in view of the legacy of
bitterness which remained from the centuries of rivalry. On the other
hand, Canadian occupation would arouse intense resentment in Newfoundland, while an American initiative would be unwelcome in both
St. John's and Ottawa. The best solution was to let the Free French
take over the islands, a view the British government consistently
adhered to throughout the next eighteen months of uncertainty. So
did Newfoundland at a later stage, but in the early summer of 1940
she inclined towards direct intervention. In an urgent telegram to
Ottawa on the morrow of Mers-el-Kébir, the Governor of Newfoundland urged that "in certain eventualities which at present seem not
unlikely, suitable military and naval action should be taken to prevent
the islands or French vessels there from hostile action against us or
British shipping." In his opinion, the presence of the *Ville d'Ys*
rendered "early action all the more necessary." The Governor added
that "we would cooperate in every possible way [with Canada] and

would be glad to be kept in touch with any action you may have in mind."*

Canadian interest in St. Pierre and Miquelon was both strategic and humanitarian. The fall of France caused something approaching panic in Canada regarding her exposed eastern seaboard. While Newfoundland was the principal worry, St. Pierre and Miquelon also occasioned concern. Both had been included within the Canadian defence perimeter at the outbreak of war, but at that time it was hardly foreseen that they might become liabilities. Confronted with an entirely new situation in June of 1940, the automatic reaction of the defence officials in Ottawa as elsewhere was to urge an immediate seizure of the French colony. C. G. Power, Acting Minister of National Defence, even intimated to the American Minister on June 29 that "if he had his way Canadian troops would occupy it."† However, the War Committee of the Cabinet had already decided two days earlier (in Moffat's words) to "take no action in the Western Hemisphere without first talking it over with us."[2] Ottawa was well aware that the prospect of Canadian military intervention in hemisphere affairs frightened the State Department only slightly less than violations of the Monroe Doctrine by other belligerents, as Greenland and Aruba had shown.‡ Clearly St. Pierre and Miquelon, which by comparison was much less important, was hardly worth the risk of incurring American wrath particularly at a time when Allied survival depended so greatly on Washington's willingness to provide emergency military aid.

*Moffat's claim,[3] based on a conversation next day (July 5) with King, that Newfoundland had been "pressing" Canada to occupy St. Pierre and Miquelon is inaccurate. What St. John's wanted was Canadian support to establish and maintain Newfoundland control of the islands, if necessary by force. Unilateral Canadian action would have created such a furore in Newfoundland that the prospects for close wartime collaboration with Canada might have been seriously prejudiced and the possibility of Union postponed indefinitely.

†The previous day, Ralston and Emerson had discussed the "Question of St. Pierre–Miquelon, particularly sustenance and [a] small force simply to exercise authority."

‡In April, 1940, Canada had proposed sending "a small defence force" (Force "X") to Greenland for the duration of the war but abandoned the idea because the State Department was "extremely anxious that no action of this kind be taken by the Canadian Government." On July 8, following a suggestion that Canadian rather than British guards might be more acceptable to the Americans as replacements for French troops in Aruba, Cordell Hull angrily insisted that "the same objection of this Government applies, although the situation would not be so acute in these circumstances." No Canadian troops were sent.[4]

At the same time, the War Committee asked for a report on the islands. On the basis of this, Rear-Admiral Nelles, the Chief of the Naval Staff, recommended on July 1 that Canada, possibly in conjunction with Newfoundland, should administer St. Pierre and Miquelon for the duration of the war in order to "deny the islands and fish products to the Germans *or the United States*." Later, consideration was given to sending the 6-inch gun cruiser HMS *Caradoc* to St. Pierre. Nelles, however, argued strongly against a policy of bluff. "Any policy which would involve such a showing of force, but leave the hands of the Senior Officer tied to such an extent that he would not be empowered to use the force in case it became necessary as proved to be the case at Oran" would weaken the Allied position rather than strengthen it. On July 6, in a second military appreciation on the islands, the Joint Planning Committee of the armed services advised that seizure of the islands would require a "superior naval force," a flight of bomber reconnaissance aircraft, and one company of troops at the most. The War Committee, however, was not impressed by the immediate military threat posed by the islands and recommended only periodic air patrols. Mackenzie King, in particular, opposed any drastic preventive action. While publicly reaffirming his earlier pledge to defend the islands,[5] he instinctively recoiled from anything involving the use of force, especially after the Royal Navy's attack on the French fleet and Vichy's diplomatic break with Britain. In the end, King's views prevailed in both Ottawa and St. John's.*[6]

On the economic side, Canada imposed no restrictions on trade with St. Pierre and Miquelon other than a system of export permits. The flow of supplies to the islands did stop for a time, but this was due to an absence of available shipping and to temporary exchange difficulties, and not to positive action on the part of the Canadian Government. Even the Vichy order warning all British ships that they would be fired on if they approached within twenty miles of any French possessions was ignored in Ottawa. St. John's, on the other hand, conscious of the presence of the *Ville d'Ys* at St. Pierre, took the threat seriously and on July 4 reacted by banning the clearance

*Only a few days earlier, King had rejected a British request to intercept a French cruiser, the *Emile Bertin*, escaping from Halifax harbour with $300 million in gold bullion aboard. Earlier, he had shared American objections to sending Canadian troops to Greenland. "Clearly our people had been a little over-zealous in preparing for a little war on Canada's own account."[7]

of all ships, including the steamer *Belle Isle*, from Newfoundland ports to St. Pierre.[8]

Following the rapid deterioration of the food situation in the islands, Canada took the initiative in seeking to restore normal trade relations. Accordingly, a joint mission such as Emerson had proposed earlier, composed of J. Hubert Penson, Newfoundland's Commissioner of Finance, and Commander J. W. R. Roy, RCN, Senior Naval Officer, Gaspé, visited St. Pierre July 17 to 20 for preliminary discussions with the Administrator on "the financial and economic difficulties" facing the islands and "related problems." These latter included the future of the fishing fleet, immobilization of the *Ville d'Ys*, and control of the cable station. What actually transpired at these meetings is a matter of controversy. Canada claimed that "a most friendly and helpful discussion" ensued, but de Bournat, at least in his reports to Vichy, painted a picture of himself standing up with "courtesy and firmness" to the almost irresistible demands of his powerful neighbours for the surrender of the trawlers. The pressure exerted jointly by the Canadian and Newfoundland representatives was, he claimed, "infinitely stronger" than that applied by Gushue alone three weeks earlier.[9]

While negotiations were still underway, Admiral Robert, Vichy High Commissioner in the French West Indies, entered the fray. On July 19, in a broadcast from Martinique, he launched a blistering attack on the Canadian Government accusing it in effect of attempting to starve the population of St. Pierre and Miquelon into submission. The Department of External Affairs, presumably with a view to the possible harmful effect of this statement on American opinion, issued an immediate and unusually strong denial which repudiated the charges as "completely untrue."

The assertion that the British (which presumably means the Canadian) authorities have stopped supplies from reaching the islands of St. Pierre and Miquelon has no basis in fact. No prohibition or restriction has been placed on the shipment of supplies to the islands.

The statement that such a blockade has been enforced because the local authorities had refused to surrender their fishing fleet is equally without foundation. No demand for such a surrender has been made, and consequently no refusal has been received.

The assertion that the French colonists have now been reduced to the choice of eating fresh or salted codfish is, of course, absurd.

In St. John's, Edward Emerson was equally categorical; Robert's charges, he retorted had no foundation whatsoever.[10]

Admittedly, the Canadian Government's carefully worded press release did not reveal quite the full story. The joint mission did not actually threaten de Bournat with sanctions, but it certainly warned him bluntly that "any deviation from strict neutrality would evoke a very strong reaction." According to Penson, "We told the Administrator that, whilst we were not trying to force upon him any change in political allegiance, the Allied Governments would be compelled to take strong economic measures if the Islands' Administration took any steps, whether under pressure or not, which gave support and help to the enemy or seemed likely to do so in our view." This was only elementary prudence in view of de Bournat's attitude. Though, outwardly at least, most cordial,

he gave no evidence of any sympathy at all for the Allied cause, of which so recently he himself was a part. Moreover, he seemed quite incapable of understanding our own attitude. He expressed surprise again and again that we were not prepared to accept mere assurances that nothing would be done inconsistent with the strict neutrality of his Government. . . . I think that both Commander Roy and myself left with the impression that the Administrator could not be regarded as a friend, and that there was a definite danger that he might yield rather easily to pressure from the German side.

—a view which confirmed Gushue's assessment of de Bournat a few weeks earlier. In particular, while de Bournat gave a written guarantee that he would not permit the Axis powers use of the territory for any purpose, he was unwilling to give anything more than verbal assurance that he would promptly report any enemy activity observed in the area. In the circumstances, Penson is clearly correct in concluding that "the real guarantee was the economic sanction, however reluctant any of us might have been to enforce it."[11]

Naturally, the Canadian Government did not want to admit this publicly; nor did it have to. Admiral Robert's charges, whether out of malice or mere ignorance, so misrepresented Canadian policy that they were easily dismissed. They attributed to the present what was at best only a possibility for the future. Actually, by this time, relations with St. Pierre and Miquelon were almost back to normal. During the previous week, Newfoundland had partially lifted the embargo on ships calling in at the islands—after assurances that they would be cordially and safely received.[12] Nevertheless, the Vichy outburst undoubtedly achieved what was in all probability its primary purpose: to commit the Allies publicly to the hands-off policy they had already decided upon privately. "Neither the Canadian nor the Newfoundland Government," the Canadian press statement concluded, "has the slightest intention or desire to interfere with the existing administration or status of the Islands."[13] In thus clarifying the situation, Robert eased the Administrator's task in his negotiations in Ottawa and Washington the following week.

The results of de Bournat's first mission to the mainland in late July were impressive.* Arrangements were made for financing purchases of food and other essential supplies in the United States and Canada and for restoring shipping services interrupted after the Armistice, thus assuring the colony's economic survival—and prolonging Vichy rule.† In return de Bournat agreed to three Canadian requests. These were, according to his own slightly dubious interpretation, "first, that the political status quo be maintained in the islands; second, that [the Department of External Affairs] be informed by telegram of any unexpected naval movements around the islands which we might observe; and third, that I do whatever I could to maintain public order in St. Pierre."[14]

This settlement suited the American temper perfectly. As already indicated, Washington was extremely sensitive to political developments anywhere in the Western Hemisphere and was determined to ensure that, if action was required in St. Pierre and Miquelon, it should be undertaken by the United States alone or the American states jointly and not by the British, the Free French, or even the Canadians on their own. Consequently, the State Department was alarmed at reports that Canadian authorities were contemplating tak-

---

*De Bournat conferred with Canadian officials and the Vichy Minister in Ottawa on July 22 and 31 on his way to and from Washington.

†Both the Resistance and the administration assumed that Washington and Ottawa were well aware of the political consequences of their policies, and were, at the very least, not unhappy with them. Free French partisans were bitter because the merchants who profited most from the revival of trade with the mainland were *Vichyards*. George Massé, in a letter to *Le Jour*, commented that "we think in St. Pierre that Canadian commercial firms should take steps to end the anti-British propaganda of their local agents."[15]

ing the islands into protective custody, and anxiously pressed for assurances that this was not the case. On July 5, 1940, Mackenzie King, who was naturally cautious even without American prompting, readily reassured the American Minister in the most unambiguous terms that there would be no unilateral Canadian occupation of St. Pierre and Miquelon, a pledge which was reaffirmed on several subsequent occasions.[16]

The Americans for their part agreed on August 1 to consult with the Canadian Government on means of co-operation immediately any danger arose which compelled them to take defensive measures in the islands. This understanding confirmed what was already implicit in RAINBOW 4, the emergency plan drawn up in May and June providing for preclusive American occupation of all Western Hemisphere possessions of defeated European nations. Under this plan, any military action in Newfoundland, and presumably in St. Pierre and Miquelon too, was to be undertaken in collaboration with Canada.[17]

United States interest in the security of these islands was also evident in the decision of the State Department in August to reopen its consulate in St. Pierre—a move which the German Embassy in Washington attributed to "American imperialism." For many years, there had been a Vice-Consul stationed in St. Pierre principally to report on the activities of smugglers, but with the ending of prohibition his presence was no longer required. "We have given careful consideration to every aspect of the matter," Sumner Welles wrote to the President in the fall of 1939, "and are of the opinion that the office should be closed." He added, "We do not see any way in which the maintenance of a consular officer in St. Pierre-Miquelon would be helpful in the enforcement of our neutrality legislation." Roosevelt agreed and the consulate closed its doors early in the New Year. Seven months later, on August 28, 1940, it was hurriedly reopened.[18]

The sudden flurry of interest which St. Pierre and Miquelon's neighbours displayed in the summer of 1940 created some uneasiness in Free French circles. As a result, late in August, Admiral Emile Muselier, Commander-in-Chief of the Free French Naval Forces (FNFL), drew the attention of the British Admiralty to his interest in the colony. His immediate concern was the fate of the fishing fleet which he was determined to keep out of the hands of both the Germans and the British. When, in September, the British requisitioned two trawlers in St. John's, Muselier lodged a vigorous protest in London. He considered that all the French trawlers should be offered the chance of rallying to de Gaulle. In the case of those tied up in St. Pierre, he proposed sending the destroyer *Triomphant* to escort them to Britain—and incidentally "to take advantage of the opportunity to take possession of the islands in the name of Free France."[19]

Meanwhile, following the second Gushue mission to the islands and the militant declaration of St. Pierre veterans on September 14, 1940, in support of de Gaulle, both the British Government and the General, then in Freetown, concluded that the time had come to attempt a coup in the islands. Four days later, the British promised economic and naval assistance to all colonies rallying to Free France and, the following day, they asked Canada to do the same in the case of St. Pierre and Miquelon. On October 11, Admiral Muselier submitted a plan of operations to the Admiralty. A week later, however, the British abruptly withdrew their support "for political reasons."[20]

One factor in the collapse of the scheme was undoubtedly the attitude of the Americans. In appealing to the Canadians for moral support, the British had emphasized that the action contemplated would, as in French Equatorial Africa and Tahiti, take the form of "an internal local movement without external assistance" and would not, therefore, violate the sacrosanct no-transfer principle. But this argument failed to impress the State Department, which re-affirmed its opposition to any outside intervention, however indirect.

Of more immediate importance in deterring the British was the crisis in relations with Vichy. While Marshal Pétain appeared to be feeling his way cautiously towards a modus vivendi with Britain through an unofficial intermediary, Professor Rougier, who arrived in London on October 22, at the same time he seemed to be slipping into much closer collaboration with Germany. On October 24, he met Hitler at Montoire and four days later appointed Laval his foreign minister.* With so much at stake, it is understandable that

*The secret Protocol drawn up at Montoire affirmed, among other things, that: "The Axis powers and France have a common interest in bringing about the defeat of England with the least possible delay. Consequently, the French Government will support, within the bounds of possibility, the measures taken to this end by the Axis

Britain was anxious, as Lord Halifax explained to de Gaulle a few days later, "to avoid any provocative action which might turn the scale against us particularly with regard to [the] crucial question of the Fleet and naval and air bases" in Africa. London did not want a repetition of the recent *débâcle* at Dakar.[21]

Although the British felt compelled to give up the idea of an early coup in St. Pierre, they had no intention of abandoning it altogether. Moreover, Vichy and Washington's views did not affect policy concerning the trawlers. Britain was still determined to prevent, if possible, their return to France with their record catch of fish. This amounted to about 20,000 tons, enough to meet half of France's annual domestic requirements of salted cod.[22] With this in mind, Raymond Gushue and F. A. J. Laws visited St. Pierre in mid-September in an attempt to persuade the trawler captains to sail their ships to a British port, charter them to the Allies for the duration of the war, sell their cargoes and permit their crews to enlist in the Free French forces, or return to France if they so wished. These efforts failed, as the officers were reluctant to commit themselves to the Allied cause because of legal scruples and the fear of reprisals against their families in France.

Matters came to a head a month later following de Bournat's return from his second mission to Washington and Ottawa with secret orders from Vichy to organize the escape of the fleet to Casablanca. Oil for the ships was provided by a tanker that sneaked into St. Pierre for this purpose. During the night of October 15, the first of the trawlers slipped out of harbour, and the rest sailed at intervals over the next two months.[23]

The Resistance promptly tipped off the British who reacted immediately by asking Canada to help intercept the ships, but Mackenzie King could see "no justification" for this.*

---

powers. The details of this collaboration in practice will be established in a special convention between Germany and Italy, on the one hand, and France on the other." In his broadcast on October 30, Pétain declared: "I have accepted the Fuehrer's invitation freely. I have not submitted to any *dictat*, to any pressure from him. Collaboration between our two countries has been envisaged. I have accepted it in principle."[24]

*A year later, Canada requisitioned the trawler *Cap Bleu* being built in Nova Scotia for the St. Pierre and Miquelon Government as well as the French freighter *Maurienne*. The *Cap Bleu* was turned over to the Free French authorities in St. Pierre in 1942.

We were not at war with France [he recorded in his diary on October 19] and were not going to precipitate a situation on this side which would make Canada responsible for [a] widening of the breach. I learned from Skelton [Under-Secretary of State for External Affairs] that Lapointe [Minister of Justice] was strongly of my view. Angus Macdonald [Navy Minister] was not too certain. Thought they would be damned for what they did or did not. Ralston [Minister of National Defence] inclined to carry out the will of the British Admiralty and left the matter up to me.

King then added: "I am positive I am right. It proves the wisdom of our maintaining strong the position of a nation making its own decisions and not having decisions made by the British Admiralty through its control of all naval forces."[25]

Despite Canada's refusal to co-operate, the Royal Navy did succeed in capturing at least two of the twelve trawlers and another ran aground, but most of them managed to reach France—not North Africa which was their original destination—where they fell into the hands of the Germans. The following April, a schooner fleet with German clearance papers again sailed for the Grand Banks. This time, however, all but two of the ships were intercepted by the British.*[26]

The presence in St. Pierre of the *Ville d'Ys*, a naval sloop of World War I vintage armed with three 3.9-inch and two 3-inch guns, was a continuing source of controversy throughout the summer and autumn of 1940. According to René Ristelhueber, the Vichy Minister in Canada, during de Bournat's visit to Ottawa in July,

The Canadian Government demanded the withdrawal of the *Ville d'Ys* whose presence was declared unceasingly to be a danger. Unfortunately, for reasons of prestige, the Vichy Government was in no hurry to settle the dispute which was becoming irritating because it kept cropping up in discussions. . . . The Canadian authorities . . . insisted on the departure of the *Ville d'Ys*. When Vichy turned a deaf ear to this idea, Ottawa suggested that the ship be disarmed and her guns taken ashore. This too was an unacceptable solution.[27]

*Earlier, in July, as a result of the Roy-Penson visit to St. Pierre, the British and Canadian governments had permitted one trawler to sail to Martinique to relieve the food shortage in the French West Indies. On December 5, 1940, as the last of the trawlers was about to escape, R. B. Hanson, Conservative Leader of the Opposition in the Canadian House of Commons, wrote to ask the Prime Minister to ensure that the ships did not return in the spring. Five months later, Hanson wrote again to express concern at the possibility of a breach of the Allied food blockade of Europe. On each occasion, King replied confidently that the Government was in close touch with the situation and was fully alive to the threat.

Actually both suggestions—withdrawal or immobilization—came originally from Ristelhueber himself who obviously considered them reasonable requests. Vichy and de Bournat, on the other hand, were reluctant to comply as they rightly feared that the withdrawal of French naval power from St. Pierre at this time would result in the colony rallying to de Gaulle. Early in September, the French authorities formally agreed "as a matter of courtesy" to send the *Ville d'Ys* away, but delayed implementing their decision for nearly two months because of the serious political unrest in the territory which came to a head shortly afterwards. Only on November 1, after Canada had held up the release of further funds and the British Admiralty had given the Vichy sloop a guarantee of safe passage to the West Indies for a limited time only, was the *Ville d'Ys* recalled to Martinique and disarmed. That same day, the Canadian Minister in Washington conferred with Under-Secretary of State Sumner Welles on possible joint courses of action in St. Pierre and Miquelon if Vichy France pursued an actively hostile policy, as seemed likely following Pétain's collaborationist broadcast two days earlier. However, the immediate crisis soon passed and, with the overthrow of Laval in December, the danger of France slipping into close alliance with Germany seemed for a while to recede. Thus, as a result of developments in both St. Pierre and Vichy, the islands ceased for a brief wintry interlude to attract the active attention of the outside world.

The question of St. Pierre and Miquelon came to the fore again in the spring of 1941 as a result of two developments. One was the intensification of the Battle of the Atlantic, and the other the fresh ascendancy of collaborationist elements in Vichy.

Early in 1941, German surface raiders penetrated farther into the northwest Atlantic and in greater strength than ever before. The pocket battleship *Admiral Scheer* and the heavy cruiser *Admiral Hipper* were on the prowl and, in May, the *Bismarck* and the *Prinz Eugen* were thrown into battle. In one two-day period in mid-March, the powerful battle-cruisers *Scharnhorst* and *Gneisenau* sank sixteen ships outward bound from Halifax within four or five hundred miles of St. John's. "As regards raiders," Churchill reported to Roosevelt following this disaster, "one great danger point is off Newfoundland, as we have a very large amount of shipping proceeding independently through this area." The submarine menace was also mounting. In March, U-boat operations were extended a further six hundred miles out to sea—as far west as 40°. As a consequence, shipping losses in the area shot up sharply, and at times British imports fell below the minimum for bare existence. In the circumstances, it was understandable that London and Ottawa should express growing concern over the possibility that St. Pierre and Miquelon might be providing the Axis with information and assistance. They would have been even more worried if they had known that, on May 17, the Vichy Minister of Colonies had sent de Bournat an "extremely urgent" telegram informing him that "the Marshal has adopted the principle of collaboration with Germany" and asking him to act accordingly.[28]

Meanwhile, on land, a major German pincer movement directed against Suez from either end of the Mediterranean appeared in prospect, with every indication that Pétain was willing to assist by opening the door to the enemy in the Levant and North Africa. The instructions sent to the French Delegate General in Syria clearly indicate Vichy's attitude at this time: "France is not in the position of a neutral Power with respect to Germany. It is not possible to treat the armed forces of Germany as hostile, but you would naturally oppose with force any intervention by the British."[29] On May 8, Vichy did in fact admit the Germans into Syria; and, four days later, Admiral Darlan, with Pétain's public blessing, conferred with Hitler at Berchtesgaden. Further negotiations ensued culminating in the Paris Protocols of May 28. These defined the supplies and facilities which Vichy was to make available in Syria, authorized the establishment of German bases in Dakar and Bizerte, and provided that the French navy would convoy German supplies in French ships across the Mediterranean to Rommel. The details of this capitulation were, of course, not available to the British and Americans, but enough was known to cause them the gravest concern. This, and the presence of the *Bismarck* in the Western Atlantic, prompted Roosevelt to declare an Unlimited National Emergency on May 27.

The repercussions of these dramatic events were felt around the world and led to a revival of interest in the situation in St. Pierre and Miquelon. In both Canada and the United States newspapers demanded that the territory be taken into protective custody. Appeals for aid from St. Pierrais themselves were also being received with increasing regularity.*[30] Newfoundland too was "much exercised" about the islands and, when Emerson visited Ottawa in April, 1941, renewed her pressure on Canada to do something about them. Even Roosevelt, unknown to his own State Department and contrary to its declared policies, "kept interrogating Mr. Mackenzie King as to what Canada intended to do about the islands." The President had been shocked by a report—which turned out to be untrue—that twenty-five German officers were arriving in the French West Indies, and immediately ordered a thorough investigation into all French possessions in the Western Hemisphere, including St. Pierre and Miquelon. "This is coming pretty close to home," he commented on April 26 to two of his cabinet members.[31]

Publicly, the Canadian Government continued to play down the importance of the islands. Twice during the latter half of May when the matter was raised in the House of Commons, Mackenzie King dismissed it with soothing assurances that the Government was "fully informed about the situation" and that there was "no occasion for concern on the part of the people of Canada in reference to either St. Pierre or Miquelon."[32] The Department of External Affairs and the Department of National Defence, however, took a rather graver view of the question and continued to press for action to protect Canada's interests. Privately, even King was not as confident as he tried to pretend. Besides, he had domestic political reasons for welcoming an increased emphasis on hemispheric defence. Accordingly, on May 16, he sought permission of the Vichy Minister in Ottawa to send Inspector Oscar LaRivière of the Royal Canadian Mounted Police to St. Pierre to survey the situation there.[33] The declared purpose of this mission was to investigate the smuggling of liquor into Prince Edward Island (which was still under prohibition), but the real motive was of course to report on political developments and

---

*"I am echoing my compatriots," said Robert Busnot, a St. Pierre businessman then living in Montreal, in May, 1941, "in asking your Prime Minister to send a ship without delay to protect our defenceless archipelago. Our colony is not fortified and it aspires to enter your great Dominion. I do not exaggerate in affirming that the arrival of a Canadian warship would be welcomed with rapture. That day would be a holiday."[34]

security arrangements. LaRivière was in fact fully briefed by Norman Robertson, Under-Secretary of State for External Affairs, before his departure.

The situation in St. Pierre and Miquelon, as Inspector LaRivière found it (May 26 to June 11), was substantially as it had been the previous summer. The one major revelation in his report concerned the existence of a powerful shortwave transmitting station in constant communication with Bordeaux and Fort-de-France. This vital bit of intelligence had somehow escaped attention in the past. It now became the major point of concern. While de Bournat tried hard to create the impression that the people were content with Vichy rule, La Rivière returned convinced that the vast majority were overwhelmingly Gaullist in sentiment. Any apparent acquiescence was due to the fact that so many of them were dependent for their livelihood on a small group of *Vichyard* merchants and officials. De Bournat assured La Rivière that he "would not, under any consideration, allow any Germans or Italians to enter the island for any purpose whatsoever." He had, he said, already refused entry to a number of Italian fishermen—although he had extended shelter and hospitality to RCAF air-sea rescue craft.* At the same time, he made it clear that he was equally determined to oppose occupation of the colony by any of its neighbours. The most he would accept was a Canadian consul—which he greatly preferred to a British or Newfoundland representative. The British Vice-Consulate in St. Pierre had in fact been closed two months earlier after de Bournat had forced Archibald Bartlett, a moving spirit in the Resistance, to resign as honorary vice-consul.[35] However, Bartlett, as Superintendent of the Western Union cable office, continued to reside in St. Pierre and promised LaRivière that he would warn Canada and Newfoundland by cable, or, if necessary, by dory of any enemy activity in the islands.

The problem of St. Pierre and Miquelon was as much political as military. The question was not only whether to intervene, but also who should exercise whatever control was required. Despite the façade of wartime co-operation, each of St. Pierre and Miquelon's

---

*The *OK Service IV*, under the command of F/O John Howell, put into St. Pierre on January 24, 1941, ostensibly to replenish her supply of fresh water. She sailed next day practically awash. RCAF officers at Dartmouth Air Station spent much of one night unloading her. Howell was a familiar figure in St. Pierre in rum-running days.

neighbours considered the islands came within its own sphere of influence. Newfoundland, as the weakest partner, was the most anxious to stake her claim. In a lengthy telegram to Ottawa on May 21, 1941, the Governor expressed the interest of his Government with uncommon frankness:

It would, we suggest, be unwise to overlook the possibility of control of United States over the islands becoming permanent if they assume it now for the duration of the War. We assume that the Canadian Government would view such an eventuality with the greatest concern. So far as Newfoundland is concerned, such a result would be truly disastrous. In the past, French control of the islands within 10 miles of our coasts has necessitated heavy expenditure in customs protective service and substantial loss of revenue in spite of all our efforts. The competition in salt cod fish industry, which has been heavily subsidized for many years, has caused us incalculable loss.

The establishment of the United States in St. Pierre and Miquelon would make it possible for them to dominate Newfoundland politically, and if they so desired, to threaten the independence of our fisheries, e.g., by establishing a fresh cod industry at St. Pierre. The assumption of civil control by the United States would raise a storm of protest of the strongest kind from our people. In view of relations between Canada and the United States there would arise in their minds a sense of betrayal by Canada of a British interest which at this particular time might have serious repercussions.

If control of the islands is to pass out of Vichy's hands we presume that we have a common desire that they become British, that is, either Newfoundland or Canada. Geographically they are as much a part of this country as any other islands that surround our coast, and in this respect bear the same relation to Newfoundland as Magdalen Islands and Anticosti do to Canada. There is easy and frequent intercourse between the two peoples. They can be administered most easily by our Government. In fact there is so little to justify control passing from Vichy to any Government but that of Newfoundland that feeling would be almost as great (though for different reasons) to our losing control to Canada as it would be if we lost it to the United States.

Under these circumstances we urge . . . that the Canadian Government use its best endeavours to ensure that if civil control of the islands is to pass from Vichy hands, that it be entrusted to the Newfoundland Government.

In his reply a few days later, Mackenzie King did his best to reassure the Governor concerning American intentions and motives. "In our opinion there is not the least likelihood of the United States

taking control of the islands. . . . We are confident that your apprehension that the United States may seize control is groundless."
He added that if it ever did prove necessary to interfere with the
political status of the colony, consideration would have to be given
to "all pertinent factors including, of course, the views and desires of
the residents of the Islands." In view of the tradition of friction
between the two territories, this Canadian qualification virtually
ruled out the possibility of a Newfoundland takeover. As Inspector
La Rivière reported a few weeks later, the population of St. Pierre
and Miquelon was not averse to control by Canadians or Americans
—"preferably the latter, for financial reasons"—but "occupation by
Newfoundland troops would not be so favourably received."

While the Newfoundland Government's reaction to the growing
American concern with St. Pierre and Miquelon was unduly alarmist,
its fears were not quite as fanciful as King seemed to suggest. Indeed,
the very day that the Governor appealed to Ottawa, Senator James
M. Mead of New York wrote Secretary of State Hull to urge the
acquisition (though not ownership) of the archipelago as a defence
base for the duration of the war.[36] Three days later, on May 24,
Major-General H. D. G. Crerar, the Chief of the Canadian General
Staff, wrote that although "as far as I can judge, they [the Americans]
would not be desirous of participating" in any Canadian operation in
St. Pierre and Miquelon, "if we do not act, they will, and I am sure
it would be preferable for us to do so." A month later, Navy Minister
Macdonald also argued for preventive Canadian intervention in the
event of open hostilities between Britain and Vichy France. "If the
Canadian Government fails to act quickly and vigorously," he insisted,
"the United States Government is almost certain to do so. Any such
action on the part of the United States would inevitably prove most
embarrassing, and the situation would be further complicated by the
position in regard to St. Pierre and Miquelon taken up by the Newfoundland Government."

There is no doubt that American interest in the islands at this
time was genuinely defensive. Although President Roosevelt's ideas
on hemispheric policy often differed from those of official Washington,
he was accurately reflecting American public opinion when he
informed the new Canadian Minister on March 12, 1941, that the
United States had no interest in acquiring St. Pierre and Miquelon

after the war. (At the same time, he invited Canada to consider the possibility of taking them over.) Even Senator Mead was adamant that the United States had "no imperialistic aspirations and that the defence of the Western Hemisphere is our sole objective."[37] Where the Americans can be criticized is in refusing to recognize Newfoundland's legitimate claim to a voice in determining the fate of the islands. As early as November 1, 1940, Sumner Welles had told the Canadian Minister that it would be undesirable to associate St. John's directly or formally with any action Washington and Ottawa might take in St. Pierre and Miquelon as Newfoundland was still virtually a crown colony.

The Americans remained, in fact, firmly opposed to outside intervention by anyone including the Canadians. Throughout the late spring of 1941, the United States repeatedly pressed Canada for renewed assurances that she would respect her undertaking of the previous summer "not to make any overt move in St. Pierre-Miquelon without full advance consultation with us." If any change in the status quo proved necesary, the most acceptable solution in Washington's view would be an international trusteeship shared by more than one American state. Commenting on this possibility in the course of a conversation in late May with Pierrepont Moffat, the American Minister in Ottawa, Norman Robertson gave it as his personal opinion that "the idea of a trusteeship was not impossible if Canada were given the lion's share of responsibility." He added, however, that " in this case Canada would probably delegate as much authority as possible to a local Free French Government."[38]

A few days later, following a further deterioration in relations with Vichy, King recorded in his diary that he feared "war with France . . . and [the] turning over of French fleet and bases to the Germans." This concern was reflected in a hardening in the Canadian attitude. That same day, June 3, Robertson reported to the American Minister that "the Canadian Government was leaning more and more towards encouraging the de Gaulle group to take over St. Pierre-Miquelon [as] that would solve all their problems without getting involved in too many technicalities." Thomas Stone, another official of the Department, went even further; he told Moffat bluntly that "Canada should take [the islands] over at once." The following month, while in Washington, Moffat warned Sumner Welles of the mounting pressure on Canada to occupy St. Pierre and Miquelon. Welles hit the roof. He immediately instructed Moffat "to tell Mr. King and the Canadian Government in no uncertain terms that they must play ball with us on that particular issue," which Moffat did in rather more diplomatic language.[39] What Washington would have said, if it had known that Canada had a top secret plan, Operation "Q", for the occupation of the islands, can only be imagined.

Canadian military action in the islands had been briefly considered, shortly after the fall of France, at the time the Americans were preparing their own plans for the emergency seizure of Martinique and Guadeloupe. Revival of the idea in the spring of 1941 stemmed in part from an offer on May 19 from Jean Callède, president of the Free French Committee in Winnipeg, to "head a small expeditionary party of Free French volunteers, all willing to be dropped by parachute or any other suitable means over the islands, seize them and protect them from enemy invasion." This particular brainwave was not, as one would expect, immediately dismissed as impracticable. Instead, it received serious consideration at the highest levels in Ottawa, mainly because it captured the imagination of Col. Ralston, the Minister of National Defence, but also, no doubt, because of the dramatic success of the German airborne assault on Crete on May 20 and the recent appalling shipping losses in the Western Atlantic. In a memorandum prepared at the request of the Minister and designed perhaps to humour him, General Crerar indicated that, "as the operation contemplated is not a capture or annexation, at least I presume it is not, the utilization of Free French would seem to have a good deal to commend it." Despite this support, Ralston failed to convince his colleagues in the War Committee of the Cabinet that the scheme was feasible, as it certainly was not. Callède's offer was accordingly declined, though the explanation given was that "the international situation does not justify such action on the part of Canada."[40]

Nevertheless, the War Committee's decision of May 27 to reject any immediate consideration of Canadian intervention did not end the matter, as the Chiefs of Staff had already ordered their Joint Planning Committee to study this possibility. Its memorandum of May 22 on "Action Necessary for the Occupation of St. Pierre and Miquelon" was necessarily pretty sketchy. It did, however, form the basis for future policy on the subject. The next day, this outline proposal was approved in principle by the Chiefs of Staff, and referred to the Joint Service Committee in Halifax for detailed operational planning. On June 6, Major-General W. H. P. Elkins, General Officer Commanding-in-Chief, Atlantic Command, convened the Committee in "most secret" session to discuss the matter. Five days later, an elaborate Appreciation and Plan were forwarded to Ottawa. The Plan, as drafted by Colonel L. C. Goodeve,* envisaged a landing force composed basically of one infantry rifle company of *Les Fusiliers de Sherbrooke*, supported by a destroyer, two corvettes, and a bomber reconaissance squadron.† In agreeing to the Plan with amendments on June 28, the Chiefs of Staff Committee laid particular stress on the importance of being ready to move on short notice. Angus Macdonald added that "the object of our occupation would be to prevent . . . the use of these islands by the enemy as a refuelling, victualling and rest base for submarines or aircraft, and as a centre for the collection and transmission of enemy intelligence."

The mounting evidence of Vichy's increasing collaboration with Germany also led the British, and even more the Free French, to reassess the St. Pierre and Miquelon situation. Early in 1941, Emile Guillot, who had recently escaped from the islands, prepared a comprehensive report for General de Gaulle on political, administrative and economic conditions in the colony. Then, in March, Captain Thierry d'Argenlieu established contact with the Resistance in the islands. He was thus able, on his return to London, to furnish Admiral Museilier with the latest information on developments there. The whole question of their liberation was then discussed at a session of

---

*Most of the officers directly involved in Operation "Q" were first World War veterans who were too old for active service overseas in the second. For many of them, the prospect of a descent on St. Pierre was the highlight of the war. After all, it was only the second occasion in history that the Canadian Army had contemplated launching a military invasion from Canadian soil. The first was the proposed Greenland expedition in April, 1940.

†The Secretary to the Canadian Chiefs of Staff proposed that, as in the case of the Greenland plan, a small RCMP detachment should accompany the expedition to assist in civil administration. He also considered that the corvettes alone would provide an adequate show of naval force. Although no organized opposition at the landing was anticipated, the unexpectedly fierce resistance of the Vichy forces in Syria following the Anglo-Free French invasion on June 8 perhaps explains why planners viewed the operation as an invasion of enemy territory. Also, intelligence sources had reported (incorrectly) the presence of an armed trawler at St. Pierre and the existence of a 4-inch gun at Cape Aigle protecting the entrance to the harbour.

the *Conseil supérieur de la Marine* early in June—on the very day that Canadian military leaders were meeting in Halifax to draw up plans for occupation of the islands. The military problems involved in a Free French take-over were not very formidable. The only Vichy warship in the area had returned to Martinique months earlier, while the local population was known to be keen to free itself from Vichy oppression. On the other hand, there were persuasive political arguments for proceeding with caution, principally fear of Vichy's retaliation against liberated territories in Equatorial Africa and the Pacific, and American disapproval. Accordingly, it was decided to wait until the political climate improved but, in the meantime, to take steps to locate Free French naval forces in the vicinity of St. Pierre and Miquelon. With this in mind, Muselier asked the British to assign the three corvettes, which the Free French had recently acquired, to convoy duty on the North Atlantic; and this was done. The Admiralty had in fact already decided, in view of the extension of submarine warfare westward, to establish a Newfoundland Escort Force under Canadian command and to include in it units of certain European allies. As a result, FNFL ships were frequently in and around St. John's within easy striking distance of St. Pierre and in close touch with the situation there.*[41]

When in July, 1941 the Free French decided to send the destroyer *Triomphant* under the command of Captain Auboyneau to the Pacific, Muselier proposed to the British that she should stop at St. Pierre on the way "to give encouragement to the island to declare for General de Gaulle." On July 9, London passed the proposal on to Ottawa, though not to Washington. Even before taking up the matter with the Americans, Canada replied asking that nothing should be done until she had had an opportunity to give the matter much fuller

---

*The Newfoundland Escort Force was formally established as a separate command on June 6, 1941—on the same day as the meetings of the Joint Service Committee in Halifax and Muselier's *Conseil supérieur* in London. Two days earlier, the first of the Free French corvettes, the *Mimosa*, had been assigned to the Western Approaches Escort Force based on Liverpool but, as a result of Muselier's representations, this order was suspended on June 7. On June 17, the *Mimosa* was allocated to the Newfoundland Force, arriving in St. John's on July 16. The *Alysse* and *Aconit* were also originally slated for service in the Western Approaches, but they too were re-allocated to St. John's (on June 16 and July 2), reaching there on August 2 and October 19 respectively. Three other Free French corvettes, the *Renoncule*, the *Roselys* and the *Lobelia* joined the Newfoundland Force in February and March 1942.

consideration.* She anticipated—correctly—a hostile reaction in the State Department. This divergence in policy between Britain and the United States put Canada in an uncomfortable position and, as so often in such circumstances, she hesitated. When representatives of the three Canadian services and External Affairs met on July 21 to discuss the situation, they were unable to reach any agreement. Ten days later, London again pressed Ottawa for an answer, but then quietly dropped the matter. While the British considered St. Pierre and Miquelon a serious threat to their ocean lifeline, they were also aware that they might "lose heavily on the deal if the Germans were able to use a successful Free French operation in St. Pierre as a lever for obtaining further concessions in North Africa."[42] Thus, the immediate opportunity passed. The *Triomphant* called in at St. John's, but sailed right by St. Pierre.[43]

Marshal Pétain's address to the French people on August 12, 1941, in which he praised Germany for her campaign in Russia "in defence of a civilization" and announced the establishment of a full-fledged authoritarian regime, produced another flutter of excitement in the press and elsewhere in Canada over the possibility of enemy use of St. Pierre and Miquelon. The day after the Marshal's speech, the Canadian Cabinet met to reconsider its stand. As a result, naval and air surveillance of the islands was stepped up, and the Vichy Minister in Ottawa was informed of the Government's concern with the possibility of misuse of the St. Pierre radio. More important, it was decided to open a consulate at St. Pierre immediately.[44]

The Department of External Affairs as well as several other government departments had been pressing for a Canadian presence in St. Pierre and Miquelon since March 1941. When Inspector LaRivière sounded de Bournat out informally on the subject early in June, he had readily agreed. In late July, Prime Minister King had also approved the idea in principle, but the actual appointment was delayed because of the inability of the Department to find "a really suitable man for a dull and difficult post." However, the August crisis speeded up proceedings. On August 19, Christopher Eberts was named Vice-Consul with the local rank of Acting Consul and charged

*Some months later, Robertson claimed that "the Canadians had twice discouraged the idea . . . that the Free French take over St. Pierre-Miquelon." This was presumably a reference to September, 1940, and July, 1941.[45]

with the responsibility of reporting "from time to time, on questions of trade, communications, navigation and shipping, and *other subjects* that may be of interest to the Canadian Government." Within two weeks, Eberts was on duty in St. Pierre.*[46]

In deciding in favour of a diplomatic approach to the St. Pierre and Miquelon problem, the Canadian Government in effect shelved preparations for a military occupation. Staff planning for this had been under way since June. On August 15, a small self-contained expeditionary force known as "Q" Force (or Queer Force) formally came into existence at Debert, Nova Scotia.[47] It consisted of "C" company of the Lake Superior Regiment, plus a number of ancillary troops and six members of the RCMP, a total of 194, all volunteers, mainly from Fort William, under the command of Lieut-Col. Herbert Cook and Major Miller Marshall. The choice of the Lakehead regiment for this task seems to have been quite fortuitous. While there have been suggestions that there was a deliberate attempt to avoid the inclusion of Newfoundlanders or even Nova Scotians in the landing force in view of the centuries of friction which St. Pierre and Miquelon had had with neighbouring territories over fisheries, this seems a bit far-fetched.†

The operational orders for "Q" Force called for its standing by to dash to Sydney ostensibly to attack and destroy a German landing force.‡ Once there, it would board two corvettes (though none was ever actually earmarked for the operation), cross to St. Pierre, land at the coal dock at dawn, seize the radio station, the telephone station,

---

*The Department of Naval Services had originally agreed to staff the post, but was unable to spare an officer in July, 1941, though it did second one following Ebert's departure in October, 1942. By that time, the Free French were in control of the islands and it seemed to the Department of External Affairs slightly less incongruous to have a naval officer, than a foreign service officer, accredited to a government which was not formally recognized (though, even in 1941, the appointment was made without an *exequator's* being issued). The first person appointed to succeed Eberts was an old sea dog and outspoken Quebec nationalist who had had close connections with many of St. Pierre's leading (and mainly pro-Vichy) citizens during rum-running days. He was quickly withdrawn as *persona non grata* with the Free French authorities and replaced by an English-speaking officer who remained in St. Pierre until the Vice-Consulate closed in October, 1944.

†*Les Fusiliers de Sherbrooke*, who had originally been slated for this "special test exercise," had earlier been expected to move into Atlantic Command, but instead were sent elsewhere.

‡Rumours that the Force was intended to defend Sydney in the event of a sudden German landing were deliberately circulated in an attempt to mislead the curious and the suspicious.

the Administrator's office and other government buildings, and over-run the defences of the island, thus "paralysing any possible resistance." Once military operations were completed, the RCMP were to take over responsibility for law and order.

Speed and surprise were considered essential to success. Accordingly, the expedition was equipped with eight motorcycles with sidecars (and two bicycles) to enable No. 4 Platoon to race through the town to seize vulnerable points before they could be sabotaged. The proposed operation was repeatedly tested in a series of practice runs around the Nova Scotia countryside. As Major Marshall writes:

I had a firegong installed in the Men's Quarters, with a switch in my room. We had no set hours for training. Consequently, I would pull the switch day or night, and away we would go. [I] had laid out flags and tapes representing the plan of attack. These were scattered all over the country. An ideal location was in the Annapolis Valley. Here [were] lots of abandoned farms, etc. We used this quite a lot. Anyway, we could get rolling in 15 minutes from the time of the alarm.

Although the troops preferred this type of training to regular army routine, maintaining morale was still not easy. For months, they were confined to barracks or subject to restricted leave. Moreover, they remained completely in the dark as to the real purpose of the force. Consequently, the commanding officer had to "spread the oil pretty thick about our crack company of the best battalion of the Canadian army being chosen for this very, very special secret operation." Moreover, "in order to keep the troops entertained, the most unorthodox and unusual types of training were introduced." This partly explains the extraordinary emphasis laid on forced marching. Even so, it is not easy to understand the need to march a mile and a half in twenty minutes with full equipment including Bren guns and ammunition. Similarly, the insistence on canned beans and hardtack for two meals and sandwiches for the third appears to have been simply a misguided attempt to bolster morale by making men miserable.

Fortunately, neither officers nor men knew that their exertions were unnecessary. The decision to despatch a consul to St. Pierre effectively rendered "Q" Force unnecessary even before it received its Operation Order on August 21. That same day, the Chiefs of State Committee recommended implementation of Operation "Q", but on August 30 the War Cabinet Committee formally decided that no military action was required, thus reaffirming its earlier stand.* Despite this, "Q" Force was kept on four hours' call for nearly a month, and then on three days' notice until it was finally disbanded at the end of January, 1942, a month after the Free French take-over. For the men involved, failure to inform them that "Q" Force had long ceased to serve any military purpose, if indeed it ever did, was not just a careless oversight; it was a cruel joke.†

For the battalion and force commanders, the real shock came with the Free French seizure of St. Pierre and Miquelon.

When the news came over the radio about 1100 hours Christmas Day, Major Marshall recalls,

Wow!! Here was I with not a soul to talk to about it. (All dressed up and no place to go.) But about 1500 hours, Col. Cook [who at long last had gone on leave] telephoned me from Port Arthur, and wanted to know if I had heard what that so and so had done to our "Q" Force. My reply was that I sure as hell did. He suggested that I quaff a few on him, which I did with zest. This was rather a sickening end to all our trouble, in training, the restrictions on leave, etc. . . . The redeeming feature of the whole episode was the willingness of the troops to put up with all the shennanigans. I think they really thought we were really due for something extra special and, if the show had come off as planned, we most certainly would have made the headlines. However, the whole bloody thing went down the drain, including 2 DSOs, 5 MCs, 5 DCMs and 20 MMs.

Part of the reason Army headquarters in Ottawa may have forgotten about "Q" Force is that every effort was made to keep its existence a closely guarded secret. Neither the Americans nor the Free French were told anything about it as both would have protested vehemently, though for very different reasons. Mackenzie King, too, seems to have been kept in the dark, possibly deliberately. His attitude to the use of force against Vichy was well known. He had consistently opposed it: at the time of the incident involving the cruiser *Emile Bertin* in June, 1940, at Mers-el-Kébir in July, at Dakar in September, and when the trawlers were escaping from St. Pierre in October. On each

---

*In response to press speculation, a Canadian Government spokesman commented on August 25 that a decision as to whether to take possession of the islands would await further development. This was the only official public reference to this possibility.[48]

†Although "Q" Force ceased to exist, Operation "Q" lived on. On January 27, 1942, General Crerar was still contemplating a military occupation of the islands by "any available units" on seven days notice.

occasion, he had argued that a resort to force would place a severe strain on national unity, especially if it provoked an open break with Vichy.[49]

Meanwhile, elsewhere in Canada, another group was secretly conspiring to seize St. Pierre and Miquelon. Five men were involved: Jean-Charles Harvey, Emile-Charles Hamel and Jean LeBret of the Montreal weekly Le Jour,* Commandant Quédrue, Free French delegate in Montreal, and Frank Paturel, a St. Pierrais resident of Montreal. All had long had an interest in the fate of the islands. In August, 1941, however, in the course of a meeting in the editorial offices of Le Jour, Paturel suddenly said: "Let's take St. Pierre and Miquelon for Free France." All agreed. Contact was quickly established with Muselier in London and, at the end of the month, Sub-Lieutenant Paul Viaud of the corvette Mimosa visited Montreal to co-ordinate plans with the group. The precise details of this so-called "officers' coup" are still a bit obscure. It was evidently conceived of as essentially a civilian enterprise, though there was provision for the use of two Free French corvettes, at least as a means of transportation. The idea was that, on arrival, a handful of adventurers would land, link up with the Resistance, and oust the Vichyards. In pursuance of their plans, Paturel and LeBret accompanied Viaud to Halifax with every intention of continuing on to St. Pierre. This proved impossible. The whole plot collapsed when the Canadian Navy ordered the Mimosa out to sea on convoy duty.[50]

The next scheme dreamed up by Paturel was even more hare-brained. It amounted to a form of privateering with a Trojan Horse twist. The plan of operations involved the use of the 6,500-ton Free French freighter Indo-Chinois. Paturel was to go ahead and make the necessary arrangements in St. Pierre. The Indo-Chinois would sail from Montreal, pick up Paturel at a secret rendezvous off the north coast of St. Pierre, and then proceed innocently into the harbour. At midnight, the crew of thirty, armed with a miscellaneous

*Published 1937–46 with a circulation of 10,000 in 1940. It was radical and unrepresentative. Many Free Frenchmen felt its support did the Gaullist cause in Quebec more harm than good. In December, 1942, the Bishops of Quebec declared that: "Le Jour is a periodical whose Christian spirit, morality and patriotism is at least questionable, and we are surprised that Christians read it." Cardinal Villeneuve denounced its editor, Jean-Charles Harvey, for his outspoken criticism of clerical education in Quebec.[51]

collection of weapons and tear-gas bombs which LeBret had collected in Montreal, would land and capture the town. Unfortunately, the *Indo-Chinois* in her various trans-Atlantic crossings did not call in at Montreal! Moreover, certain members of the Montreal group bragged about the plan so openly that it ceased to be a secret. In any case, Muselier appears to have opposed the idea. Although paper plotting continued in Montreal right up to the arrival of Muselier in Canada in December, thinking in London was proceeding along more realistic lines.

A year earlier, Free French headquarters in London had hoped that local Gaullists in St. Pierre would, on their own, succeed in effecting a peaceful overthrow of the regime in the islands. However, following the failure of attempts to force the Administrator to agree to a plebiscite, it became evident that external assistance would be required. At one stage, it seemed possible that a locally engineered coup with a minimum of outside help might suffice, but by the autumn of 1941 it was apparent, at least to leaders in London, that nothing less than a full-scale military take-over was needed.

On October 13, 1941, General de Gaulle decided that the moment to rally the islands had come. Accordingly, he wrote to the British Foreign Secretary to ascertain his views on the subject. In his reply a week later, Anthony Eden undertook to take up the question (for the third time) with the Canadians and later the Americans. "You will realize," he stated, "that the geographical position of these islands prevents our assenting to any operation involving a change in the *status quo* without the express agreement of the Canadian and United States Governments."

Despite this, de Gaulle pressed ahead with his plans. He discussed the matter fully with Admiral Muselier and arranged "in principle" that he should carry out the operation, if circumstances permitted, during a tour of inspection of Free French naval units. These had been conveniently and deliberately massed in western Atlantic waters. Whether de Gaulle had assumed that American approval would be forthcoming in due course, or whether at this stage he had already decided to act in any case is not clear. The latter seems more likely. Certainly, René Pleven, who had only recently returned from a mission to Washington, was of the opinion that the islands would have to be taken by surprise. As he commented somewhat bitterly, "Welles and his school think they know better than our British allies, and even ourselves, about France."[52]

Meanwhile, in September, shipping losses in the Atlantic had once more begun to climb and, in October, the first U-boats moved into the Newfoundland coastal area. Under heavy pressure from the Royal Canadian Navy, Ottawa finally concluded that something would really have to be done to exercise effective control over the operations of St. Pierre's shortwave radio transmitter. As Eberts reported on September 19, 1941, in one of his earliest despatches,

> It is impossible to ascertain what information the main station is sending out to France, Martinique and New York, as all confidential messages are, of course, given to it in cypher, and only the Administrator and his Secretary, Mr. Charles Cormier, handle cypher messages. It is not believed here that the Administration would report convoy movements even if it should receive word of them, and I do not think that any St. Pierre vessels go south into the shipping lanes. I feel, however, that this question can only be settled satisfactorily if an experienced telegraphist is employed to take down every message leaving the station over a period of a month or two, so that these messages can be sent to Ottawa to be broken down.

Presumably the information received from the British (on October 21) concerning the aspirations of the Free French also served to spur the Canadian Government into action. In any case, the very next day an interdepartmental committee composed of representatives of External Affairs, Naval Services, the Royal Canadian Navy, and the Foreign Exchange Control Board met to consider the matter.

The problem was to work out a plan which would meet the essential security needs of the situation and yet prove acceptable to the Americans.* The solution finally proposed arose out of two ideas which the State Department had advanced earlier. The first was a hint which Sumner Welles had dropped the previous July when he suggested that, rather than occupy St. Pierre and Miquelon outright, Canada might negotiate an *ad hoc* agreement with the Administrator governing the operation of the radio transmitter. The second was the principle of stationing foreign inspectors in the islands. A year earlier, the United States had demanded and received the right to post

---

*Not everyone in Ottawa was willing to accept an American veto. According to Moffat, Thomas Stone was all for saying, "To Hell with consulting the United States. This is a war measure and is none of America's business." Stone was passionately pro-Free French.[53]

observers in all French colonies in the Western Hemisphere to ensure that they remained neutral and demilitarized. This privilege had been exercised in Martinique but not yet in St. Pierre and Miquelon.[54]

The plan recommended by the committee of Canadian officials was accepted by the War Committee of the Cabinet on October 29 (at the same time as it rejected the British request for approval of a Free French take-over). As further developed in the course of the next few weeks, this scheme called for the early despatch of a number of Canadian civilian technicians (or possibly a joint Canadian-American team) "to pre-censor all incoming and outgoing wireless and cable messages and to supervise all radio transmitting stations on the islands." A senior official would precede or accompany them to explain to the Administrator the reasons for the Canadian action. Brigadier Georges P. Vanier, titular Minister to France, was first chosen (on November 26) for this mission, though it was eventually decided to send Thomas Stone instead because of the latter's special knowledge of economic warfare and censorship questions. On arrival at St. Pierre, the Canadian spokesman was to point out that it would be in the interests of the islands to co-operate in dispelling any suggestion that the radio station was being used to broadcast information about Allied ship movements. He would also indicate to de Bournat "the consequences of his doing anything more than registering a formal protest."* At one stage, the Department of External Affairs also considered enlisting the support of Cardinal Villeneuve of Quebec to encourage the Administrator to be reasonable.

There was no question of negotiating with de Bournat, as Sumner Welles had originally envisaged; there was not sufficient time for that. As Robertson explained, "the matter had been allowed to drag until now [the Canadians] were faced with the need for sudden action."† If the Administrator refused to co-operate, as seemed prob-

---

*On August 24, following a lengthy strike among Cape Breton coalminers, the Department of National Revenue prohibited the export of coal to St. Pierre and Miquelon as none could be spared for export. This inevitably caused considerable hardship in the islands. Although there was no political motive behind this decision, it served to remind the territory of its dependence upon Canadian goodwill.[55]

†Robertson undertook on November 3 not to make any approach to de Bournat "for at least 24 hours" in order to give the Americans time to consider the proposal. That same day, a U-boat was spotted 85 miles southeast of St. Pierre. A rash of sub-sightings and ship sinkings occurred in Newfoundland waters, October 25 to November 4.

able, this would be regarded as *"prima facie* evidence that the suspicions with respect to . . . the transmitting stations . . . are well founded." In this event, Ottawa, and it was hoped Washington too, would cut off the supply of funds to the islands "until starvation did the trick." In addition, force might have to be used. This in turn would render the continuation of diplomatic relations with Vichy "most problematical."[56]

When Norman Robertson first outlined the Canadian proposal to Pierrepont Moffat on November 3, it evoked no enthusiasm and considerable apprehension. The American Minister pointed to the "dangers" involved and warned that Canada appeared to be "embarking lightly on this demand without quite realizing what the consequences would be." Robertson then inquired whether the United States would prefer occupation by the Free French as advocated by the British. Faced with this harsh choice, the State Department acquiesced in the Canadian plan. Five days later, it informed the Canadian Legation orally that the plan "had been noted and we had no comment to make." According to John Hickerson, who handled Canadian affairs for the Department, this cryptic reply was "intended and so understood by the Canadians as constituting a green light for them to go ahead." Robertson's relief when this reply was received "at long last" indicates the sense of urgency he felt at this time.[57] The United States lent further support to the proposal when Canada raised the issue at a special meeting of the Permanent Joint Board on Defence in Montreal on November 10, and even indicated that she would be prepared if necessary to join Canada in exerting economic pressure on the Administrator to comply with the Canadian demand.[58]

With this assurance, the Department of External Affairs drafted a formal memorandum on the subject for submission to the Prime Minister and the War Committee of the Cabinet. This proposal assumed that some modification of the status quo was imperative and that action by Canada was greatly to be preferred to either of the other alternatives: to allow Free French naval forces to liberate the islands, or "to connive at and internally create a de Gaullist overturn." Leaving the initiative to the Free French "would relegate the problem to one of domestic French politics, would not allow any charge of British imperialism vis-à-vis the French Empire to gain ground nor raise questions under the Monroe Doctrine." On the other hand, there was the question of relations with Vichy in general to consider. Moreover, "many people in the Government [in Ottawa] . . . felt that they would not even trust the Free French in so vital a strategic position with a wireless just a few miles removed from [Allied] convoys."[59]

The Department pressed the Prime Minister for an early decision, but this proved impossible for two reasons. The first was the fresh crisis which blew up over Pétain's abject surrender on November 18 to demands by Hitler and Darlan for the immediate recall of General Weygand, Delegate General in French Africa. This raised anew the spectre of large-scale infiltration of German forces into North Africa, and reinforced all King's natural instincts to avoid any Canadian initiative. Then there was the critical illness of Ernest Lapointe. This not only absorbed a good deal of Mackenzie King's time, but also delayed consideration of the St. Pierre and Miquelon situation by the Cabinet. As the senior Quebec minister in the Cabinet, Lapointe was consulted as a matter of course on all matters affecting French-speaking Canadians, a precaution which was particularly important at this time because of the recent revival of pro-Vichy sentiment in Quebec.*[60]

The Prime Minister was unable to turn his attention to St. Pierre and Miquelon until after Lapointe's funeral on November 29. During the next four days, the War Committee debated the question at length. Two points in particular prolonged the discussion. The first concerned the advisability of threatening de Bournat with economic reprisals if he failed to comply. Some members argued that this form of pressure would take some time to become effective, whereas the danger to Allied shipping was an immediate one. There was also the possibility that de Bournat might use a Canadian ultimatum as a pretext for openly aiding the enemy. Finally, there was the fear that the refusal over an extended period of time to release supplies needed by the poor people of St. Pierre and Miquelon might have undesirable repercussions on public opinion at home. For all these reasons, it was decided to delete any specific reference to the possible application of economic sanctions.

Secondly, Mackenzie King continued to question the wisdom of even a show of force. As he noted in his diary for December 1, he

---

*Lapointe was a warm admirer of both Pétain and Weygand, but he disliked and distrusted de Gaulle. So did King, who said that de Gaulle reminded him of Colonel George Drew, an arch political foe.[61]

took strong exception to any action of the kind, pointing out that this was a very critical moment as between Vichy and Britain. That today Pétain was being crowded more than ever by Hitler and was actually meeting with either Hitler or Darlan*; that a seizure of a Vichy possession by the Government of Canada was all that was needed to give Darlan an excuse to turn over the French fleet to Germany which is what all who are anxious to save the situation becoming worse were seeking to avert.

Not all his colleagues agreed. A month earlier Robertson had estimated that "a large, if not predominant, group in the Cabinet" favoured occupation of St. Pierre and Miquelon, if efforts at persuasion failed; and this was still the majority view. King, however, warned that, if the War Committee approved such a dangerous policy, "I would wish to have the minutes record that I was distinctly opposed, believing that the course was entirely wrong." His diary adds that: "Once I took this position the others came around to agreeing to have the proposed course submitted to the Governments of the United States and Britain, and awaiting their comments thereon before taking any action."[62]

A month later in the course of a conversation with the American Minister, the Prime Minister commented further on his attitude to armed intervention in St. Pierre and Miquelon. By that time, the Free French had seized the islands and the subsequent uproar seemed to justify his fears. According to Moffat, King said,

this was the only problem on which he [King] and Robertson had materially differed. Robertson and Stone had cooked up a plan of sending Stone to the islands to take over the radio. He had approved Stone's going but had absolutely vetoed the corvette [as an instrument of coercion, not as a means of transport]. He felt that if Robertson and Stone had had their way, they rather than Admiral Muselier, might have upset the equilibrium with repercussions all over the world. He thought that the realization of this had sobered them and that they had learned a valuable lesson without cost.

In King's opinion, history had again vindicated his caution. As he proudly noted in his diary on Christmas Eve, "Fortunately, I have fought from the beginning against attempting anything against St. Pierre and Miquelon by force. I have kept up the fight at each meeting of the War Committee and the record is perfectly clear."[63]

*Actually, Pétain, Darlan, and Juin conferred with Goering, not Hitler, at Saint-Florentine that day.

Actually, the outcome of the debate was something of a compromise. The revised Canadian proposals, drafted by King personally and formally submitted to Churchill* and Hull early in December for their comments, contemplated the landing of a "versatile detachment of ratings" in charge of a petty officer to protect the four technicians and ensure that there was no interference with the performance of their duties. This may not have amounted to an overt use of force, but it certainly constituted a "show of force," to which King had also voiced objection. Moreover, it was more than the Americans were prepared to accept at this stage. The State Department felt that, before anything quite so "drastic" was "even considered," an attempt should be made to see if economic pressure might not produce the desired result. Washington was more optimistic than Ottawa concerning the efficacy of the economic weapon, especially if de Bournat were "led to believe that his acquiescence under protest might avert more drastic action."[64]

The day after Pearl Harbor, State Department officials outlined a counter-proposal, which subsequently received the approval of Hull and the President. This involved a three-stage approach to the Administrator, the final two stages to be invoked only if he should prove recalcitrant. No American personnel were to participate. The operation was to be entirely Canadian, although it was to have American diplomatic backing.

There was no difference of opinion on the initial step to be taken. A senior Canadian representative would interview de Bournat and tell him "in a friendly manner that there were rumours that the wireless station was being employed in a manner inimical to our interests, especially through the transmission of cypher and code messages. It could be represented to him that while doubtless these reports were unfounded, he would wish to give no possible cause for apprehension." De Bournat would then be invited to admit the civilian Canadian radio inspectors. In the "likely event" that he refused, he would be reminded that St. Pierre and Miquelon depended for its economic existence on funds controlled by Canada and the United States, and warned that the Canadian Government was

---

*King's telegram (December 4) was Canada's formal reply to the British notes of July 9 and 31, and October 21 concerning Free French readiness to rally St. Pierre and Miquelon.

"prepared to hold up the release of further funds until wireless transmissions were effectively supervised, and that they had good reason to believe that the Government of the United States would take parallel action."

The Americans felt that there was a "good chance" that the mere threat of starvation would cause de Bournat to reverse his decision. But if, like the defiant Governor of beseiged French Somaliland, he remained obdurate, he would be solemnly warned, probably that same day, that if he transmitted any message of assistance to the enemy, or any messages at all in code or cypher, he would be held "responsible for any consequences which might follow." The State Department conceded that "any departure from these conditions could, if necessary, provide an occasion for the despatch of Canadian personnel to the Islands."[65]

Thus the Americans, even more than Mackenzie King, came to the disagreeable conclusion that a resort to force in some form might ultimately prove unavoidable if other means of persuasion or coercion failed. Both were agreed, however, that armed intervention should be limited to controlling the radio station.* There was no intention of occupying the islands or otherwise interfering with their administration. On the other hand, it does not seem to have been fully appreciated in Washington, or in Ottawa either, how profound an impact the presence of even a few Canadian military personnel would be likely to have on local opinion in St. Pierre and Miquelon. It is doubtful in such circumstances if Canada could have remained aloof from internal politics.†

Once the Americans had come around to accepting a modified version of the Canadian plan as a "reasonably satisfactory" solution to the problem, they were eager that Ottawa should press ahead with it as quickly as possible. It was now London's turn to delay proceedings. Britain's slow response was probably due mainly to preoccupation with the Far Eastern crisis; but she was also most anxious not to

---

*According to Moffat, Roosevelt "hoped that Canada would try suasion as a first move, but if suasion failed and force were necessary he hoped it would be confined to gaining control of the wireless."[66]

†A few weeks earlier, Robertson had been "inclined to feel" that economic sanctions alone might suffice to touch off a local coup. "If the public in St. Pierre realize that economic or financial help was being denied them because of the Administrator's policy, they might well take matters in their own hands, depose him and declare for de Gaulle."[67]

provoke Vichy while the outcome of the offensive in Libya remained in doubt.[68] For a critical week and a half, therefore, Mackenzie King's telegram soliciting Churchill's early approval of the scheme remained unanswered. Eventually, on December 15, he replied rejecting the Canadian proposal on military and political grounds. In the view of the British Government, it was not enough simply to supervise the radio station. As long as Vichy retained any control at all in St. Pierre and Miquelon, it would continue to constitute a threat to Allied shipping in the area. Churchill went on to reiterate the view which the British had consistently advocated and which de Gaulle had again urged on him only a few days before. This was that the Free French should be authorized to take over the islands, as indeed they were about to do anyway. The situation which the Americans had most feared now loomed up as a frightening possibility.[69]

On December 9, 1941, Admiral Muselier arrived in St. John's, Newfoundland, and immediately took up with the Governor and members of the Commission Government the question of rallying St. Pierre and Miquelon. Edward Emerson, the Commissioner for Defence, amongst others, heartily approved of the project. Certainly he preferred it to occupation by the Canadians.

At this stage, Muselier contemplated carrying out the operation in a few days' time, but before doing so he felt he ought to sound out Canadian and American opinion. As Pearl Harbor had occurred only two days earlier, he was anxious not to precipitate an unfavourable Vichy reaction elsewhere in the world or otherwise to increase the burdens of his hardpressed Allies. Accordingly, before setting out for Halifax, he cabled de Gaulle that, in view of the "new general situation," he would "proceed immediately to Ottawa to get [the] agreement [of] Canada and America," and asked him in turn to request formal British consent.*[70]

*While in St. John's, Muselier was the guest of Rear-Admiral Murray, RCN, who commanded the ships of the Newfoundland Force. One evening during dinner, Emerson complained that it was impossible any longer to obtain French Vermouth, whereupon Muselier offered to take him to St. Pierre and Murray volunteered to accompany them. Next morning, as the Free French ships were about to depart, Murray returned to the banter of the previous evening and laughingly suggested that

De Gaulle was furious. He had given Muselier carte blanche to carry out the operation if the opportunity presented itself, but hardly expected him to give the game away like this. In the words of one of Muselier's critics in London, this "untimely step" had "botched everything." Certainly, de Gaulle felt there was "no change in the situation" justifying Muselier's actions. American agreement was "desirable, but not indispensable since this was merely an internal French affair." Nevertheless, as the secret was now out, de Gaulle felt "obliged to warn the British in order to avoid the appearance of concealment." On December 10, he reluctantly wrote to Churchill to inquire whether he had any objection to this *"petit coup de main."*[71] The British, of course, had none but, as we have seen and as de Gaulle had feared, they asked him (on December 15) to postpone the operation for thirty-six hours while the approval of Washington and Ottawa was sought. The British clearly assumed that this would be readily granted now that the United States was a full belligerent in the war.[72]

That same day, Admiral Muselier reached Ottawa and immediately raised the issue of St. Pierre and Miquelon with the Canadian authorities and the American Minister.* The response from the Navy and the Department of External Affairs was encouraging. Angus L. Macdonald and Admiral Nelles welcomed the idea warmly. Norman Robertson, Lester Pearson, and Thomas Stone, though not Mackenzie King, were also personally in favour of it.[73] Indeed, even before Muselier's arrival, officials in Ottawa were beginning to have second thoughts on their earlier plans concerning St. Pierre and Miquelon.

---

it "might not be wise to let you go near St. Pierre with those three corvettes," to which Muselier replied, "I have told you I will go straight to Halifax." Two weeks later, when Murray went to Emerson's home for Christmas dinner, Emerson appeared at the door, rather belatedly tying his tie, exclaiming, "He's done it. He's gone there without us." Emerson was so delighted at the news that, as soon as he had heard it via the bush telegraph, he cabled his congratulations to Muselier, the only Allied leader to do so. Publication of the telegram by the Free French proved so embarrassing that he later felt compelled to explain publicly that his message had been purely "personal and private."[74]

*Muselier, along with Commander de Villefosse and Lieutenant Savary, were met in Montreal by P. J. A. Cardin, the senior Quebec minister in the Cabinet, who accompanied them to Ottawa where they were entertained at luncheon by the Governor-General. Muselier also called on the Minister of National Defence for Naval Services (Macdonald), the Government leader in the Senate (Dandurand), the British High Commissioner, the American Minister, the Chief of the Naval Staff (Nelles), and the Under-Secretary of State for External Affairs (Robertson), as well as the members of the Free French Committee.[75]

The Canadian Government would probably still have been prepared to go along with the American modification to its own scheme
if it had been pressed to do so. Nevertheless, it never formally
accepted them, and Robertson at least remained dubious about certain
features. In particular, he feared that de Bournat would refuse to be
intimidated, and might "stage a sit-down strike in which he would
not use his wireless, at least with any code message." This would
immobilize the senior Canadian official, and, more important, the
corvette. (Moffat thought this was being "unduly apprehensive.")
Moreover, there were growing doubts in the Department of External
Affairs on the wisdom of the whole approach. Churchill's warning
that any action by Canada might embroil her in an embarrassing
political situation did nothing to ease Canadian anxiety. In any case,
it seemed to many that the time to act had passed. As Moffat observed,
"The general feeling here is that the St. Pierre show has been hashed.
It has been talked over so much and so often, and so much time has
elapsed since it was first proposed in early November that it is
becoming progressively harder to justify as an emergency measure."*
In the circumstances, the simplest thing to do seemed to be to let
Muselier carry on. With this in mind, the Department had already
begun to consider whether an attempt might usefully be made once
more to persuade the Americans to reconsider their attitude towards
recognition of de Gaulle, in view of their new status as belligerents.[76]

Admittedly, not everyone in Ottawa had been won over to the
Free French point of view. Hugh Keenleyside, for one, had not. In a
conversation with Moffat on December 15, he complained bitterly that
"Norman Robertson had gone off on a tangent" and that "if we ever
toyed with the idea of encouraging de Gaulle to seize the islands,
we had long since moved away from it." Keenleyside saw "no excuse
for further procrastination" and favoured "acting and acting quickly"
along the lines of the American plan. Mackenzie King was another

---

*Ottawa was also less inclined to act after having talked to Muselier. As Robertson
expressed it, if Canada was going to take over the radio transmitter, he wished she
had done so before the Admiral had visited Ottawa. Stone felt the same way and
actually asked to be relieved of the responsibility of heading the mission to St. Pierre
owing to his "personal relations with Admiral Muselier." He had already been
provided with the necessary "full powers" to treat with the Administrator. Vanier
was then reinstated as the Canadian envoy. On December 19, Moffat expressed the
fear that "more and more people are getting to know about the plan and, if they
[the Canadians] do not hurry, so will the Governor of St. Pierre and Miquelon."

who had not changed his mind. He told Pierrepont Moffat that he agreed "one hundred percent with our point of view." On the other hand, he admitted that he was having "great trouble" convincing some of his Cabinet colleagues that the question of the regime in St. Pierre and Miquelon was "mere chicken feed" compared with the bigger issues involved. They were so distrustful of Vichy that they could not see that it was "our duty to play for the highest stakes." He also found the attitude of Robertson and Stone equally incomprehensible and irritating.* All were agreed, however, that the determining factor in Canada's attitude to Muselier's proposal should be the reaction of the United States.[77]

Confirmation of American opposition was not long in coming. Roosevelt strongly disapproved of action by the Free French and favoured Canadian control instead on the grounds that it would produce "fewer adverse repercussions." Hull, for his part, viewed the possibility of a clash between Vichy and de Gaulle "with something like horror."[78] The British and Canadian Governments thereupon accepted the American veto as decisive. The British also reiterated their objections to the Canadian plan,

We fully appreciate the reasons in favour of this proposal [London informed Ottawa on December 18]. There is, however, always danger it might arouse hostility among the Islanders. Moreover, our military advisers feel nothing short of occupation of Island by British or Allied forces would really meet the case from military point of view. This course, however, now seems ruled out by United States attitude. . . . In the circumstances, it seems wiser not to take any action for the time being.

The Free French too, agreed to respect Washington's wishes. On December 17, the views of the American Government were conveyed to Muselier in Ottawa and to de Gaulle in London, both of whom agreed reluctantly but definitely to call off the operation, or at least defer it.[79] "The President's view," the British assured the Canadians next day, "has been represented to General de Gaulle who agrees that proposed action should not, repeat not, now be taken." Yet that very day, just as Muselier was preparing to leave Ottawa, after having been completely rebuffed by the Americans and then suddenly and inexplicably recalled to England, he received secret orders from de Gaulle to proceed at once to St. Pierre and Miquelon "without

*This was December 17, King's birthday, always a difficult day for his staff.

saying anything to the foreigners." The General undertook to accept full responsibility for the consequences.*[80]

This deliberate act of defiance has been almost universally denounced as "unwarranted," "unlawful," "high-handed," "outrageous and inexcusable." Even Admiral Muselier accused de Gaulle of acting like a "dictator" in allegedly issuing the order without consulting the members of the French National Committee, while Colonel Pierrené, Free French Delegate in Ottawa, commented simply, "He is crazy." Nevertheless, Muselier decided, albeit with an apparent heavy heart, to obey out of a sense of duty to de Gaulle and to resign only later after his return to London. The alternative—refusal and immediate resignation—would, he felt, have led to the disintegration of the Free French Naval Forces. He continued to insist, however, that prior agreement from Washington and Ottawa was both desirable and possible, and that no Canadian occupation was imminent.†[81]

How is this apparent breach of faith to be explained? The immediate cause of the *volte-face* was a confidential tip from the Foreign Office concerning Canadian intentions which de Gaulle received a few hours after he had undertaken not to go ahead with the operation.‡ He at once considered this scheme an outrage which dramatically altered the whole complexion of the problem. Formal protests were lodged with Eden, Hull, and the Canadian High Commissioner in London, but the situation called for more than words. "As soon as a foreign intervention on French territory was in question," he records in his *Memoirs*, "no hesitation seemed to be permissible."[82]

In the meantime, the Canadian Government had reassessed the situation in the light of continued American objections to Free French

---

*De Gaulle later admitted that, on December 17, he "gave the British Government to understand that [his National Committee] would be ready to give up, for the moment, any action against St. Pierre and Miquelon." In his agreement of August 7, 1940, with Churchill, de Gaulle had undertaken to accept "the general direction of the British High Command."

†Moffat reported that "the Canadian supposition is that when the unconfirmed reports of Pétain's resignation reached [Muselier] he decided to take the bit in his own teeth regardless of American or Canadian wishes." There is no evidence to support this interpretation of Muselier's actions.

‡De Gaulle understood that Canada intended to destroy the St. Pierre radio station, not supervise it. He also appears to have thought that the Foreign Office was quietly giving him the go-ahead signal. Muselier learned in Ottawa that some thought had been given to letting the Canadians deal with the problem, but he was apparently not aware that a plan was under active consideration.[83]

action and renewed British opposition to Canadian intervention. On December 19, Ottawa definitely decided to postpone its plan "for the present." Many, if not most, of the Cabinet were impressed with the British argument, based on bitter experience in Syria and elsewhere, that any tampering with French territory would be bitterly resented by all Frenchmen—Gaullists and Vichyites alike—as an unwarranted infringement on the sacred sovereignty of France. This was confirmed by Muselier's own solemn warnings while in Ottawa, and reinforced by de Gaulle's angry protests.*

The British and Americans were informed of the Canadian decision (on December 22)—but not de Gaulle, presumably because the Canadian plan was still thought of as being on a twenty-four hour basis. However, whatever the reason, de Gaulle could with some justification complain that his Allies had not treated him with complete frankness.[84]

It should be realized that the Free French viewed the Canadian plan, not in isolation, but as part of a nefarious plot to neutralize the whole French overseas empire piecemeal and thus endanger, as de Gaulle expressed it, "the whole of the very future of our country as a Great Power." Indeed, at that very time, an American admiral was negotiating the renewal of an agreement with Admiral Robert, the Vichy High Commissioner for the French West Indies, providing for the maintenance of the status quo in the territory under his jurisdiction. As General de Gaulle recounted later, on hearing that Admiral Horne had been sent to Martinique "to settle the terms for the neutralization of our possession in America," "I was all the more determined to gain control" of St. Pierre and Miquelon and "decided to act at the first opportunity." Thus, paradoxically, the Horne-Robert agreement of December 17 provoked the very thing it was intended to prevent.[85]

De Gaulle's decision, therefore, was not as reprehensible as it seemed, especially to those unacquainted with his motives or incapable of understanding his fierce insistence on France's sovereign rights. Nevertheless, one may legitimately wonder how sincere his original undertaking really was, whether in fact the Canadian plan was not

*As early as October, 1940, de Gaulle had warned Washington that any unilateral occupation of St. Pierre and Miquelon under the Act of Havana would "cause profound grief to all Frenchmen." He offered instead to occupy it himself "in cooperation with the American Fleet."[86]

simply a convenient excuse for releasing him from his pledged word. His original intention had apparently been to seize the islands by surprise; and it was only Admiral Muselier's calculated indiscretion forcing him to consult his Allies which upset this tidy plot.* Even after this, although fully anticipating an American refusal, he twice urged Muselier to act immediately. Thus, on the morning of that critical day, December 17, a few hours before his apparent acquiescence in the American veto, he cabled that, "we shall be able to undertake nothing at St. Pierre and Miquelon if we wait for the permission of all those who say they are interested. . . . The only solution is an action on our own initiative." His order to Muselier the next day does not, therefore, seem to have been a sudden impulse. On the contrary, he appears to have welcomed the opportunity of creating a crisis in order to clarify the unsatisfactory nature of Free French relations with the United States. "Perhaps, on my side," de Gaulle later admitted, "I provoked it in order to stir up the bottom of things, as one throws a stone into a pond." If so, his wish came true. The pebble caused a tidal wave.†[87]

There is one other possible explanation of de Gaulle's decision. Muselier was an individualist whose forceful personality evoked either intense devotion or deep distrust on the part of his associates. So strong indeed were the feelings against him in certain Free French circles in London that, in January, 1941, some of his enemies, on the basis of forged documents allegedly smuggled out of Occupied France, had engineered his arrest and imprisonment by the British on charges of high treason. De Gaulle, too, had frequently found him a difficult colleague, most recently in September, 1941, during a bitter dispute over the composition of the French National Committee, and had for some months been trying to post him abroad. Muselier had no illusions concerning the motive which inspired these suggestions. Nevertheless, despite his chronic ill-health—his doctors had in fact prescribed a six weeks' rest cure in a "warm dry climate"—he readily

---

*Ten years earlier, de Gaulle had written that to build up one's prestige it was indispensable "to keep for oneself some secret surprise which might at any time intervene."[88]

†According to one Free French observer in London, "De Gaulle suspected the existence of an understanding in regard to our Atlantic possessions between the United States and Vichy. . . . It was decided therefore to throw a stone into the frogpond. If the frogs croaked, he thought, it would be because an agreement had been concluded. . . . And how the frogs did croak!"[89]

Arrival at St. Pierre, December 24, 1941. Admiral Muselier on board
Mimosa salutes during playing of the *Marseillaise*

l. to r., Lieut. Savary, Admiral Muselier, Lieut.-Cdr. de Villefosse
on board *Mimosa*, approaching St. Pierre and Miquelon

The town of St. Pierre

Muselier and Savary (civilian dress) at opening of school for boy seamen St. Pierre, January, 1942

General de Gaulle and Admiral Muselier take the salute in London,
July 14, 1940

General de Gaulle inspects first group of Free French volunteers
from St. Pierre and Miquelon to arrive after liberation, January, 1942

Gilbert de Bournat, Administrator of St. Pierre and Miquelon, in his office, 1940

Voting in the plebiscite, December 24, 1941

accepted the St. Pierre and Miquelon assignment. Then, on the eve
of his arrival in Ottawa, a mischievous and totally inaccurate article
written by Geneviève Tabouis appeared in the London *Sunday
Dispatch*. This suggested that Muselier intended to negotiate with
Washington concerning collaboration in the Pacific war and official
recognition of the Free French movement—something which he had
no authority to do. De Gaulle promptly cabled Muselier asking him
to return to London but, two days later, reconsidered the matter and
ordered him to St. Pierre instead. It is just conceivable—and this possibility occurred to Muselier—that, when the strength of American
opposition became apparent, de Gaulle decided deliberately to force
Muselier into the hornet's nest in the hope that he would be so badly
stung that he could be easily dispensed with. If it ever had been de
Gaulle's intention to break Muselier in this way, his machiavellian
scheme misfired. The resulting American fury was, in fact, directed
against the General and not the Admiral.*[90]

*This line of reasoning assumes that the violence of the American response was
predictable. De Gaulle realized that some reaction was "inevitable," but felt that
"the worst to be normally expected was a little ill-humour in the offices of the
State Department."[91]

4

LIBERATION

On December 22, 1941, Admiral Muselier sailed out of Halifax with three corvettes, the *Mimosa*, the *Alysse*, and the *Aconit*, the submarine cruiser *Surcouf*, and some 360 Free French sailors and marines. His destination was St. Pierre, 365 miles to the northeast.

Before Muselier's departure, Commodore "Jetty" Jones, the senior Canadian naval officer on the Atlantic Coast, had questioned him concerning his plans. Muselier had responded by producing a copy of the orders he had issued to his commanders detailing the naval exercises to be carried out at sea. He made no mention of St. Pierre and Miquelon and Jones, unlike Murray in St. John's two weeks earlier, did not raise the question. The conversation ended with Commodore Jones apparently completely reassured, though whether he chose to appear deceived or was simply slightly naive is still not entirely clear; the latter seems more likely. Thus, without having to lie openly about his intentions, Muselier obtained the necessary permission to sail, and also Jones's firm promise to censor any references in the press to the Admiral's movements.[1]

Once safely out to sea, Muselier went through the motions of carrying out manoeuvres. These consisted principally of a communications exercise by means of which he managed secretly to pass new operational orders for the assault on St. Pierre to his flotilla—without arousing the suspicions of the British naval liaison officers serving on his ships. Even this pretence was soon abandoned when, as a result of heavy weather, he was forced to heave to and, incidentally, head in a direction which took him to St. Pierre. At this point, Muselier's conscience began to trouble him. On the evening of December 23, therefore, he signalled his change of course to London in order, as he said, to give the British an opportunity to intercede with de Gaulle to cancel the operation if they so desired. This was an unnecessary precaution as the British had of course already cracked the Free French codes. As a result, the Admiralty at least, and probably the Foreign Office too, should have been well aware of what was happening. Neither did anything about it.[2]

Although elaborate security precautions were taken to avoid a repetition of the Dakar disaster, efforts to maintain secrecy were not fully effective. On December 18, one Free French leader in Montreal —accounts differ as to the identity of the culprit—deliberately tipped off the New York Times about the expedition, for a price. As a result, Ira Wolfert was assigned to cover the story. Within two hours, he was on his way to Montreal armed only with a set of long woolen underwear. He eventually caught up with Muselier's party at the Lord Nelson Hotel in Halifax at five o'clock on the morning of their departure. Although everyone hotly denied any knowledge of an alleged mission to St. Pierre and Miquelon, Wolfert managed to bluff them into believing he knew more than he did and, by threatening to publish the story in full, to blackmail them into taking him along. In the end, he was virtually kidnapped, smuggled into the Naval Dockyard on the floor of a taxi, put on board the Alysse, and locked in a cabin until she sailed a few hours later.[3]

Meanwhile, following further leaks, rumours of the impending operation began to circulate in Montreal. These reached the ear of René Ristelhueber, the Vichy Minister in Ottawa, on December 17 and again on the 23rd. However, on each occasion, his fears were laid to rest when, following inquiries in the Department of External Affairs, he was solemnly assured that there was no substance to the stories.*[4]

More disturbing to Muselier as he ploughed northward through heavy seas were recent reports that the fast cruiser Emile Bertin was about to escape from Martinique for an unknown destination,

---

*At the time Robertson gave his second assurance, Muselier was already in occupation of St. Pierre and Miquelon. When Robertson learned of this a few hours later, he rushed over to the French Legation in great embarrassment to explain to Ristelhueber that the news had come as a complete surprise to him. Ristelhueber was convinced that Robertson, while not unhappy at the outcome, had at least acted in good faith, but he suspected that the naval authorities in Halifax, and perhaps elsewhere, had deliberately "closed their eyes" to what was happening.

conceivably St. Pierre. If she had succeeded in eluding the American naval net and reaching St. Pierre and Miquelon first, this would have ended all hope of liberating the islands.*[5]

In the event, the operation went off without a hitch. The force arrived off St. Pierre early on the morning of December 24, and entered the harbour at dawn without being detected, thanks to a gendarme on lookout duty who ran out of coal for his stove, went into town to procure some more, and decided not to return that night. Within twenty minutes, it was all over without a drop of blood being shed or a shot being fired or indeed resistance of any kind.[6]

Baron de Bournat later claimed that the coup came as no surprise to him. He was, of course, aware of Admiral Muselier's presence in the Western Atlantic and, as a result, had posted sentries at observation points around the island (though on the night in question only one remained, and he went home early). But he also insists that his suspicions were further aroused when, on the eve of the take-over, Christopher Eberts, the Canadian Consul, invited him and the American Consul, Maurice Pasquet, to dinner. "These two consuls and their wives were charming," de Bournat recounted twenty years afterwards,

and we spent a pleasant evening [actually playing roulette] which prolonged itself to a rather late hour. Ordinarily, this type of social evening ended between midnight and one o'clock in the morning. But these two consuls, who no doubt were aware of the impending arrival of Admiral Muselier on the following morning, contrived ways and means to detain me with them. In fact, they succeeded in doing so until 4:30 in the morning [two o'clock would be more accurate]—no doubt saying to themselves that, when the fleet arrived, the Governor would be in bed, and hence this would be a much easier way to get him. However, this stratagem aroused my suspicions. I went home at 4:30, but I did not go to bed! I shaved and, when at six o'clock in the morning the fleet sailed in, I was already on my way to the office. . . . Immediately, I telephoned orders to the police station for them not to use the two machine guns which were our only means of defence for the territory.[7]

It is hardly necessary to say that de Bournat's charges of complicity are both completely untrue and utterly ridiculous. Eberts and Pasquet

---

*The rumours regarding the *Emile Bertin* were untrue. On the other hand, the aircraft carrier *Béarn* intended to put to sea, December 10 to 20, 1941, until Washington insisted it remain at Martinique.[8] See page 38.

knew nothing of Muselier's plans in advance and would not have conspired with him if they had. The whole fanciful tale is, however, a revealing commentary on the strange world of distrust and suspicion in which de Bournat moved.

Admiral Muselier's first concern, once the landing had been completed, was to establish the legitimacy of his regime by means of a plebiscite. De Bournat had refused demands for this for over a year. Muselier, on the other hand, not only welcomed an appeal to public opinion, but let it be known that he would withdraw immediately if the people repudiated the Free French at the polls. However, there was little danger of this; the enthusiastic welcome they had received made the outcome obvious. Voting took place on Christmas Day on St. Pierre and on succeeding days on the other islands. The results were decisive: 783 voted to "Rally to Free France" and only 15 for "Collaboration with the Axis Powers." Muselier therefore rightly claimed 98 per cent support for the Gaulle.[9] (Table II)

TABLE II

	St. Pierre (Dec. 25)	Ile aux Marins (Dec. 26)	Miquelon (Dec. 28)	Total
Raillement à la France Libre	651	63	69	783
Coopération avec les Puissances de l'axe	11	0	4	15
Spoiled ballots (bulletins blancs ou nuls)	140	3	72	215
Ballot Cast (votants)	802	66	145	1013
Abstentions	188*	0	27	215
Registered electors (inscrits)	990	66	172	1228

*Ristelhueber says there were only 977 electors present (présents) in St. Pierre and therefore only 175 actual non-voters. Pasquet said there were only 815 to 820 eligible voters, or a maximum of 20 abstentions; Wolfert agrees. Voters were required to strike out one of the two choices.

Vichy apologists have challenged this verdict on a variety of grounds, none of them very substantial. The reason they have been so anxious to cast doubt on the validity of the vote is clear: it was the first significant expression of public opinion in any territory which had been under Vichy domination. (The plebiscite in French Oceania in September, 1940, came too early and took place too far away to make much of an impact.) The outcome had, therefore, a significance which ranged far beyond the confines of the tiny colony.

As might be expected, the most extreme attack came from de Bournat himself. On his return to Vichy, he bluntly accused Muselier of having "faked" the figures. Not only had fully 35 per cent of the electorate abstained,* he asserted, but "more than half of the rest remain loyal to the government of Marshal Pétain."[10] These claims are preposterous; in any case, why, if he was so confident of support for Vichy, had he consistently rejected popular demands for a plebiscite? Even Admiral Robert, de Bournat's superior in Martinique, conceded that the results were "more or less representative of the opinions of the population." The conduct of the plebiscite was, in fact, scrupulously honest, even to the extent of disenfranchising those who had recently enlisted in the Free French forces. Apart from these, all male residents over the age of eighteen, except the former Administrator and one other (Henri Morazé), were eligible to vote.† Although some *hésitants* may have been influenced by fear of losing their jobs, no attempt was made to intimidate the electorate. The balloting was secret and the counting open. In St. Pierre, Emile Gloanec, senior *conseiller d'administration* and last mayor of the town, presided over the proceedings. The whole operation was closely scrutinized from beginning to end by an unofficial American observer, Ira Wolfert, who has testified to the completely free and fair nature of the plebiscite.[11]

Interpreting the results presents a more difficult problem.[12] Although it is impossible to dispute the fact that the action of the Free French in liberating St. Pierre and Miquelon from Vichy rule had the whole-hearted approval of the vast majority of the population, it is not easy to determine the real strength of the opposition, principally because the ballot did not permit voters the opportunity to express a preference specifically for the maintenance of the status quo. This omission was deliberate, the result of a personal decision on the part of Muselier himself. In this, he was no doubt partly influenced by a desire to maximize his majority. As he pointed out later, in explaining his success, "It is only necessary to know how to state the question."[13] However, the wording of the ballot can be defended

*The figure of 35 per cent includes those who spoilt their ballots (17.5 per cent) as well as those who abstained (17.5 per cent). In the plebiscite held in Canada four months later, the abstentions rate *alone* was 29 per cent and in Nova Scotia amounted to nearly 50 per cent.

†The voting age was lowered from 21 to 18 to include all those of military age, but the pre-war practice of restricting the franchise to men was retained.

on more legitimate grounds. After all, Pétain *had* publicly accepted a policy of collaboration with Hitler. This was an unpleasant fact which local *Vichyards* were loathe to admit. Consequently, only a handful of them were prepared to vote for "Collaboration with the Axis Powers." The majority either struck out both alternatives or stayed away from the polls.

It does not follow that all 430 registered voters who failed to cast valid ballots were *Vichyards*. Not at all. Some illiterate fishermen who were obviously pro-de Gaulle evidently misunderstood the procedure and failed to mark their ballots at all. Others in their enthusiasm spoilt theirs by scribbling sentiments such as *"Vive de Gaulle"* or *"Vive la France Libre"* on them.* Moreover, the abstentions included St. Pierrais serving in the Free French forces who thereby lost their right to vote.

Critics of the plebiscite have also alleged that the people of St. Pierre did not have time fully to reflect on the issues involved, that they were swept off their feet by a momentary wave of emotion. Consequently, it is argued that the vote in Miquelon three days later was a more accurate reflection of the true state of public opinion throughout the islands. Certainly, the fact that nearly half the voters in Miquelon spoilt their ballots represented a setback for Free France. Even Muselier conceded this, though he attributed it to the intrigues of priests and merchants, and to American hostility, rather than to reaction against, say, the arrest of de Bournat (which does seem to have influenced some people). There is, however, a simpler and more convincing explanation of the vote in Miquelon which has little to do with either ideology or international politics. The Miquelonnais are a proud, independent, and rather conservative people who have traditionally looked upon the wealthier and more sophisticated St. Pierrais with a certain air of suspicion. As a result, it is not uncommon for the two communities to vote very differently. Even the high proportion of spoilt ballots was not something new; in the last elections for the *Conseil d'Administration* in 1939, well over 50 per cent of the ballots in Miquelon were declared invalid.[14] Consequently, the outcome of the voting there cannot be compared with results elsewhere. Nor, in view of the lengthy and heated debate on the issue of Vichy *versus*

*Some ballots indicated curious preferences, for example, *"Vive Pétain et de Gaulle"*, *"Vive Henri IV"*, *"Vive Jeanne d'Arc"*, and *"Vive Clemenceau."*

Free France during the preceding year and a half, is it possible to argue that the people of St. Pierre made up their minds on the spur of the moment.

The available evidence suggests that the *Vichyard* element was limited to 250, or at the very outside 300 electors. This means that, if all eligible voters had cast valid ballots, the Free French majority would still have been an impressive 75 to 80 per cent. This conclusion is not out of line with the view which the American Consul expressed at the time that even a more neutrally-worded ballot would have produced approximately 75 per cent support for de Gaulle, or with Muselier's estimate that on arrival 70 per cent of the population was pro-Gaullist, 10 per cent Vichyite and 20 per cent undecided.*[15]

The second task facing Admiral Muselier was to secure the territory against internal subversion and external aggression. The number of convinced collaborators on the islands was small, perhaps twenty in all (including fifteen subscribers to *Gringoire*, the notorious fascist weekly published in Paris). They were reinforced by an active group of *Vichyards* who acquired new confidence now that, as one of them said, "we've got President Roosevelt on our side." Encouraged by the prospect of imminent American intervention, they created a serious nuisance; they met secretly, circulated pamphlets and false rumours, spread disaffection among school children and Free French volunteers, organized demonstrations, and indulged in occasional acts of violence. The core of this opposition centred on the church, the Chamber of Commerce, a majority of whose members promptly resigned, and the expatriate officials, some of whom, including all three doctors on the islands, refused to serve under Muselier.[16]

There was no wholesale purge of the administration. Originally, all officials—including de Bournat—were invited to remain at their posts, and many did. However, a few hostile officials who did not resign voluntarily were dismissed or transferred, and their positions filled either by Frenchmen who had recently arrived with Muselier's

*Nevertheless, Sumner Welles wrote disparagingly of the "apparent acquiescence of the inhabitants." In the October, 1945 elections in St. Pierre and Miquelon for the French National Assembly, de Bournat ran second in a field of five candidates, receiving 500 votes or 23 per cent of the total. (He then retired from the race.) The Gaullist candidate polled 893 votes (42 per cent) and went on to win with 1058 votes (49 per cent) on the second ballot. This was the first election following the introduction of women's suffrage. It is doubtful if these figures have much relevance to the situation in the islands four years earlier.[17]

expedition or, more often, by local residents. These latter were generally, but by no means always, members of the Resistance, including
some, like Henry Humbert, who were re-appointed to posts from
which they had previously been removed by de Bournat.[18] The more
notorious Vichy officials were arrested, among them the Administrator,
the islands' judge (Emile Macé), and the heads of the radio telegraphic service (René Delort), the health service (Bertrand Gau),
and the public works department (Jean Liorel). In the eyes of the
Resistance leaders, all had committed political crimes of one sort or
another. Most were quickly released, but three officials, two of them
doctors, remained under house arrest in the country for more than a
year. Another favourite target of the underground, Aubert de la
Rüe, a Swiss geologist employed by the Vichy administration to prospect for silver and iron, was also exiled to Langlade for over a year,
after which he was deported to Canada.* He was variously accused
of propagating Vichy ideas (which he undoubtedly did), spying for
the Germans, or simply milking the colony's meagre Treasury.[19]

In addition to officials, a few St. Pierrais *notables* were taken into
protective custody for a few days immediately after the liberation.
One of them, Henri Morazé, was later rearrested and confined to his
summer home on Langlade for a lengthy cooling-off period. Morazé
was reputedly St. Pierre's wealthiest citizen, having amassed his
fortune during the *temps du whiskey* when he became well-known
to customs officials and the police in the United States, Canada, and
Newfoundland. The reason that he was singled out for special treatment was not because he was considered particularly dangerous, but
because he was incapable of controlling his tongue. Despite warnings,
he insisted on denouncing de Gaulle, the British, and the war at the
top of his voice in the main square of the town. For the rest of the
Vichyards, the threat of incarceration sufficed to deter them. On one
occasion, Muselier called in thirty of them and laid down the law in
unmistakeable terms. "If your opposition does not cease immediately,"
he warned them sternly,

I will find myself, to my great regret, compelled to use against you the
sanctions laid down and applied by those [Vichyites] whom you admire.

*Aubert de la Rüe charges that the delay in obtaining permission to enter Quebec
was due to the Canadian consul's political partisanship for Free France. There is no
truth in this allegation.

So, if all agitation does not end within twenty-four hours, I will regret-fully intern fifteen of you, named here, in the old barracks. You are aware that this barracks has been fitted up to receive inmates. It is surrounded with barbed wire. It will be known henceforth as the *Hôtel des Notables.* If, after this first precaution, the agitation continues, fifteen other members of your group, named here, will join their friends. *Au revoir, messieurs.*

As a further precaution, Muselier ordered two trucks armed with machine guns to patrol the streets to reassure the Gaullists and intimi-date the *Vichyards.*[20]

Originally, Muselier had planned to appoint Frank Paturel, a St. Pierre businessman who had been living in Montreal, as Administrator —until the local Free French leaders raised objections. As a result, Alain Savary was named to the post. He was a remarkable twenty-three year old lieutenant in the Free French Naval Forces who re-turned after the war to represent the islands in the National Assembly in Paris. De Bournat himself, due to the illness of his step-daughter, was allowed to remain in the governor's mansion—until his supporters organized a demonstration outside (which was dispersed by a naval detachment). He and his wife were then transferred to a tugboat in the harbour, where they remained for a month, except for two visits to the house of the Canadian Consul for baths. Later, they were moved to a luxurious villa in the country. As de Bournat feared reprisals from those he had so recently oppressed, he specifically asked to have Free French sailors as guards rather than local militiamen, and this request was granted. Three months later, de Bournat was repatriated to unoccupied France. He would have preferred to go to Halifax, where his step-daughter was attending school, but, fortun-ately for Canada, the Free French refused him permission. As it was, St. Pierrais *émigrés* caused quite a bit of trouble in Quebec in the course of the next couple of years.[21]

With de Bournat out of the way, the Apostolic Prefect—a dignitary with the appropriate name of Poisson—assumed the unofficial leader-ship of the *Vichyards.* At the outset, relations between Admiral Muselier and Monseigneur Poisson were friendly but, with the re-vival of opposition confidence, the latter's attitude changed. Poisson joined in the manifestation outside de Bournat's residence, mixed religion and politics in his sermons, and despatched a priest to Mique-lon to organize the anti-Free French vote there. Then, on December

27, he told Muselier bluntly that, after three days of observation, reflection, and prayer, he had concluded that, "I cannot in all conscience recognize you as the legitimate government of St. Pierre. Your military take-over of the territory and your plebiscite are wrong in practice and in principle and do not entitle you to govern. You are an occupying force. You are not a legitimate government either in law or in fact." Later that day, Poisson repeated this denunciation of the Free French in a declaration posted on the door of the cathedral. This dramatic challenge was evidently an attempt to court arrest. However, Muselier, though provoked, refused to make a martyr of Poisson. Instead, he pleaded with him earnestly to reconsider his stand and at least to remain neutral. When this failed, he cut off for a time Poisson's salary and allowances and those of other clergy, all of whom, with the single exception of the *curé* of Ile-aux Marins,* backed their bishop.[22] Although the church did not accept the authority of the Free French regime, it was quite willing to accept its subventions.

Two weeks after this incident, there was a fresh crisis in relations between church and state when, in announcing a special mass for Muselier's former chief of staff killed in Libya, Monseigneur Poisson pointedly omitted the traditional tribute, *mort au champ d'honneur*. Muselier immediately rose in his pew and marched out of the church in protest, followed by a substantial body of the congregation. He also ordered all church schools to close for fifteen days and seized certain church premises. At the same time, in London, de Gaulle approached the representative of the Vatican in an effort to end the cold war.[23] Officially, the opposition of the clergy ceased on January 20 but, even after that, a majority of them, including Poisson, refused to co-operate fully with Muselier.

On the whole, the Free French were remarkably indulgent with the antics of their opponents, thanks in large measure to the restraining influence of Muselier and Savary. Despite occasional public cries of "De Bournat to the stake!" there was none of the nastiness which followed in the wake of the liberation of France three years later. Certainly, there was nothing remotely resembling the lurid tales

---

*Father Lebris, who is still at Ile aux Marins and still an ardent Gaullist. Prior to the occupation, Father Pichon, Father Pallussière, and Father Legallo had been, like the bishop, pro-Vichy; the other priests were neutral.

broadcast by Vichy radio describing St. Pierre and Miquelon as "bathed in blood," with de Bournat and Bishop Poisson both shot, and "a thousand refugees" fleeing for their lives. As this propaganda was demonstrably false, it tended to defeat its own purpose and expose the local *Vichyards* to ridicule. In the end, Muselier managed to win many of his opponents over to his cause. On the eve of his departure in mid-February, a delegation of *Vichyards* waited upon him to shake his hand and apologize for the stand they had taken earlier.[24]

The external threat was potentially more serious than the problem of internal security though, as we have seen, the two were related. The danger was twofold: either Admiral Robert in Martinique might attempt to recapture the colony, or the United States might do it for him—incredible as that might seem.* [25] Neither threat materialized, but both were possibilities. On one occasion, a report that the *Emile Bertin* was in the area caused the Free French an anxious few hours. Equally disturbing was the information received on New Year's Day that American troops were boarding landing craft at Norfolk, Virginia, headed for St. Pierre. Fortunately, this turned out to be an amphibious exercise quite unrelated to St. Pierre and Miquelon.†[26]

Whatever happened Muselier was determined to fight to the bitter end—even if ordered to evacuate the islands by de Gaulle himself. "There is no power in the world," he declared defiantly, "that can remove either me or my men alive from these islands. For honour's sake, I will resist any navy of any power or any combination of navies. . . . Here we are, and here we shall remain."‡[27]

Accordingly, Muselier hastily erected rudimentary defences throughout the territory, organized three mobile "combat groups" and a small home guard, improvised four armoured cars, manned and armed two tugboats and various smaller craft including two high-powered motor launches—legacies of rum-running days—constructed a makeshift harbour boom, extinguished all lighthouses, and banned

*One report, dated December 31, claimed that Otto Abetz, German Ambassador in Paris had been summoned to Berlin to discuss "the possibility of inducing Vichy to dispatch the French fleet to defend Vichy's interests at St. Pierre and Miquelon." According to this account, the Germans considered that there was nothing to prevent France from protecting her interests in the Western Atlantic as she had in Syria.

†Commander de Villefosse told Ira Wolfert that he would personally see to it that, if the Marines did land, Wolfert would be the first American shot. Muselier told Pasquet on December 26 that it would be "repulsive to him to have to fire on American ships" as his wife was a descendent of Lafayette.

‡On another occasion, Muselier responded to reports of an American attack by echoing General Cambronne's classic retort at Waterloo: "*merde.*"

air and naval reconnaissances near the islands.[28] Nevertheless, it was obvious that the islands were in no position to put up more than a token resistance. The *Surcouf* and the corvettes were no match against a cruiser or battleship attack. In any case, they remained under Canadian operational control and over-all American command. Besides, on December 26, both the *Alysse* and *Aconit* returned to convoy duty, as Muselier had previously promised, and the other warships sailed shortly afterwards.[29]

In January, 1942, the Western Atlantic suddenly became an active theatre of war and, despite his own difficulties, Muselier was anxious to afford the Allies all the help he could, even to the extent of completely denuding St. Pierre and Miquelon of naval protection at times. Early in February, in the course of one such mission, the *Alysse* succumbed to a torpedo attack, and sank; four months later the *Mimosa* suffered a similar fate.* The whole situation was extraordinarily paradoxical: while the Free French were protecting the American and Canadian coastline, guarding Allied ships, and offering them shelter from enemy submarines, they were at the same time preparing to ward off a possible American attack and struggling to overcome the effects of a partial economic blockade.[30]

The serious economic plight in which Muselier found St. Pierre and Miquelon on his arrival was greatly aggravated by the sudden end to the flow of funds from Vichy accounts in North America. Naturally, neither the French Ambassador in Washington nor the French Minister in Ottawa was willing to authorize the release of credits for the use of the Free French administration in the islands. Moreover, General de Gaulle himself refused to touch Vichy money. Muselier did try to draw upon the existing funds in the Administrator's account in Halifax, but the Canadian Government would not approve this procedure. As a result, it was not until August, 1943,

---

*On February 18, 1942, a month after leaving St. Pierre, the *Surcouf* was rammed by an American freighter in the Caribbean and went down with all hands, including Commander Blaison. Thus, three of the four ships in the original expedition were lost within six months. Five St. Pierrais (but fortunately not Lieut.-Cdr. Pépin-Lehalleur) went down with the *Alysse* on February 8 and seventeen with the *Mimosa* (and Commander Birot) on June 9. The *Aconit* (Lieut-Cdr. L. V. Levasseur) avenged these losses by sinking two German submarines (U432 and U444) on one day in March, 1943. News of the corvette sinkings touched off renewed *Vichyard* agitation in St. Pierre. One businessman was placed under house arrest and several women were fined for seditious utterances. Angry Free French sailors also smashed the windows of several *Vichyard* shops—the sole incident of this sort.[31]

when Canada officially recognized Free French authority in St. Pierre and Miquelon, that this money became available. In the meantime, however, the new administration was authorized (on January 21, 1942) to open a second account of its own in a Halifax bank.

The shortage of foreign exchange was most critical during the early weeks after liberation. Despite frantic telegrams to de Gaulle urgently requesting a minimum of $80,000 from the *Caisse Centrale de la France Libre*, little immediate assistance was forthcoming from London.* Consequently, the islanders were compelled to live a precarious hand-to-mouth existence, making use of whatever financial resources they could lay their hands on. Some temporary relief was obtained by pooling the pay of the crews of the Free French ships and by tapping the personal savings of local residents—voluntarily except in the case of detainees and speculators. Additional sums were realized by disposing of the colony's remaining cache of liquor and stocks of salted cod.[32] But the most celebrated source of revenue came from the sale of overprinted postage stamps. Responsibility for this undertaking was entrusted to Marcel Benda, a Free French hanger-on associated with the Montreal *Le Jour*. Whether through ignorance or otherwise, he botched the operation badly, creating something of a scandal in philatelic circles. Moreover, part of the proceeds undoubtedly found their way into the pockets of some of those on the inside. The whole sorry mess was not cleaned up until the arrival in March, 1942, of Henri Gauthier, a qualified philatelist and Free French leader from Ottawa.†[33]

Early in January, the formidable difficulties facing the fledgling regime in St. Pierre and Miquelon were increased when, at Washington's insistence, an Allied embargo was imposed on the shipment of military stores and certain other supplies to the islands. The British reluctantly accepted this harsh measure as the best way to forestall more positive American intervention. Even Free French personnel including doctors and welfare workers were barred from travelling there. Admittedly, there were no restrictions (other than financial)

*Muselier suspected that de Gaulle was deliberately holding back. The Free French National Committee eventually provided 84 per cent of the colony's 1942 budget.

†Stamps worth $60,000 on the market were sold at their face value for $7,000. The remainder with a face value of $3,000 were sold by Gauthier for $34,000. Another series, specially surcharged "Oeuvres sociales" with a face value of $8,000 were (according to Muselier) sold on behalf of the newly-established Committee on Social Assistance for nearly $100,000.

on Free French corvettes stocking up in St. John's, Sydney, or Halifax with supplies of food and fuel which were then unloaded at St. Pierre. But, when Muselier requested the assistance of the Canadian naval authorities in moving certain stores from St. John's to St. Pierre, Ottawa refused. It also diverted to Saint John, New Brunswick a consignment of urgently needed supplies aboard the Free French ship *Indo-Chinois* destined for St. Pierre and Miquelon. As Robertson explained to Moffat in February, 1942, the Canadian Government took the view that it "should not act as though Admiral Muselier would remain in occupation of the islands." Consequently, communications with him were "limited to purely practical questions involved in escort and patrol duties." The Royal Canadian Navy found these restrictions increasingly embarrassing. On the one hand, it depended on the Free French for vital naval support. Yet, it found itself unable to offer full cooperation in return. Even its urgent request of February 19 for permission to post a naval liaison officer to St. Pierre was rejected in Ottawa "for the time being, while the situation in the islands is straightening itself out."

Throughout this trying period, Admiral Muselier remained remarkably understanding of Canada's diplomatic difficulties. "I feel satisfied," Christopher Eberts reported in early February, "that he realizes that Canada has very good reasons for continuing to recognize the Vichy Government, and he is anxious to see his Movement act with proper discretion in its dealings with the Canadian Government." Accordingly, the Consul recommended that Muselier be invited to Ottawa and given a full explanation of the limits of Canadian cooperation, and an assurance that steps would be taken to prevent "the recurrence of further incidents which could be interpreted as unfriendly."

Muselier himself was anxious to visit Ottawa (and Washington), but the Canadian Government did not welcome the prospect as it feared provoking "a first rate publicity sensation." To avoid a direct snub, it offered to send a plane to St. Pierre to facilitate the Admiral's speedy return to Britain. However, Muselier was by now so angry at Canada that he refused.* Although he appreciated the reasons

---

*He left instead by corvette on February 13, 1942. He spent three days in St. John's recovering from a severe cold and bronchitis and ten days at Gander waiting to catch a plane overseas, before finally reaching London on February 28. While in St. John's, Muselier was again the guest of Admiral Murray, to whom he apologized profusely for having broken his pledged word.

for Canadian policy, he was nevertheless infuriated by the various indignities to which he was subjected. At one point, he accused the Canadians of "treating us like negroes." He also became increasingly peremptory in his demand that the *Indo-Chinois* cargo be handed over. Finally on February 3, he threatened, not unreasonably, to withdraw his corvettes from convoy duty—after meeting the most recent Canadian request for a Free French escort for three ships bound from Louisburg. Mackenzie King, however, continued to hesitate, in view of the delicate state of relations with Vichy, "to take any step, however small, that might rock the boat." It was only as a result of a direct British request and Washington's acquiescence that Ottawa relented. On February 11, the civilian supplies from the *Indo-Chinois* were released and, the following month, the ban was lifted completely.[34]

Meanwhile, rather than wait upon events, Admiral Muselier attempted to shape them in the only way he could: by appealing over the heads of the Department of State to the sense of freedom and justice of the American public. His efforts to publicize his case may not have been decisive in determining the course of the crisis, but they undoubtedly had some influence on the outcome. This success was partly the result of the very active *Service de Presse et d'Information* organized by Jean LeBret of the Montreal *Le Jour* immediately after the liberation. More important though was the sympathetic response which the Free French cause struck in the hearts of the American people, and the strong support of the American press.

The inclusion of Ira Wolfert in the expedition was a stroke of good fortune that Muselier exploited to the full. Wolfert had merely to pick up his pen and sixty newspapers across the North American continent from the *New York Times* down accorded him headlines. Later, with the arrival of a number of other newsmen, the propaganda campaign became even more effective. St. Pierre and Miquelon's most enthusiastic advocate was the New York *Post*, a liberal tabloid with a long history of opposition to State Department appeasement of Vichy. Partly as a newspaper stunt and partly to embarrass Hull, the publisher of the *Post* dreamed up a scheme to bring a delegation from St. Pierre and Miquelon to Washington to plead its case with the Government. With this in mind, George Britt visited the islands in early January, 1942. He returned with three volunteers, all veterans of the first world war—Henry Humbert, Louis Plantegenest, and Emile-Léon Boissel, a fisherman—who after some delay managed to see Samuel Reber of the State Department and Eleanor Roosevelt at the beginning of February. They also made a number of radio and press appearances. However, communications with the mainland were so slow that, by the time the mission arrived in the United States, St. Pierre and Miquelon had faded from the front pages of the newspapers and was ceasing to concern even the diplomats. Consequently, the delegation did not have the impact on public or official opinion that it would have had a month earlier.*[35]

Admiral Muselier had two other objectives in St. Pierre and Miquelon: to improve the lot of the common people and to organize the islands' contribution to the Allied war effort. By the time he sailed from St. Pierre on February 13, 1942, he was able to look back with justifiable pride on the accomplishments of the Free French administration in both of these spheres. In this he was assisted by a remarkable group of able officials headed by Alain Savary who were determined to turn St. Pierre and Miquelon into a Free French showpiece and who gave the colony perhaps the best government it has ever had. The most notable innovations were in the field of social policy where a number of highly progressive measures were adopted. These had immense popular appeal—except within the traditional governing clique, who were suspicious of any change in the status quo and treated Muselier's reforms as one more grievance against the Free French.

In a period of under two months, Muselier greatly expanded the colony's social services, particularly the public health and child welfare facilities, trebled the advances paid to fishermen for their catches and encouraged them to establish a co-operative, set up several trade schools, increased relief payments, reduced hospital fees, and lowered the price of bread. His most striking success was in expanding employment. At the time of his arrival, there were 181 registered unemployed; two weeks later this number had been cut by more than half. The balance were soon absorbed, and before long

---

*Another development which contributed to projecting a favourable image of St. Pierre and Miquelon at a later date was the production of the Warner Bros. documentary "Little Isles of Freedom," directed by Victor Stoloff, written by Dorothy Thompson, and narrated by Charles Boyer.

an acute labour shortage developed. The explanation of this remarkable achievement was Muselier's policy of enrolling almost every available person in some form of war service. In addition, he launched an ambitious public works programme. His major prestige project was the construction of an air strip, a rather questionable undertaking at the time, but one which has since proven a valuable asset in stimulating the tourist trade.[36]

Muselier also banned the usual festivities associated with the *carnaval* season as a reminder of the sufferings of the French people, and closed the cafés and liquor stores during the mornings. Moreover, he demanded a new standard of morality in business and administration, clamped down on private profiteering and abuses of foreign exchange regulation, and attempted to suppress the petty smuggling which had so long been a part of the life of the islands. Similarly, imports of luxury goods were forbidden and pleasure driving prohibited.[37]

As in the First World War, the war effort of the tiny colony after December 1941 was impressive. It consisted principally of strengthening the home defences of the islands, offering the Allies a naval base, supplying them with fish, and sending a substantial contingent of men and women overseas. Recruiting began immediately after Muselier's arrival and at first more people came forward than could be accommodated on the ships available. In fact, a total of 456 men—about one-third of the male population of military age—and about fifty women volunteered for active service before the introduction of conscription in January 1944, and over three hundred (including those who had earlier escaped via Newfoundland) served overseas in the army, navy, or air force. Twenty-seven of them "Died for France," twenty-three at sea.

This record is all the more remarkable when one remembers the pressing problems of domestic and international politics which beset St. Pierre and Miquelon in the stirring days following its liberation. It was only by the exercise of the greatest ingenuity, by careful management, and by enlisting the sympathies of the overwhelming majority of the population that the colony managed to survive these few critical weeks during which the outside world was trying to make up its mind what to do with this pawn in the game of power politics.

5

ANGER

The international controversy generated by the seizure of St. Pierre and Miquelon passed through four more or less distinct phases during which diplomatic activity centred, first on the demand for prompt Canadian action to eject Muselier by force (Christmas Day), then on the restoration of the status quo ante by more acceptable means (the next week or so), thirdly on the neutralization of the territory (the next month), and finally on the winding up of the *affaire*.

The immediate reaction among most Americans, Britons, and Canadians to the news of the landing was enthusiastic. Here at last was a crumb of cheer after the depressing events of the previous two weeks. Moreover, as the *New York Times* commented, "The bloodless investiture of these surprised islands by four little warships . . . was accomplished with a display of style and manners in the best tradition of Alexandre Dumas."[1] In official circles in London and Ottawa, the coup was greeted with surprise and embarrassment—but not displeasure. Foreign Office officials and navy chiefs in both capitals were secretly overjoyed.* Thomas Stone of the Department of External Affairs told Moffat frankly that it was "a good thing that the blister had been broken, even if in an irregular fashion." Mackenzie King, too, though initially "terribly annoyed as well as distressed," let Hull know how "relieved and pleased" Canada felt. In St. John's, the Commissioner of Defence, L. E. Emerson, quickly cabled his congratulations to Muselier. Among American officials in Newfoundland, the instinctive reaction was to welcome the change. The US Army

*De Gaulle speculated that "the English are pleased with our action, first for reasons of maritime security, and then because of the dangers of American encroachments on their own American possessions."[2] There is no evidence that the second motive was important.

base commander recommended that the Free French be allowed to remain, and in St. John's a jubilant American consular officer joined a member of the Canadian High Commission in celebrating the coup.³

In Washington, the official reaction was very different. What Ira Wolfert called "the nicest Christmas present the world got that year" struck one State Department official as a "hell of a Christmas present." Cordell Hull in particular was positively livid with anger. He had only recently been stabbed in the back by the Japanese, and was in no mood to suffer a second humiliation. Accordingly, he denounced the occupation in an inflammatory press statement which immediately transformed an otherwise trivial incident into an *affaire*. "Our preliminary reports," the Secretary of State declared on Christmas afternoon, "show that the action taken by three so-called Free French ships at St. Pierre-Miquelon was an arbitrary action contrary to the agreement of all parties concerned and certainly without the prior knowledge or consent in any sense of the United States Government." He then added: "This Government has inquired of the Canadian Government as to the steps that Government is prepared to take to restore the *status quo* of these islands."⁴

The phrase which immediately caught the press and public's attention and aroused their ire was the reference to the "so-called Free French ships." Hull was responsible for this as he had personally inserted the offensive phrase in the original statement drafted by Samuel Reber, the Department's French desk officer. Whether Roosevelt agreed to this description is not clear. Hull asserts twice that his statement had the "full approval" of the President, but Sumner Welles insists that Roosevelt "thought the Department's statement ill-advised and said so flatly." According to Norman Davis, the President considered that "the Christmas Day communiqué about St. Pierre-Miquelon with its reference to 'so-called Free French ships'" was Hull's "one mistake" in his handling of the whole crisis. A number of Hull's advisers were also critical of his choice of words. Welles termed it "exceedingly unfortunate" (though he blamed Reber unfairly for proposing it), Dean Acheson thought it "silly," and Reber feared it might be "misconstrued." Lester Pearson in Ottawa considered it "one of the worst things" the Americans had done in the whole affair.⁵

The inclusion of the word "so-called" was nothing less than a gratuitous insult, and may have been meant as such. Although Cordell Hull has vehemently denied that this had been his intention, his public explanation some three weeks later—it was scarcely an apology —was both belated and feeble, and appeared to be simply an attempt to stem the flood of letters and telegrams of protest, some of them addressed to the "so-called Secretary of State." One telegram was signed by fifty prominent American citizens, including Frank P. Graham, Walter Millis, Reinhold Niebuhr, Carl Sandburg, and Helen Keller. In his defense, Hull claimed that he had merely sought to avoid blaming the Free French National Committee for what might have turned out to have been simply unauthorized piracy on Muselier's part. This is possible, but not quite plausible. A strained interpretation of Moffat's telegram to the State Department on Christmas morning could conceivably have led Hull to this conclusion. On the other hand, if this had been Hull's intention, a different wording would have conveyed the meaning better. In any case, Admiral Muselier's Proclamation, published on the front page of the *New York Times* that morning, stated explicitly that he had acted on General de Gaulle's orders.*⁶

The second point to note concerning the statement is that Hull denounced the Free French action as "contrary to the agreement of all parties concerned." The allusion here to an alleged agreement is obscure. Admittedly, de Gaulle had promised to postpone his planned seizure though, as we have seen, he considered himself no longer bound by his pledge once he had learned that the Canadians, with American encouragement, were themselves plotting to upset the status quo.† But the evidence also suggests that the agreements which Hull principally had in mind were not with the Free French at all but with Latin America and Vichy: namely, the Havana Act of 1940 on the disposition of European colonies in the Americas in general, and the recent Horne-Robert and Roosevelt-Pétain understandings on the status of French possessions.⁷ How Hull contrived to accuse

*The New York *Herald Tribune*, in a bitterly sarcastic editorial, commented that, "If in the future one refers to the 'so-called American State Department' it will now be understood that no reflection is intended upon the Americanism of Secretary Hull and his assistants, merely a doubt as to the adequacy with which they are discharging the functions of the Department of State."

†Two days later, in a Note to the State Department (which Atherton refused to accept), de Gaulle emphatically insisted that he had "no knowledge" of any "agreement of all parties concerned."⁸

de Gaulle of violating agreements to which he was not a party, and
to which he took strong exception, is something of a mystery.

By the same illogical process, Hull also seems to have considered
Canada almost equally culpable. In the course of a telephone conversation with Moffat on Christmas Day, he referred to Canadian pledges.
"I pointed out," Moffat records, "that there had been no pledges but
merely an understanding as to policy. He replied that in the first
place Mr. [Hume] Wrong's conversation with Mr. [Ray] Atherton
[on December 22] virtually involved a pledge, that in the second place
whether it was a pledge or an understanding was merely a quibble,
that in the third place, on the basis of our meeting of minds, the
United States had reached an agreement with Admiral Robert which
had now been breached." Accordingly, Canada ought to feel bound
by the agreement and obliged to take steps to enforce it. Indeed,
"Canada had perhaps greater responsibilities than anybody else,"
Hull asserted in the same conversation, "partly because of geography,
partly because of her understanding with Admiral Muselier. In any
event [he concluded] we must ask Canada to repair the damage and
to do so at once."[9]

Hull might also have added that his emphasis on Canada's special
responsibilities in the matter also reflected the widespread suspicion
in Washington that Ottawa was more deeply implicated in the plot
than it was prepared to admit (though it was surely illogical to suspect
Canada of complicity with Muselier and at the same time expect her
to agree to expel him). As two leading Washington newspapermen
reported: "When the smoke cleared, it seemed apparent that Muselier
. . . had set sail from Halifax with the approval, or at least the connivance, of Canadian authorities." President Roosevelt even seems to
have thought that Canada had supplied Muselier with the ships with
which to carry out the operation—until Mackenzie King disabused
him of this fantastic idea.[10]

Pierrepont Moffat too, jumped to the conclusion that he had been
double-crossed. On hearing news of the coup early Christmas morning, he immediately telephoned Thomas Stone, a close personal friend
for years, and bitterly accused him of bad faith.* Although Moffat

*Stone was singled out as the chief Canadian villain. Some months later, Moffat
reported that "Ray Atherton is particularly suspicious of Tommy Stone whom he
considers bitterly anti-American under the facade of individual friendliness." The

states that he satisfied himself later that morning that there was "no possible collusion between the Canadians and Admiral Muselier," it is doubtful if he was ever completely reassured.[11] There was also a personal reason which helps account for Moffat's "somewhat hectoring impatience" on St. Pierre and Miquelon. For him, the whole affair was personally embarrassing. He had always prided himself on his success in keeping Canada in line; naturally, therefore, he feared that his apparent failure on this occasion might adversely reflect on his professional reputation. As one senior External Affairs official noted at the time, "Mr. Moffat is very ambitious and it is probably his anxiety to impress Washington with his ability to get things done in Canada that leads to the occasional displays of impatience when he does not get immediate and favourable action in response to his demands."*

The State Department communiqué did more than denounce the Free French seizure. On the personal insistence of Cordell Hull, it proposed a restoration of the status quo and invited Canada to do the dirty deed. Faced with what amounted virtually to an American ultimatum to expel Muselier by force, the Canadian Government backed by public opinion reacted sharply. "In our view," Lester Pearson commented, "the conduct of the State Department in this matter is entirely inexcusable." He added, however, that "we know Moffat well enough here personally to tell him exactly what we think about the way his colleagues handled this matter." Thomas Stone, in particular, took his educational responsibilities in this respect seriously. In a frank conversation over eggnogs with Moffat Christmas evening, he bitterly denounced American policy over a whole range of issues and accused Washington of "asking Canada to put out de Gaulle after a plebiscite had been taken in his favour, . . . thereby impugning the honesty or value of the plebiscite, . . . disavowing and discouraging the Free French and . . . asking Canada to run the risk of coming to physical blows in the event that Admiral Muselier should offer forcible resistance."[12]

Equally objectionable to Ottawa was the manner in which the

Vichy Minister in Ottawa cleared the Canadian Government of collusion, but not the Royal Canadian Navy. Savary says "the Canadian authorities did not know anything of our plans when we left Halifax."

*Moffat's attitude at this time gave rise to a departmental ditty entitled "Sur le Pierrepont. . . ."

American approach was made, particularly as this was but the latest in a series of recent diplomatic incidents.* When Moffat first heard about the proposal, he suggested that the matter be discussed with Mackenzie King on his arrival in Washington the next day. Hull, however, said "that was not quick enough, that the situation was so urgent that the Canadians should start steps this very afternoon." Moffat then asked Washington to withhold any public statement on the matter until he had taken it up with the Canadians, but Hull ignored this advice, much to Moffat's consternation, and rushed into print with a statement containing the offensive sentence calling on Canada to remedy the situation—without the courtesy of informing Ottawa first.

This press release had a profound effect on Canada's attitude to the whole affair. While the Government had from the first been reluctant to become the "whipping boy" for the Americans or to humiliate the Free French, up to this point it had been prepared to do what it could to ease the situation, provided, of course—and here we again encounter one of the prime determinants of Canadian foreign policy—the British were also agreeable. All this changed with the publication of the Hull bombshell. Immediately afterwards, Robertson telephoned Moffat "in great perturbation" to protest at the contents of the communiqué and to complain that the Americans had not "played the game." "His whole attitude," Moffat noted in his diary, "had changed from one of helpful cooperation to one of most reluctant cooperation." Henceforth, Canadian policy appeared to the Americans to be casual and unconcerned, if not downright obstructive.[13]

After a further long-distance telephone conversation Christmas afternoon with James Dunn, the State Department's Adviser on Political Relations, which closed on the belligerent note, "Muselier must go, and go shortly," Moffat sought to appease the Canadians and encourage them to work out a formula which would save de Gaulle's face. Accordingly, Hugh Keenleyside drafted a statement, but when Moffat saw it he was shocked. "It was so bad," he wrote in his diary, "and so completely divergent from all we were asking that

*"United States-Canadian relations present a very difficult problem indeed in present circumstances." (Pearson, January 9, 1942). Only a week before the seizure of St. Pierre and Miquelon, Washington had excluded Canada from the Rio Conference of American Foreign Ministers.[14]

I pled with [Thomas Stone] to issue nothing at all rather than a statement which placed our positions further and further apart." Moffat also reiterated the Washington view that "Muselier would have to get out of the islands, [and] the status quo would have to be restored."

Lester Pearson immediately reported to Prime Minister King, who by this time was in Montreal en route to Washington, that the Americans had renewed their "ultimatum demanding we should take action immediately." According to King's account, Pearson was "obviously greatly disturbed" and felt the situation was "critical."* The Prime Minister then consulted two of his defence ministers, Ralston and Macdonald. "We agreed [King reports] we could not take action without thereby implying that we had been responsible for what the Free French had done. Also that until the President and Mr. Churchill agreed on the action to be taken, we could not take action without precipitating a new situation for which we would be wholly and solely responsible."† Accordingly, they drafted a revised statement which specifically denied any Canadian responsibility for the Free French occupation and ruled out any immediate Canadian intervention: "We decline to commit ourselves to any action or to take any action pending [agreement with both the United Kingdom and the United States]. In the circumstances . . . the Canadian Government cannot take the steps requested to expel the Free French and restore the status quo in the islands."[15]

From the American point of view, this new draft was not much better than the earlier version. In the end, therefore, the Canadian Government decided not to issue any public statement, though the Prime Minister did tell reporters on his way to Washington that Canada was not a party to any agreement to maintain the status quo and that he considered it mainly a matter for Frenchmen to settle among themselves.[16]

On arrival in Washington, Mackenzie King went straight to the

---

*Pearson himself recorded that "St. Pierre and Miquelon gave me one of the busiest and most exciting Christmases I have ever had. I was at the Office all day and until 1:30 A.M."

†King felt that "the best thing to do was to tell the Americans to themselves order the Free French out," though this "raised the question as to who is in command in that area." Moffat had earlier told Dunn that, in his considered judgment, if action against the Free French proved necessary, the Canadians would find it "less embarrassing" if the Americans did it than have "the onus thrust upon them."

State Department. Both there and later at the White House, he emphatically repudiated the suggestion that Canada was in any way responsible for the actions of the Free French. He reminded Roosevelt, Hull, and Churchill (who had also arrived in the American capital) that Canada had followed a consistent policy with regard to these islands of acting only on the basis of agreement with Britain and the United States, and stressed that she would continue to do so. Accordingly, there could be no question of Canadian action until Washington and London had settled their differences.

From the first, the response of the press in Canada to the liberation of St. Pierre and Miquelon was generally enthusiastic. This was particularly true of French-language newspapers—with the notable exceptions of *Le Devoir* of Montreal and later *Le Droit* of Ottawa, both of which were frankly hostile, partly because of the association of *Le Jour* with the expedition. In Quebec City, *L'Evénement-Journal* considered Free French control "logical, prudent and beneficial," *Le Soleil* expressed "lively satisfaction," and even *L'Action Catholique* considered that "everybody is delighted." Editorial opinion and news presentation in Montreal newspapers was also favourable. Whatever initial hesitation there may have been was quickly overcome as a result of Hull's angry Christmas Day statement.[17]

Curiously, this outburst had the opposite effect on the English-language press, providing temporarily a "cold douche on enthusiasm." Thus, the *Ottawa Citizen* quickly concluded on December 27 that "Washington is probably right" (though even it did not go so far as to advocate the expulsion of Muselier). According to one Free French press analyst in Ottawa at the time, "This [reaction] indicated clearly how powerful is the influence of Washington and what it thinks in forming editorial opinion in Canada. I believe it even surprised many editors themselves to see how quickly Canada's public opinion became uncertain, hesitant and inclined to follow the thinking in Washington. The result was that many Canadian commentators abstained completely from discussing the subject." This setback in press support for Free France proved short-lived. Any lingering faith in the infallibility of American policy-makers was finally shattered when Churchill addressed the Canadian Parliament on December 30. As Pierrepont Moffat observed on New Year's Day, "although public sympathy has been from the beginning with the

Admiral," prior to Churchill's speech, "there was a willingness to recognize that [Muselier's] move might have such far-flung repercussions . . . that some form of accommodation . . . might be a wise move." However, since then, public opinion in Canada had "swung as a virtual unit against any form of compromise. Led by prominent members of Parliament and echoed by the press, Mr. King is being petitioned to take no part in any policy that would savour of a rebuff to General de Gaulle."[18]

Although the State Department was undoubtedly in deadly earnest in inviting Canada to evict Muselier by force, and on her own, regardless of the wishes of the people of St. Pierre and Miquelon, it was difficult for others to treat the idea seriously. Indeed, it was so unrealistic and unreasonable a request that it survived barely a day. In view of the strong reaction of the Canadian Government, and King's continued opposition to any resort to force,* the Christmas Day scheme was quickly dropped in favour of a "formula" which would achieve the same ends by more acceptable means. As first worked out by Cordell Hull on December 26 and 27, with some assistance from Mackenzie King,† this called for Muselier's voluntary withdrawal, the restoration of Vichy authority (but not of de Bournat), and either the closing down of the radio station or the posting of Canadian and American personnel to St. Pierre, to control broadcasting.‡ No one would be censured; the whole incident would be dismissed as due to confusions and misunderstandings. In fact, the Free French were to be warmly praised for their part in making agreement with Vichy on proper supervision of the radio station possible.[19]

*It is not clear whether King (or anyone in Ottawa) was aware that "Q" Force was still standing by to move on short notice. Not that this would have made any real difference. A force of under two hundred men could not have dislodged Muselier. Operation "Q" had assumed that there would be no organized resistance.

†Although Roosevelt and Churchill had asked Hull and King to work out a "satisfactory practical solution" and King discussed the matter with Hull at length, the result was in no sense a joint proposal as has sometimes been suggested. Hull says King "seemed more or less acquiescent, without expressly saying so" to his approach. King says he did not receive an actual copy of the State Department formula though he was "just as glad that the matter should be kept between Britain and the U.S." Pickersgill says King "passively but stubbornly objected to any proposal to restore the status quo ante."[20]

‡For texts or summaries of the several successive proposals, see Appendix B.

No one outside the State Department (with the possible exception of Mackenzie King) was particularly enthusiastic about this plan. Certainly the Free French, though they were not informed of it, let alone consulted, would have rejected it out of hand. It seems inconceivable that the State Department should ever have thought de Gaulle would now abdicate in favour of Vichy, and accept the nefarious Canadian plan when this is what had triggered the affair in the first place. Moreover, to do so would have exposed his followers to the certainty of merciless reprisals. The Canadian consul had already reported that the immediate reaction of at least two leading *Vichyards* to Hull's Christmas Day rebuke was to threaten revenge on Free French supporters.

Nor did the Hull proposals appeal to the British. While they deplored the behaviour of de Gaulle, they had consistently advocated Free French control of St. Pierre and Miquelon as the best solution to the problem politically and militarily, and now felt strongly that, with Muselier established there, he ought to be allowed to remain. Above all, nothing should be done to disavow de Gaulle, a point which was also stressed in Ottawa.[21]

Hull considered this attitude of the British incomprehensibly irresponsible, and said so in unmistakable terms. In the course of "a blunt conversation" with Churchill at the White House on December 26, he "indulged in some plain speaking," apparently with some assistance from Mackenzie King. At this stage, Churchill was prepared to contemplate a Free French evacuation simply to appease Hull and thus dispose of the matter as quickly as possible. According to King, the British leader even agreed to "take de Gaulle by the back of the neck . . . and bring him to his senses."[22] However, Churchill's attitude soon stiffened when the Foreign Office objected strenuously to any move to oust Muselier from the islands. Moreover, the Prime Minister was finding Hull's intense preoccupation with "this departmental point," amid gigantic events, a trifle tedious.*[23] On December 30,

---

*Hull on the other hand claimed it was the British who were making a mountain out of a molehill. He told the British Minister in Washington on January 8 that: "I wonder whether the British are more interested in a dozen [sic] or so Free Frenchmen, who seized these islands, and the capital they can make out of it primarily at the expense of the United States Government, than they are in Singapore and in the World War situation itself. I have neither seen nor heard of anything from British spokesmen in the last few days that would indicate to me that there existed a World War compared with the Saint-Pierre-Miquelon situation."

he let fly in a typically Churchillian oration before the Canadian
Parliament—in the presence of both the Vichy Minister and the Free
French representative, Colonel Pierrené. With obvious relish, he
heaped contempt upon "the men of Vichy" who lay "prostrate at the
foot of the conqueror," and lavished praise on those Frenchmen "who
would not bow their knees and who under General de Gaulle have
continued to fight at the side of the Allies."*24

This "highly incendiary" outburst caused Hull to explode. Even
prior to this, he had been in a fearsome rage, but now, as a result of
this "violent diatribe" as he called it, his anger quickly assumed (in
Robert Sherwood's words) "hurricane proportions." The speech confirmed his suspicions that the British were "really behind" the seizure
and that they were now "fomenting . . . for British benefit the bitter
agitation" being directed against the State Department. He could
imagine no other explanation for the spontaneous wave of indignation
which swept the American people than that Churchill had deliberately turned his press agents loose. As Sherwood records, "Nothing
could convince Hull that the British had not double-crossed him."25
Something of Hull's bitterness towards the Prime Minister may be
sensed in a malicious memorandum sent to the President on December
31 in which he urged Roosevelt to work out a solution to the problem
with Churchill provided he is "disposed to talk with you, or rather
let you talk with him."

The press campaign that Cordell Hull complained about was widespread and surprisingly violent, possibly because, for many Americans,
the issue involved in St. Pierre and Miquelon was a simple question
of principle—appeasement.† The New York Herald Tribune found
Washington's attitude "very unpleasant," a "strange web of contradic-
tions," indicative of "befuddlement and want of courage." "The moral
victory," it predicted, "will lie with the Free French cause—which

*Thus Churchill, as Robertson observed, had completely "boxed the compass"
within a period of four or five days. Robertson assumed that Churchill's Ottawa
speech was intended to "prevent the Free French movement from falling to pieces
under Allied criticism." Pearson noted that "Mr. Churchill reacts somewhat differently in Washington under American pressure than in Ottawa."26
†According to press surveys, roughly 70 per cent of the nation's editorial writers
welcomed the Free French seizure initially, 70 per cent later supported the State
Department's criticism and, following Churchill's Canadian speech, 64 per cent
condemned Hull. Thus, over a third of the newspapers vacillated radically in their
views.27

is our own." The New York *Post*, in a series of daily front page editorials, charged that in the past the State Department had tried "cajolery, bribery, blindness and stupidity in bidding against Hitler for Vichy's support. Now it is trying treachery." The *Washington Post* sympathized with those who were "bewildered by the psychology of men who wage war with their right hand and appease with their left." Even the *Christian Science Monitor*, though regretting the confusion the Free French had created, feared that the Hull ultimatum to Ottawa may have given Vichy the "notion that the United States can be made an unwitting agent of pro-Axis interests."

A number of widely syndicated columnists also joined in the general hue and cry. Dorothy Thompson described the conduct of "certain Striped Pants in the State Department" as "perfectly terrible." Walter Lippman referred to the affair as "lamentable," a "fiasco," "this blunder, this little diplomatic Pearl Harbor," and Anne O'Hare McCormick called it "unfortunately handled." Major George Fielding Eliot reminded his readers that "no satellite power of the Axis has done as much to aid the Axis as has Vichy France." The condemnation by influential radio commentators such as H. V. Kaltenborn, Raymond Gram Swing, and Elmer Davis was equally harsh.[28]

The Secretary of State was particularly sensitive to this wave of criticism since it was a novel experience for him thus to be attacked. In the past, he, almost alone among members of Roosevelt's Cabinet, had been virtually immune from public abuse and ridicule, and he did not take kindly to it now. In vain, Hull begged Churchill (on January 2) to say "just a few little words" of appreciation for his Vichy policy, but the Prime Minister was quite unrepentant. Nor was Roosevelt, to whom Hull turned next, any more sympathetic. Indeed, he had told his Secretary of State only the day before that it was "inadvisable to resuscitate this question." While at the outset he had been inclined to support Hull, at this stage he simple shrugged his shoulders over the whole affair and hoped it would die a natural death.* Robert Sherwood even suspected that he derived "a certain amount of mischievous pleasure from the spectacle of his esteemed old friend . . . learning at last how it felt to be the target of wide-

---

*Sherwood states that Roosevelt "refused to make any reference to the St. Pierre-Miquelon incident" in his State of the Union Message to Congress on January 6 because "he believed the whole thing would quickly blow over and be forgotten. He was wrong."

spread criticism." Hull was so exasperated by Roosevelt's refusal to back him up or take him seriously that he eventually pencilled out a note to the President tendering his resignation. It was never sent, but the fact that he could actually consider such a step is dramatic evidence of the extraordinary extent to which this incident dominated —and warped—his thinking.* [29]

Thus, Cordell Hull found himself rebuffed on all sides: by the British, the Canadians, the American people, even the President. But perhaps the unkindest cut of all was the ingratitude of Vichy. It alone welcomed Hull's Christmas Day statement and, although "rather skeptical" about the extent to which Washington would be prepared to back up its brave words, eagerly exploited it to the full. On December 30, Admiral Darlan alleged that the Germans had already used the seizure as "an argument for the entry of Axis troops into Africa in order that it might be protected against a similar invasion."†[30] (He also threatened that, if the United States did not keep her promises concerning St. Pierre and Miquelon, he would arrange with the Japanese to have them occupy the Pacific islands that had rallied to Free France. Early in February, he did in fact conclude an agreement to co-operate with the Japanese in capturing these territories.)[31] Vichy

---

*Hull himself states that St. Pierre and Miquelon was "one of several factors" inducing him to resign, the "principal" one being the state of his health. After a conversation with Norman Davis, Moffat recorded that Hull had been "hurt to the quick by several episodes. The first was the unfounded accusation in the press that he had failed to tip off the Army and Navy as to the seriousness of the situation in Japan. The second was the St. Pierre-Miquelon issue, where he felt that Churchill had double-crossed him and that the President had supported Churchill. The third was when Sumner Welles changed his instructions [at the Rio de Janeiro Conference] without consulting Washington. . . . Norman Davis had prevailed upon him not to resign in anger and, above all, not to resign on the St. Pierre-Miquelon issue. Finally the Secretary decided to resign on the ground of ill-health. He went through every known test and the Doctor pronounced him absolutely fit, merely suffering from nervous exhaustion."

†Langer says that it is "altogether likely" that Darlan's references to alleged German pressure was "mere camouflage, but of course one could not tell." Hytier suggests that, in contrast to the State Department's "disproportionate fear of Vichy reactions," Vichy, while annoyed, does not "seem to have taken the affair tragically" and that its protests were "certainly made in large part to reassure the Germans." Muselier had considered the pre-liberation plan for Canadian supervision of the St. Pierre radio station a much more dangerous precedent for Germany to follow in such vital places as Casablanca and Dakar. The Canadians had also realized that their plan "might be interpreted by Vichy as an effort by Canada to take control if not possession of the islands . . .; and that Vichy might seek to find in the incident . . . an excuse to hand over the French fleet to Germany as a means of protecting French colonial possessions."

spokesmen everywhere echoed the demand for the "immediate re-establishment of the status quo ante." Only then could the question of control of the radio station be considered. Any thought of an early replacement for de Bournat was, however, ruled out.* On one occasion, on December 30, when Gaston Henry-Haye, the French Ambassador in Washington, was preparing to launch into a lengthy recital of French rights, Hull cut him short. It was more than he could take. "At a moment," he protested with understandable bitterness, "when I am being subjected to every sort of abuse, even in this country . . . the only reply I receive from you is a stump speech about the greatness of the French nation. Soon it will be too late to handle this matter on its merits and in a proper spirit because of its explosive possibilities."[32] This proved to be the case.

Negotiations during the early days of 1942 over the future status of St. Pierre and Miquelon were complicated and confused. As Harry Hopkins observed, "Hull really wanted to take the whole thing up through diplomatic channels, but the President insisted on handling it with Churchill."[33] Yet these two war leaders, unlike the Secretary of State, were too preoccupied with other pressing matters to give the islands more than passing attention. Moreover, Roosevelt and Churchill did not share the exaggerated fears of imminent disaster which drove Hull to urge a speedy restoration of the status quo.

Cordell Hull's anxiety to effect a quick settlement was also due to the continued public outcry against his "appeasement" policies. Popular passions, which he described as "rabid," had been further inflamed as a result of Churchill's outburst in Ottawa. As the New York *Herald Tribune* commented editorially, the Prime Minister had "certainly blown all question of St. Pierre-Miquelon and Washington's 'so-called Free French' through the dusty windows of the State Department." The Secretary of State, as already indicated, reproached Churchill severely (on January 2) for this further humiliation, but failed to persuade him to undo any of the damage. Moreover, when Hull asked Roosevelt to "bring his own personal influence

---

*The Vichy Note of December 27 included insulting references to "Gaullist mercenaries," "ex-Admiral Muselier," etc. A similar Note to the Canadian Government provoked Robertson into speaking to Ristelhueber "with some asperity."

with Churchill to bear to produce a straightening out of this ano-malous situation," the President flatly refused.[34]

Later that morning, Hull worked out with the Vichy Ambassador a modus vivendi designed to "save the face of the French on the question of sovereignty." Although this proposal had the strong sup-port of Henry-Haye, it evoked only qualified approval from Vichy. Its spokesmen demanded amongst other things that the Canadian Government, like the American Government, should formally under-take to respect the sovereignty of the territory. The reaction of Admiral Robert in Martinique was even more belligerent; he still harped on the point that Washington should acknowledge that it was "obligated to obtain the reestablishment of French sovereignty over St. Pierre Miquelon."[35]

On January 2, Cordell Hull reported to the President on his dis-cussions with the French Ambassador that morning. At the same time, he proposed that, pending the conclusion of a final settlement, Roose-velt and Churchill should issue an interim statement "to quiet steadily spreading rumours and reports very damaging to the British-American situation"—by which he meant to take the heat off the State Depart-ment. The departmental draft which Hull sent to the White House assured the world that an agreement satisfactory to all concerned would not be difficult, gave implied approval to continued American diplomatic relations with Vichy, and ended with the bland assertion that there should be "no occasion for confusion or misunderstanding since there is complete cooperation and understanding" among the United States, Britain, and Canada on the matter.[36]

The next day, the President and Prime Minister drew up a tri-partite declaration of their own, and forwarded it to London and Ottawa for their approval. It emphasized that while the three govern-ments viewed "this incident as on a very small scale compared to what is going on all over the world," it did raise certain problems related to the safety of Allied shipping in the North Atlantic and "existing international commitments" (which the Americans had with Vichy and Latin America). The statement continued:

Accordingly, the three Governments have agreed that the principle that these islands are to be regarded in the present phase as demilitarized and out of the war shall be maintained. All armed forces will be withdrawn, it being understood that at the same time adequate steps shall be taken to assure that no radio station situated on the islands shall be used contrary to the interests of the United Nations. The local inhabitants will be left in full exercise of their rights of domestic self-government. . . .

This document incorporated some of Cordell Hull's ideas and phrases, but owed rather more to a draft Churchill and Lord Halifax had put together on New Year's Day.* In addition, it introduced an idea which the President had toyed with some time earlier, of letting the St. Pierrais manage themselves until the end of the war. The Free French would still withdraw, but the Vichy French would not return. This was the major departure from Hull's previous approach.†[37]

Monday, January 5 was another bad day in the life of Cordell Hull. The British, the Canadians, and the French all raised objections to the various proposals presented to them. From Hull's point of view, the Vichy French reservations were the most reasonable as he was still emotionally committed to allowing them to reassert their sovereignty over the islands.

The attitude of the Canadians was much more disturbing, especially as the State Department had assumed that Mackenzie King had already accepted the Roosevelt-Churchill formula. It came as something of a shock, therefore, to learn that this was not quite true. King's concern was with the domestic political implications of any demand for a Free French withdrawal. With the reaction of the Canadian public and press, as Moffat noted, "still bad," the proposed agreement was bound to be "most unpopular" in the country.‡[38] Consequently, before giving his final approval, the Prime Minister wanted to be absolutely certain that it had the full support of both Churchill and the Cabinet in London as well as of his own War Committee—which was not meeting for another two days. Above all, it was of the "utmost importance" to have firm British assurances that Muselier would

*According to Pierrepont Moffat who heard the story only at third hand, the purpose of the British formula was to "set forth the circumstances of the seizure, protect the collateral position of the Havana Act, and then leave the Free French in occupation."

†Hull makes no mention of the Roosevelt-Churchill draft, but instead charges that the President "did not press [my] statement upon his visitor, nor did Mr. Churchill agree to it." Two days later, in sounding out the reaction of the French Ambassador to the Roosevelt-Churchill declaration, Hull claimed it as his own. Moffat thought the statement "extremely adroit."

‡Moffat wrote on January 5 that the Canadian press was "being fed so much on propaganda from everywhere that the Free French will remain in possession that the ultimate announcement is going to come as a shock. The Canadian public is not capable of seeing the bigger issues involved and certainly the Government has not taken steps by way of preparation to point out the bigger issues."

depart peacefully; his fighting speech only the day before had scarcely been encouraging in this respect. King also insisted there should be no possibility of reprisals against de Gaulle's partisans in the islands. Finally, he felt that, as the Allies were giving up a great deal under the formula, the timing of the announcement should be "at their pleasure and not at that of Vichy." Certainly, it should not come first from the Vichy French—or the Germans. Ottawa had already been embarrassed by a mischievous broadcast from Berlin earlier that day announcing the eviction of Muselier.*

The Secretary of State was in no mood to countenance Canada's dragging her feet any longer. He was "so annoyed with the adverse publicity and the deliberate attempts of troublemakers to sow trouble" that he had decided that the time had come to issue the Roosevelt-Churchill statement. And having made his own mind up, he demanded "immediate" Canadian compliance. According to Moffat, Hull "directed me to put all the persuasion of which I was capable [to bear on the Canadian Government] to get a clearance this evening." (It was then six o'clock.) When Pierrepont Moffat reminded James Dunn of King's reservations, Dunn "swept these aside as of no importance and said that speed was of the essence if we wanted to get an apparent alignment of front. If it was not forthcoming, the Secretary would probably have to issue a unilateral statement in which he would set forth in his own words the position taken by Mr. Churchill and Mr. King." Robertson was "most unhappy and said that he could not possibly agree to the statement on such short notice." Eventually, after a hectic series of long-distance telephone consultations and under great pressure, Mackenzie King reluctantly gave in and undertook to accept anything the British and Americans could agree upon.†

*"The St. Pierre and Miquelon affair has been settled, it was officially announced here [Vichy] Monday [January 5]. It was declared that the United States authorities saw to it that Admiral Muselier and his forces evacuated both islands. An official French communiqué has been prepared for Monday night."

†Writing four days later, Pearson commented that, "we are not out of the woods yet, though the earlier and wilder plan of Washington to use us to drive the 'so-called Free French' . . . out has been abandoned. However, there is very little we can do to influence American policy on this matter. I am afraid they do not treat our views with any great deference or respect and I am also afraid that we have ourselves partly to blame for this. Great Britain will have to fight the battle for the Free French and it looks as if we will have to accept any arrangement agreed to by Great Britain and the United States. Mr. Churchill was very sound on the matter when he was in Ottawa and his speech in the House of Commons in his references to Vichy was very helpful though it infuriated the State Department."[39]

At long last, Washington seemed to have achieved three-power agreement. Even Churchill had approved the declaration and, to Americans unfamiliar with the operation of the cabinet system, this seemed sufficient to bind the British. It came as a distinctly unpleasant surprise, therefore, when a message arrived that evening from London proposing three changes, one of which "cut straight across" Hull's negotiations. The Secretary of State was so upset that he went home indicating that "in all probability, he would issue a unilateral statement on the morrow." Actually wiser counsels in the Department prevailed and there was no repetition of his Christmas Day blunder. Hull, however, did not easily forget this latest act of obstruction. Three days later, "speaking as I had seldom spoken to the representative of a friendly nation," he lectured Sir Ronald Campbell, the British Minister, at length on his opinion of Britain's conduct throughout the *affaire*.[40]

Meanwhile, the State Department had prepared a new draft agreement on January 8 which incorporated some of the improvements suggested by the British and Canadians. This provided that:

1. The islands are French and will remain French [a point Eden insisted on].
2. To avoid any potential threat to the shipping of the governments concerned, the use of the wireless station on the islands will be subject to the supervision and control of observers appointed by the American and Canadian Governments and attached to their respective consulates.
3. The islands shall be neutralized and demilitarized and shall be considered out of the war.
4. The present Vichy Administrator shall be withdrawn for the period of the war; the appointment of an Administrator shall be withheld for the same period, and the administration of the islands shall be left in the hands of the Consultative Council.
5. All armed forces will be withdrawn. . . .[41]

This proved to be Hull's last great effort to find a basis of agreement among the contending parties.

Although the various proposals worked out in Washington during the first week of 1942 differed in emphasis and, in some respects, in principle, they all dealt with three issues: security, sovereignty, and demilitarization.

Provision for adequate supervision of the St. Pierre radio station was the overriding concern of the Allies. It was also in a sense the simplest problem to deal with. Washington and Ottawa had agreed on a solution a month earlier before the Free French take-over, and it only remained to work out the details. London continued to feel that control of the islands and not just of the radio transmitter was necessary, but it did not press the point. At one stage (December 26), President Roosevelt suggested that the Canadian Government appoint a commission composed of representatives of Vichy France, Free France, and Canada to look after the station. This idea was thoroughly unrealistic and never seriously pursued. Instead, negotiations proceeded on the basis of Hull's proposal to send "three or four experts of Canadian nationality" to St. Pierre.* Subsequently, it was decided that these technicians should be called naval observers and be attached to their consulates, as in Martinique, in order to "save the face of the French on the question of sovereignty."

Although Vichy vehemently denied that the St. Pierre broadcasts posed any threat to Allied shipping, it quickly recognized the need to give in to the Americans on this point. At the same time, it asked that the Allies merely control the station and not close it down. While agreeing to end broadcasts of weather bulletins and to submit messages *en clair* to censorship, Vichy wanted to retain the right to "strictly limited use of the wireless for transmission of messages of a purely administrative order" in code. The Free French later were to take an even stronger stand. They insisted that the Canadian and American "liaison agents" should merely co-operate with the station management and not exercise control over it.[42]

The intense preoccupation of Frenchmen of all political persuasions with the forms of sovereignty was even more apparent in the lengthy discussions concerning the future administration of St. Pierre and Miquelon. Vichy was determined to reinstate the former Administrator in office both in order to symbolize its restored authority and also as a tribute to his "courageous attitude in the face of the Free French invaders." As evidence of Vichy's continued confidence in de Bournat,

---

*This was subsequently amended to "three or four experts, preferably Canadian," then "two or three Canadians and an American," later one or two Americans and one or two Canadians, and finally (according to one account) two Americans and a Canadian. De Gaulle was prepared to accept "at most one Canadian and one American."

Marshal Pétain had promptly bestowed his personal *Francisque* medal on him and elevated him to a higher rank in the *Légion d' honneur*, actions which even Hull considered distinctly unhelpful at that critical juncture.[43]

Cordell Hull had originally been quite agreeable to allowing de Bournat to continue as Administrator—until Mackenzie King during his visit to Washington told him bluntly (and repeatedly) that this was "impossible," that de Bournat was "pro-Axis and his wife a German," and that his return would probably provoke civil strife. Hull eventually accepted the force of King's arguments and informed the French Ambassador that de Bournat would have to go as he had made himself "personally offensive to Canada and to some of the people of the islands." Vichy could still name his successor, but he would have to be someone whose "conduct and attitude would be broad enough and impersonal enough to be free from reasonable objections" on the part of the Allies or any considerable number of the local population. Hull had in mind a St. Pierrais who had managed to "eschew politics" and could thus provide "peaceful and nonpartisan" government. In the autumn of 1940, Canada had suggested Emile Guillot, the senior judge in the islands, as a possibility, but he was no longer in St. Pierre.

At first, Vichy rejected outright any suggestion of replacing de Bournat as he had done such "a brilliant piece of work." Moreover, it claimed there was no local inhabitant competent to fulfil the duties of Administrator satisfactorily. The most Vichy was prepared to do was to recall de Bournat to Martinique temporarily for consultations —after he had been allowed to resume office for a "brief period." He would then return to St. Pierre on the armed merchant cruiser *Barfleur** to "confirm the restoration of French sovereignty in these islands." A few days later, the Vichy Government relented slightly and indicated its willingness to name an acting Administrator in place of de Bournat who would be "actually removed though not officially recalled." By then, however, it was too late to consider a compromise in these terms. The Allies were now not prepared to accept any Vichy appointee.[44]

*The *Barfleur* was a modern 4,300-ton banana ship, 315 feet in length. At the outbreak of war, it had been converted to an auxiliary cruiser and armed with seven 5.9-inch guns, two 3-inch guns, and two anti-aircraft guns. It had been based on Martinique since the fall of France.

On January 3, Roosevelt and Churchill decided that the islanders should be allowed to rule themselves under a system of "domestic self-government" modelled on that traditional American folk institution, the "town meeting."[45] What this would mean in practice was not made clear, except that a local Consultative Council would take the place of the Administrator for the duration of the war.* The British, backed by the Canadians, insisted that the council should be a more representative body than the *Conseil d'Administration* elected in 1939 in which the Free French element was a minority. Hull, however, was greatly upset by the suggestion that there should by a new council elected by the people themselves.†

Although General de Gaulle naturally welcomed the prospect of democratic reforms, he opposed the attempt to grant autonomy to the islands. Instead he demanded that Savary should remain as Administrator and also that the Consultative Council should be "under the orders" of the French National Committee in London. He quickly saw in the proposal for territorial self-government a sinister Anglo-Saxon plot to dismember the French Empire. Although this universal and recurring French suspicion was almost completely groundless, it is worth noting that what Cordell Hull and Roosevelt were advocating (according to Professor Langer) was "really an American-Canadian-British trusteeship, though the phrase had to be avoided" in view of the Havana agreements of 1940 (which provided for collective trusteeship by the American republics of European possessions in the Western Hemisphere).[46]

The fundamental Free French objection to the State Department

*This had the advantage of avoiding the need to choose between Vichy and Free France. Another alternative was a second plebiscite under neutral auspices. There was considerable speculation in the press over this possibility, but the idea apparently received little encouragement in official circles. Whatever the outcome, it would have been embarrassing to the Department of State.[47]

†The problem largely solved itself as over half the membership of the *Conseil d'Administration* changed after the liberation. Previously it had consisted of four ex officio members (Gilbert de Bournat, Emile-Raoul Macé, Léon Bourroult, and Alexandre Paret) and seven elected members. Of the latter, three were *Vichyards* (Henri Claireaux, Jean Legassé, and Auguste Maufroy), two were Free French (81-year-old Emile Gloanec and Henri Paturel) and two were more or less neutral (Henri Epaule and Léonce Claireaux). Muselier removed the first three officials appointing Alain Savary and Félix Arago, two FNFL officers, and Emile Sasco, who was neutral, in their places. The three elected *Vichyards* resigned and were automatically succeeded by their elected alternates (*membres suppléants*). Two of these were Free French (Léonce Dupont and Pierre-Louis Sérignac) and the third was neutral (Albert Grimeaux).[48]

proposal of January 8, was the provision that St. Pierre and Miquelon should be "neutralized and demilitarized," and "considered out of the war." This was completely unacceptable to General de Gaulle as it would defeat his whole purpose of bringing French territories back into the war. He was willing to issue a statement that the French National Committee had "no intention of keeping its ships at St. Pierre and Miquelon" and that they would "shortly resume their normal functions, which is to attack the enemy wherever he is to be found." But he insisted that the local home guard should continue in the territory to protect it from attack.*[49]

Although negotiations with Vichy France began immediately after Christmas, the Free French were not brought into the picture until three weeks later. The principal reason for this was the belief in Washington that de Gaulle, by his actions, had forfeited whatever rights he once had to be consulted on St. Pierre and Miquelon. There was also the practical problem of how to persuade him to retire peacefully. The Americans wanted no part in this, though they certainly expected the British and the Canadians to do their duty. The Canadians too were anxious to leave the responsibility to others. Fortunately, Churchill undertook to compel the Free French to comply. Yet it was one thing to get de Gaulle to agree and another to get Muselier to act. Mackenzie King, in particular, rightly had grave doubts whether the Admiral would obey an order from the General to evacuate the islands. Once installed in St. Pierre and Miquelon, Muselier considered himself bound by his French sense of honour to remain. And, as his rage at his treatment by the Americans (and Canadians) mounted, his determination to defy all challengers—even de Gaulle—increased. On December 30, Muselier had in fact cabled de Gaulle that if the latter sent him an order to evacuate, he "could not carry it out."[50]

Churchill finally managed to convince his Cabinet colleagues to approve the Hull formula of January 8. This they did only with the greatest reluctance since, as the official British history recounts, "it

*One Ottawa press report suggested that Canada might be asked to assume responsibility for the protection of the neutrality of St. Pierre and Miquelon. The *Alysse* and *Aconit* had already returned to ocean convoy duty on December 26, 1941. The *Mimosa* sailed early in January, and the *Surcouf* in mid-January.

seemed absurd, after the behaviour of the Vichy authorities at Dakar and Syria, not to allow General de Gaulle to occupy territories which in fact welcomed him." However, while agreeing "to try to persuade General de Gaulle to accept the compromise, they were unwilling to compel him to do so," greatly to the annoyance of the State Department which evidently considered insistence on Free French consent as unnecessary, if not obstructionist. It fell to Anthony Eden to inform the Free French leader of the Allied decision. This, the embarrassed Foreign Secretary did on January 14. As could be expected, General de Gaulle promptly rejected the scheme out of hand. Eden then warned that the United States was contemplating the despatch of a powerful task force—he mentioned a cruiser and two destroyers—to St. Pierre in addition to exerting continuing economic pressure. When asked what he would do then, de Gaulle replied:

The Allied ships will stop at the limit of territorial waters and the American Admiral will come to lunch with Muselier, who will be delighted.
But if the cruiser crosses that limit?
Our people will summon her to stop in the usual way.
If she holds on her course?
That would be most unfortunate, for then our people would have to open fire.

"I can understand your alarm," de Gaulle added when Eden threw up his arms in despair, "but I have confidence in the democracies."*

It is not clear whether this frank exchange was merely a bluff and, if so, who was bluffing: the British, the Americans, or the Free French. Churchill certainly reported to London that the President was threatening to despatch the battleship *Arkansas* (then at Argentia only 75 miles away)† to eject Muselier by force if necessary, and his savage telegram reporting this caused "utter consternation" in Ottawa when read to a startled and angry War Committee of the Cabinet on January 14. The Canadian Government feared that any such action would produce a violent public reaction, particularly in Quebec.[51]

*One curious feature of the situation was that, in accordance with a British *aide-mémoire* handed to General Catroux on September 18, 1940, the British Government was obligated "to defend against all attack by naval forces, colonies which rallied to the Free French movement."

†The *Arkansas* was at sea on convoy duty from December 25 to January 2 and at Ship's Harbour, Argentia, January 2 to 21.

Churchill's message, when leaked to Washington by Norman Robertson, also occasioned considerable surprise in the Department of State. Cordell Hull immediately informed the American Minister in Ottawa that: "One thing the President has consistently opposed is any idea of sending armed ships to the islands. Every time the President and the Secretary have talked about the islands, the Secretary has assured him that the State Department has not even considered such a solution. The Secretary had no reason to believe and does not believe that the President's position has changed in any way." Certainly, in arguing on New Year's Day against attempting to restore the status quo, Roosevelt had told Hull that "we cannot afford to send an expedition to bomb [Muselier] out." On the other hand, Robert Sherwood states categorically that Roosevelt did tell Churchill that "he might send the battleship *Arkansas* to drive the Free French by force out of the tiny islands, or he might establish a blockade to starve them into submission." In any case, whatever the truth regarding its attitude to the use of force, Washington did nothing to discourage the British from holding the threat of US military intervention over the heads of the Free French. Hull specifically instructed Moffat not to pass on his message (quoted above) to the Canadians "for fear that it would reach the British and perhaps complicate matters."* Moreover, Professor Langer, the author of the authorized explanation of the State Department's Vichy policy, is extremely critical of British weakness in the face of the General's intransigence. He charges that while the British may have intended "to thump de Gaulle over the head," they "hardly went beyond a light slap on the wrist."[52]

De Gaulle's own report of his encounter with Eden agrees substantially with this assessment. He admits Eden "put up a show of insisting" on the American proposal, but says he was convinced that this "small piece of blackmail" need not be taken seriously. Nevertheless, de Gaulle did undertake to accept a modified statement subject to three secret reservations. The net effect of these would have been to keep St. Pierre and Miquelon in the war and firmly in Free

---

*The Canadians may have intercepted the message anyway. Moffat in the course of this telephone conversation with Atherton in Washington commented on the security situation: "I used to know the man who listened in to my conversations but I think he has been changed and I am not sure whether they listen in when I telephone from the house."

French hands. The only real concession he was prepared to make was the acceptance of Canadian and American radio officials in a liaison, not a controlling, capacity. De Gaulle was as stubborn as Pétain when it came to safeguarding French sovereignty against Anglo-Saxon encroachments.[53]

After his interview with Eden, General de Gaulle was confident that the State Department had "now shot its bolt" and that the crisis was "nearing its end." In fact, the very next day the Foreign Office informed him that the three Governments were "giving up any communiqué for the moment." However, a week later, on his return to London, Churchill personally took up the question with de Gaulle in a final effort to dispose of it once and for all. While accounts differ as to what transpired at this meeting—Muselier even going so far as to accuse de Gaulle and René Pleven of concocting forged minutes*—it is at least clear that Churchill "insisted with the greatest force" that, in order to save the face of the State Department, the Free French should publicly accept a compromise formula worked out by Eden following his meeting with de Gaulle.† This new draft communiqué was noteworthy principally for its omissions. It made no mention of neutralization or demilitarization, of any prohibition on recruitment, of a withdrawal of armed forces other than naval vessels, or of the status of the Free French administrator. Canadian and American officials would be sent to St. Pierre but only to "assist" in the operation of the radio station. In substance, then, it met most of de Gaulle's previous objections. Moreover, the obligations imposed on the Free French were intentionally more apparent than real. As Churchill and Eden pointed out (according to the de Gaulle account), once the communiqué was published, effective control would remain with Savary and "nobody would bother any more about what was happening in the islands"—provided the Free French did not crow about their victory. On the strength of these verbal assurances, de Gaulle agreed not to press his three points, but balked at final acceptance of the plan without consulting the members of his National

*Muselier quotes both de Gaulle's account of the meeting and a resumé of what purports to be the official British minutes which indicate that de Gaulle was compelled to make far greater concessions than he was prepared to admit to Muselier. The resumé appears to be at best highly inaccurate.[54]

†Sir John Dill told Moffat in Ottawa on January 19 that (in Moffat's words), "It was perfectly absurd not to make de Gaulle toe the line and Churchill intended to do it."

Committee, which included Muselier.* While the Committee was favourably disposed to a quick settlement in the interests of "re-establishing friendly relations with the United States, and above all out of personal consideration for Churchill," it is not certain whether it ever gave its formal consent. Muselier gave the plan his qualified approval, though he asked that a decision be held up for a few days to enable him to return to London for consultations. De Gaulle had his own reasons for wanting to play for time. He felt that the longer he delayed, the better the deal he would get and that if he could hold out long enough the State Department would simply wash its hands of the whole affair.[55]

This in fact is what happened. While Roosevelt was apparently willing to settle for the Eden plan and ignore the inevitable protests from Vichy, Hull preferred to accept the *fait accompli* rather than provoke Vichy further and perhaps risk reviving a public debate on the question. It was clear to him that Pétain would not agree to the latest compromise communiqué† and, therefore, it "would not be of assistance to us in holding the Vichy Government to its assurances" regarding the French fleet, North African bases, and French colonial possessions. Moreover, as Ray Atherton observed, the aims of State Department policy towards St. Pierre and Miquelon which earlier had been "considered essential," now had "far less application." The Rio de Janeiro conference of American Foreign Ministers, about which so much concern had been felt in Washington, had ended without any embarrassing discussion of the issue. Also, in spite of Hull's heroic efforts, Vichy was moving into even closer collaboration with Germany. Finally, the intense U-boat activity off the Atlantic coast of the United States dramatized the potential menace of the islands from a security point of view. Accordingly, on February 2, three days before he went on sick leave, Hull wrote the President suggesting

*Churchill reported to Roosevelt on January 23 that "after a severe conversation" de Gaulle had "agreed to the communiqué . . . without any acceptances by us of his proposed secret conditions. He feels it necessary to consult Admiral Muselier who is a member of the National Committee but I understand that I am to receive final assent of Free French tomorrow."

†Hull says the Vichy Government did agree to the January 8 plan, whereas Langer says that Vichy was "prepared to assent, though it wanted the administrator to stay on at least for a while, presumably for the sake of appearances." Actually, it seems that Vichy never fully and formally accepted any of the American plans, and was not even given the text of the January 8 formula.

somewhat belatedly that "further negotiations or discussions of the matter be postponed for the period of the war." This recommendation was received with relief.[56]

The universal desire in Allied capitals to allow the whole affair to die a natural death was painfully evident in the reaction to Vichy's pathetic last-minute efforts to keep interest in the issue alive. Early in February, René Ristelhueber urged Robertson to put pressure on London to accept the American proposals, but quickly concluded that it was hopeless to expect any positive action from the Canadians. This was confirmed two days later, when the French Minister finally managed to obtain the appointment with the Prime Minister that he had been pressing for since Christmas. Mackenzie King, too, was no help at all. "There are some things," he told Ristelhueber, "one could do no good by injecting oneself into . . . [and] this was one." He added that he had "enough to worry about without taking on unnecessary troubles." In desperation, Ristelhueber turned to Pierrepont Moffat and begged him to press the Canadians to take a "more realistic attitude," only to receive a polite brushoff. Moffat advised him that "all conversations with any parties at interest should be concentrated in Washington and not carried on piecemeal elsewhere." A month later, Admiral Darlan despatched a formal note to Washington concerning "the situation created by the landing of dissident forces at St. Pierre-Miquelon." It pointed out that, since January 13 and "despite several *démarches* made to the State Department by Monsieur Henry-Haye, the Federal Government has not made known its views on the question and simply advised the French Government not to make any declaration with regard to the matter until the settlement of the incident." Vichy then urged the re-establishment "without further delay" of its authority in St. Pierre and Miquelon and asked if the Department of State would kindly inform it "as soon as possible as to its final position in this respect."[57]

By this time, however, as Moffat noted during a visit to Washington, the issue was "dead as a doornail." Towards the end of March, the State Department finally replied to a request from its consul in St. Pierre for guidance regarding the attitude he should adopt towards the Free French administration. The Department advised that, although the status of the islands had not yet been "finally determined," nevertheless it was desirable to "take into account the *de facto* situation. There is no reason why your personal relations with the Free French officials should not be maintained upon the most cordial basis." Later, during Churchill's and Mackenzie King's visit to Washington in June 1942, the Canadians indicated an interest in legitimizing the Free French regime, but Cordell Hull made it clear that "in no circumstances" did he want to discuss the matter.[58]

So in the end, nothing was done. No communiqué was issued. The blockade was lifted and the restrictions on overflights removed (on August 1, 1942). The official status of the islands remained unsettled, but the Free French continued in unfettered control. And St. Pierre and Miquelon relapsed once more into the obscurity from which it had emerged for a few hectic weeks.*

*Sherwood is incorrect in asserting that "in the end, the semblance of Vichy sovereignty on St. Pierre and Miquelon was restored." So is Alfred Cobban in claiming that the Hull formula of January 8 was implemented.[59]

6

ISSUES

The debate over St. Pierre and Miquelon revolved around five principal issues: the extent to which the colony constituted a military threat, whether the Monroe Doctrine had been violated, the soundness of the State Department's Vichy policy, the strength of support for de Gaulle in France, and the personalities of the chief protagonists: Cordell Hull and Charles de Gaulle.

There was no denying the strategic location of St. Pierre and Miquelon: it was situated at the entrance to the Gulf of St. Lawrence, uncomfortably close to the main trans-Atlantic convoy route and only 115 miles from the American advanced air and naval bases on Placentia Bay, where Churchill and Roosevelt met to draw up the Atlantic Charter in August, 1941. Thus, in unfriendly hands, the colony could menace the security of the northwest Atlantic area. The islands could, in fact, be considered as Canada's Quemoy and Matsu, or Cuba.

As early as December, 1936, the War Plans Division of the War Department in Washington surveyed the possibilities of a base in St. Pierre and Miquelon but advised against it on both political and military grounds. However, in March, 1940, interest in the islands was revived and General Marshall's attention drawn to their significance for hemispheric defence. In particular, St. Pierre's small but excellent, ice-free harbour offered possibilities as a base for light naval vessels and seaplanes. Nevertheless, once again, the Army planners felt that the potential military value of the islands was "insufficient when weighed in the light of political and economic considerations, to justify their acquisition." Moreover, Newfoundland obviously offered better prospects as a northern anchor for the Atlantic naval patrol. Consequently, when Argentia became available six months later, interest in Washington in a base at St. Pierre collapsed.[1]

St. Pierre's value as naval base was clearly apparent during the German submarine offensive along the east coast of Canada in the spring of 1942 when it played a not insignificant role as a shelter and rendezvous for Allied merchant ships and escorts. This led to renewed discussion in Canada of the defence potentialities of the islands, especially as a supplementary supply base for warships shepherding slow convoys. In August, a Canadian naval team visited the territory along with the American vice-consul in St. John's, and reported that St. Pierre offered "a most valuable potential base for light surface ships" as well as promising repair facilities. However, the Chief of the Naval Staff in Ottawa was less impressed; in any case, the Royal Canadian Navy was in danger of acquiring too many secondary bases. Consequently, no action was taken, apart from appointing a Canadian Naval Liaison Officer to St. Pierre to deal with "the increased scale of naval cooperation between Fighting French and Canadian forces operating from the Gulf of St. Lawrence."[2] Canadian ships continued to use St. Pierre on an emergency basis—it was always a popular port of call for thirsty sailors—but no shore installations were established. Similarly, nothing came of various proposals to develop an RCAF flying boat base at St. Pierre or to utilize its airstrip, then under construction, as an alternative landing field for light aircraft.

The fall of France raised the spectre of Axis occupation of European possessions in the Western Hemisphere. With this in view, the Americans hurriedly drafted an emergency plan RAINBOW 4 which envisaged military co-operation with Canada in the defence of the northwest Atlantic area. Yet at no time did these islands figure directly in German war plans. They were too small and their resources too limited to serve Axis purposes; certainly there was no question of their being used as a springboard for attacking Newfoundland or the mainland. Berlin had, in fact, neither the means nor the incentive, nor even the ambition, to occupy St. Pierre and Miquelon outright, with or without the acquiescence of Vichy.[3] As the Royal Canadian Navy's Director of Plans Division wrote, in a brief appreciation of the problem on June 30, 1940, "It is difficult to see any reason for occupation of the islands by the enemy since even if he landed a garrison he could not maintain it for long without command of the sea. . . . If the enemy should have control of sea communications, he would hardly waste his time on a couple of barren and uninviting islands when most of our coastline and that of Newfoundland would be his for the taking."*

The Chief of the Naval Staff and the Chief of the Air Staff concurred in this assessment. Nevertheless, in the crisis of the summer of 1940, both felt that the only way to be sure of denying the facilities of the islands to the Germans was to occupy them, a view which the Minister of National Defence shared. Shortly afterwards, Commander Roy, RCN, was sent to St. Pierre to survey the situation on the spot. His report was reassuring respecting the teritory's limited usefulness to the enemy. Accordingly, for this and other reasons, mainly political, it was decided not to pursue the question of protective occupation at that time.

The only credible threat was that the odd Axis submarine might exercise its rights under international law to use St. Pierre's port facilities. As Angus Macdonald, the Canadian Navy Minister wrote in June, 1941, "the possibility of German ocean-going submarines using these islands, not necessarily for refuelling, but merely for the opportunity of rest, recreation and carrying out running repairs, cannot be eliminated."† There were, in fact, occasional allegations that the territory was serving as a haven for U-boats, or that supplies provided by Canada and the United States were finding their way to submarines lying off shore. Perhaps the most fanciful account of all was the story that "crews of U-boats which had surfaced in the fog offshore swaggered into town on murky nights in their turtle-neck sweaters and black, rakish uniforms to buy supplies." Such reports were wholly without foundation, and at the time were rightly greeted with scepticism in Ottawa and elsewhere.[4] Yet the threat, however slight, could not be dismissed completely, particularly with the increase in enemy activity in the Western Atlantic in late 1941. On

---

*There was, throughout the summer of 1940, great concern in Ottawa and Washington over Newfoundland's lack of defences. According to Stimson, Roosevelt talked to King at Ogdensburg on August 17 about the danger of a German "attack by way of the St. Lawrence or northeastern coast of Canada, where sudden attack was very likely."[5]

†On February 20, 1942, a German submarine off Martinique landed a seriously injured officer. The United States demanded immediate "categorical assurances" that "under no circumstances or condition" would French authorities again permit Axis vessels or aircraft to enter French ports or territory within the Western Hemisphere.[6]

the other hand, as long as the United States remained neutral, the presence of Germans in or near the islands was, if only for political reasons, an extremely remote prospect.

As we now know, Hitler was convinced that the Kaiser's fatal error was forcing the Americans to declare war. He was determined not to commit the same blunder if at all possible. Accordingly, he was firm in resisting, sometimes under great provocation, all suggestion for action in the Western Atlantic which might prejudice the continuance of American neutrality. On several occasions during 1940 and 1941, Admiral Raeder proposed, with the full sanction of the German Foreign Office, the mining of the approaches to Halifax harbour and the stationing of submarines in Canadian territorial waters, but each time Hitler intervened personally to veto the scheme because of the "psychological effect" it would have had on the United States. The Navy was in fact ordered not to seek any engagements in the Pan American security zone (which extended as far north as Halifax) or to stop, search, or sink American ships outside that zone.[7]

As the activities of the American neutrality patrol became less and less neutral and as U-boats pushed farther and farther westward in search of their prey, pressure mounted for a relaxation of the restrictions previously imposed. In February and March 1941, surface raiders took a toll of twenty-one ships within a few hundred miles of St. John's. However, it was not until the autumn of 1941 that submarines were permitted to operate in Newfoundland coastal waters, and the Allies sustained their first losses there. In mid-October, four U-boats of the Incendiary Group appeared in the congested shipping areas near Cape Race and the Strait of Belle Isle, and quickly sank five ships.[8]

The entry of the United States into the war altered the picture dramatically. To the great relief of Admiral Doenetz, the German Navy was suddenly relieved of the crippling restrictions under which it had chafed for so long, with results that were immediately and tragically apparent. During January, 1942 alone, twelve ships succumbed to U-boat attacks in the Canadian coastal zone, some within sight of St. Pierre and Miquelon—without the loss of a single submarine—while a further twenty-one were torpedoed in the Gulf of St. Lawrence region between May and October. Fortunately, by this time St. Pierre and Miquelon were in Allied hands. It is impossible, therefore, to know whether the enemy would have made any direct use of the islands if they had remained under Vichy control. The risk of his trying would, however, have increased considerably. Canadian nerves were jittery enough during the fateful summer of 1942 and it seems unlikely that the Canadian Government would have been able to resist military opinion and public pressure to do something about the situation. As it was, the territory proved to be an asset rather than a menace.[9]

American and Canadian service chiefs were interested in St. Pierre and Miquelon during the spring and summer of 1940 because of their general concern for the defence of the whole northeast coast of the continent. Once it had been concluded that the islands would not be likely to be of much military value to anyone, interest shifted. Much more serious than the threat of direct German use of the islands was the very real possibility that they might be used to communicate vital information to the Axis. This was the danger that exercised the democracies throughout 1941. There were three aspects of the problem: the cable station, the fishing fleet, and, above all, the St. Pierre radio.

St. Pierre's overseas cable connections created a good deal of confusion and needless suspicion right up to the end of Vichy rule. Two submarine cables passed through St. Pierre. The first was the Western Union Telegraph Company's line from North Sydney, Nova Scotia, to Newfoundland and on to Penzance, England. This presented no real difficulty as its terminals were in Allied territory. Moreover, as a result of the Penson-Roy mission of July, 1940, de Bournat had agreed not to remove Archibald Bartlett as superintendent of the Western Union Office (though de Bournat did force Bartlett's resignation as honorary British vice-consul). Bartlett was a Free French supporter, as was Gustave Roblot, the chief telegraphist, but most of the company's employees were *Vichyards*, especially Mathurin Lehors, the chief electrician and a favourite target of the Resistance press.[10]

The French Cable Company's lines caused more concern as they ran from Orleans, Massachusetts through St. Pierre to Déolan near Brest in occupied France. During the great submarine earthquake that shook the Grand Banks on November 18, 1929, this cable was so badly damaged that it was finally abandoned, and the St. Pierre station closed down. Nevertheless, after the fall of France, the British feared that the cable link might be restored. To avert this danger, the CS *Cambria* sailed from Halifax on August 7, 1940, cut the cable, rerouted it around St. Pierre, and diverted the western end into Halifax. The original intention had been to run the trans-Atlantic section to Land's End but, because of mid-ocean breaks in the cable and the difficulty of working off the French coast, the operation was never completed. Nevertheless, as far as St. Pierre and Miquelon was concerned, the threat of direct cable connections with France had been removed.[11]

A second danger stemmed from the presence in and around St. Pierre and Miquelon of fishing trawlers and other craft able to observe Allied ship movements and, in some cases, broadcast reports on them. The departure of the metropolitan fleet in the fall of 1940 reduced the risk considerably, but its return the following spring with the approval, if not at the instance, of the German authorities, at a time when the Battle of the Atlantic was being intensified, created renewed alarm. One intelligence source even suggested that the purpose of the expedition was specifically to wireless information on ships' sailings to the Germans. The area around Newfoundland was so congested with shipping that the mere thought that "a fishing smack sailing one hundred miles from St. Pierre could bring back and put on the wireless vital information" concerning Allied convoys was, according to Moffat, enough to "terrify" at least one senior Canadian official (Thomas Stone). Accordingly, steps were taken to intercept the French vessels and all but two fell into the Allied net.[12]

The greatest threat to Allied security, however, came from St. Pierre's powerful shortwave station. This had been built in 1939 as part of a communications network to enable Air France to undertake trans-Atlantic flights. Its manager, René Delort, was fanatically pro-Vichy. On November 10, 1941, following the resumption of the U-boat offensive in the autumn, the Permanent Joint Board on Defence at the prompting of its Canadian members warned that "the existence on the Islands of an uncontrolled and high-powered wireless transmitting station constituted a potential danger to the interests of Canada and the United States."[13] This was one point on which opinion, particularly in naval circles but also in the State Department and other foreign offices, was unanimous.[14]

There seems little reason to doubt that this "obnoxious radio station," as Churchill called it, did aid the Axis considerably, but the precise extent of its aid is still a matter of dispute. One Canadian spokesman is alleged to have said that, "If one of our citizens were to tell the enemy what the Vichy station has been telling him, he would be arrested for treason." Certainly, the meteorological reports from St. Pierre were of direct benefit to the Germans. The mere fact that the number of daily weather broadcasts increased sharply immediately after the Armistice suggests that outside influences were at work.[15]

Whether any other information was passed on to the Germans has never been definitely established. Admiral Robert terms Churchill's reference to the possibility of the St. Pierre radio secretly signalling to U-boats a "supposition tendancieuse et malveillante," while Ambassador Henry-Haye stated publicly that the station was used "only for fishermen." However, we now know that, on December 3, 1941, Darlan had volunteered to supply the Germans with intelligence concerning British naval movements in the Atlantic, and Muselier later asserted that the secret files of the station provided clear proof that movements of Allied warships had been signalled to Vichy and, from there, leaked to the Germans. Certainly, this would have been easy as the main Allied convoy route from New York and Halifax passed close to St. Pierre and Miquelon, and ships from Quebec came within sight of the islands.*[16] Moreover, the stream of messages which poured forth in code gave legitimate grounds for suspicion. As early as July 22, 1940, the Vichy Minister of the Colonies issued confidential instructions to de Bournat to use code "only for very secret transmissions" and to send such messages in "V.N. marine code as known to the German and Italian authorities." The Canadians monitored all broadcasts but, as late as November, 1941, there was still at least one code they had not cracked.[17]

Even if there was no direct assistance afforded to the enemy in the

---

*The newly-appointed Canadian vice-consul reported in September, 1941, that, while it was impossible to ascertain what information the radio was sending out, it was not believed in St. Pierre that the Administrator would report convoy movements even if he should receive word of them. He also said that he did not think that any St. Pierre vessels went south into the shipping lanes. Nevertheless, the RCMP did devote a good deal of attention to the activities of one pro-Vichy shipowner, August Maufroy, whose tug, the Béarn, was under repair at Pictou, Nova Scotia that fall.

critical Battle of the Atlantic, the St. Pierre station was, as Churchill points out, certainly spewing "Vichy lies and poison throughout the world."* Moreover, Sir Desmond Morton who, as Personal Assistant to the British Prime Minister, was in a position to know, states categorically that St. Pierre was "one of the chief means whereby the Vichy and German Governments were able rapidly to communicate instructions in cypher to their agents and supporters in the Western Hemisphere, and to receive secret information in return." Clearly, in Vichy hands, St. Pierre and Miquelon was a serious security risk. De Gaulle's action was therefore, as Sherwood has noted, "in conformity with Allied military policy and sound policy at that."[18]

Throughout 1940 and 1941, whenever the question of the liberation of St. Pierre and Miquelon (or any other European possession in the Western Hemisphere) arose, the invariable and automatic response of the American Government was that any change in the colony's status, even unilateral Canadian occupation, would violate that sacrosanct principle of American international law: the Monroe Doctrine. It was precisely to obviate this danger that Cordell Hull had convinced the other American republics at Havana in July 1940 to adopt his proposals for the Provisional Administration of European Colonies and Possessions in the Americas. This envisaged temporary collective trusteeship for orphaned colonies threatened with Axis aggression. "If a non-American *State*," the convention reads, "shall *directly or indirectly* attempt to replace *another* non-American State in the *sovereignty or control* which it exercised over any territory located in the Americas, *thus threatening the peace of the continent*, such territory shall *automatically* . . . be submitted to a provisional administrative regime." The administering authority would be "one or more American States" who would be subject to the overriding control of an Inter-American Commission for Territorial Administration composed of representatives of each of the American republics. Prior to January 8, 1942, when the convention came into force, the functions of the Commission were to be exercised by an interim

*There were negotiations between the French Government and Western Union both before and after the fall of France concerning the installation of a transmitter to beam propaganda to the United States. However, the State Department intervened and the proposal was dropped.[19]

Emergency Committee in Washington set up under a related document, the Act of Havana.*[20]

This arrangement was clearly intended to exclude Canada, at least from Caribbean territories. She was not invited to Havana or entitled to sign the Convention. Moreover, even before the conference met, one American official asserted flatly that Canada would not share in any trusteeship for places like Martinique because "Canada would be representative of the British Empire, not of the Americas." On the other hand, the spokesman considered it conceivable that Canada might participate in a trusteeship body for St. Pierre and Miquelon. In fact, immediately after the conference, Washington promised to consult with Ottawa in future on any matter involving the defence of the islands including, by implication, protective custody. Three months later, on November 1, Sumner Welles agreed to a Canadian suggestion that rather than involve the Latin American republics directly in St. Pierre and Miquelon, the United States and Canada should work out a joint policy between themselves, possibly utilizing the Permanent Joint Board on Defence for the purpose. Welles added, however, that "the other American countries would [still] have some concern about what might be done regarding St. Pierre and Miquelon and that the United States Government would accordingly have to inform them of whatever action the United States and Canada might contemplate." Thus, although St. Pierre and Miquelon was formally covered by the Havana agreements, it was from the first regarded, like Greenland and for the same geographical reasons, as rather different from European possessions in the Caribbean.[21] It is significant that the April, 1941 agreement, legalizing the military occupation

*The preamble to the Convention states:
   That any transfer, or attempted transfer, of the sovereignty, jurisdiction, possession or any interest in or control over any [European colonies in the Western Hemisphere] to another non-American State, would be regarded by the American Republics as against American sentiments and principles and the rights of American States to maintain their security and political independence . . . .
   That the American Republics . . . reserve the right to judge whether any transfer or attempted transfer . . . has the effect of impairing their political independence even though no final transfer or change in the status of such region or regions shall have taken place.
Both Pétain and de Gaulle protested against the Havana decisions at the time, suspecting that they masked annexationist designs.[22] In May, 1941, de Gaulle relented a little and rather surprisingly offered to collaborate with the American republics in establishing provisional regimes in St. Pierre and Miquelon and the French Antilles, provided French sovereignty was preserved.

of Greenland, makes only incidental references to United States "obligations under the Act of Havana."[23] Neither then nor later did the State Department make any move to refer the question of Greenland to the inter-American emergency committee, let alone constitute a provisional administration as provided for under the Act.

Following the seizure of St. Pierre and Miquelon, Cordell Hull promptly pointed to the Havana Act as ground for his opposition. Whether the Act was ever applicable to St. Pierre and Miquelon, it clearly was not applicable in this case, as the Free French action involved a change of government, not a transfer of sovereignty. It was, as Mackenzie King indicated on Christmas Day, simply a domestic struggle between rival groups of Frenchmen. This claim was hotly disputed by Hull who contended that the coup was "not a controversy between fellow Frenchmen as far as this hemisphere is concerned," since "the de Gaulle group is not recognized by virtually any country [actually by none] in this Western Hemisphere." The logic of his reasoning here is not readily apparent. The Secretary of State also argued that it was really a case of British intervention, with the Free French only tools of British imperialism.* It was not until February 13—after Hull had gone on sick leave—that Sumner Welles publicly conceded that the Havana accords did not apply to the St. Pierre and Miquelon situation, though the next day a State Department spokesman carefully explained that the American republics still reserved the right to apply the Convention to the islands. In other words, while it had not been invoked on this particular occasion, it apparently could have been if there had been a threat to the political independence of St. Pierre and Miquelon or to hemispheric peace and security.[24] Even with these qualifications, Hull's original position was pretty well repudiated. In particular, his argument that the Free French coup threatened continental peace was quietly forgotten. "To let the de Gaulle occupation continue unchallenged," Hull had insisted during a heated exchange with Lord Halifax, "would mean that de Gaulle would probably undertake to capture other French colonies, such as Guadeloupe and French Guiana† and that further-

---

*Earlier in 1941, Hull had expressed the view that any Vichy attack on Free French territory in Africa would be "tantamount to a civil war." Logan states at one point that the Havana accord "unquestionably applied in this unhappy incident," and in another that the coup did not involve a technical change of sovereignty.

†Certainly this continued to be Muselier's hope. In September, 1940, he had

more Admiral Robert . . . would probably take his large cruiser and go up and relieve St. Pierre and Miquelon, *et cetera, et cetera* . . . ." The fact that Hull did not at any time take steps to implement the Havana agreement suggests that he was not completely convinced by his own oratory.[25]

Hull also claimed that the seizure of St. Pierre and Miquelon was in conflict with another provision of the Havana Convention which specified that "by virtue of a principle of American international law, . . . the acquisition of territories by force cannot be permitted." Apparently there were fears in Washington that Muselier's action might create a dangerous precedent which, for example, Argentina might use to occupy the Falkland Islands, or Brazil, to take over French Guiana.[26] Yet this provision of the Convention was obviously not intended to cover the use of force to overturn regimes, a common occurrence in Latin America. Once it is accepted that the Free French action was an internal matter, Hull's argument collapses. Admittedly, someone unfamiliar with the French colonial mentality might contend that this was not a domestic affair as Muselier was an outsider as far as St. Pierre and Miquelon is concerned, but then so was de Bournat.

The liberation of the islands was even less a violation of the spirit of the Monroe Doctrine and its corollaries spelled out at Havana. These had been intended to foster continental security and prevent the spread of alien European political concepts among liberty-loving American peoples. One of the resolutions adopted at Havana had specifically called on the American Republics "to eradicate from the Americas the spread of doctrines that tend to place in jeopardy the common inter-American democratic ideal." It was a curious perversion of the original purposes of these doctrines, therefore, to invoke them to justify reimposing on St. Pierre and Miquelon an authoritarian regime which the people had decisively rejected in a democratic vote, and forcing them against their will back into virtual collaboration with the enemy. It was also contrary to the principle reaffirmed in the Act of Havana that "peoples of this continent have the right freely to determine their own destinies."

Another aspect of the St. Pierre and Miquelon situation which

---

planned to take over the French West Indies, but postponed the operation on American advice. He now regarded St. Pierre and Miquelon as only the first step in an ambitious program to liberate Martinique, Guadeloupe, French Guiana, Reunion and Madagascar in that order.[27]

agitated the State Department was the anticipated reaction in Latin America. In July, 1941, Sumner Welles warned that any Canadian occupation of the islands would "play havoc with our own Latin American policy." Even to send radio technicians to St. Pierre, as proposed in November, 1941, might embarrass the United States in her relations with her sister republics to the south. After the liberation, Cordell Hull claimed in one of his more explosive encounters with the British Ambassador that, unless the status quo were restored, "the whole basis of the good neighbour policy . . . would be repudiated by the United States with the unthinkable repercussions of injury that would occur through Latin America."[28] Two days later he wrote the President predicting "ominous and serious developments. . . . The developments revolving around . . . the South American and Rio Conference situation are calculated to be very materially affected to our disadvantage if the fact goes out to the world that the British Government was really behind this movement and we abandon our own policies without serious protest, *et cetera, et cetera.*" Accordingly, the American Government pressed vigorously for a settlement of the issue before the opening of the Conference of American Foreign Ministers at Rio de Janeiro on January 15, 1942, so as to avoid the danger of having it raised there. Actually, far from sending shivers up and down the coast from Rio Grande to Patagonia as the alarmist had feared, the Latin Americans never evinced the slightest interest in St. Pierre and Miquelon. At Rio, it was not even discussed.* The excessive fears of the State Department appear to have been mere figments of its fertile imagination, if not simply rationalizations of its policy.[29]

The United States was also anxious lest the Free French action in St. Pierre and Miquelon should upset the uneasy naval status quo established in the French Antilles. Washington was understandably jittery, in the immediate post-Pearl Harbor period, over the defence of the Caribbean and the Canal Zone. Its concern had already led to a hurried exchange of letters between Roosevelt and Pétain and to the

---

*Muselier is incorrect in claiming that: "During the Pan-American Conference, Sumner Welles had done everything he could to secure adoption of a resolution requesting that St. Pierre and Miquelon be managed by the Americans and the Canadians."

famous Horne-Robert agreement dealing with the movement of ships of the French West Indies squadron.

In return for Vichy's explicit undertaking "not to allow the departure of any French naval ships from Martinique or from any other port in the Western Hemisphere," President Roosevelt had written Marshal Pétain on December 13 what Leahy called "another of those courtesy notes" stating that Pétain could "rest assured that the Government of the United States under present circumstances and in view of the instructions which you have issued to Admiral Robert will continue to give full recognition to the agreement reached by our two governments [in November 1940] involving the maintenance of the *status quo* of the French possessions in the Western Hemisphere."[30]

Admiral Leahy in Vichy confesses that he had "no faith in the ability of the Marshal" to live up to his part of the bargain. The American service chiefs, too, were most unhappy with the existing arrangement. They deeply distrusted Admiral Robert, and would have preferred to give Martinique and Guadeloupe one hour to surrender and then "hit them with everything at once." Although Hull admitted Robert was "very pro-German," he asked merely that the French ships should be disarmed and American inspection teams admitted to confirm that this had been done. Even this demand Darlan flatly refused to concede. In fact, all Rear Admiral Horne, USN, could obtain when he visited the tough and resolute Admiral High Commissioner in Martinique on December 17 was a signed confirmation of the Robert-Greenslade gentleman's agreement of November, 1940.* This did not even go as far as Darlan's assurances five days earlier. Its terms have never been published, but in essence Robert agreed that: (1) French warships at Martinique would not go to any ports other than ports in the French West Indies and French Guiana. [St. Pierre and Miquelon was not mentioned.] (2) Four days advance notice would be given of movements of the aircraft carrier *Béarn* and the cruisers *Emile Bertin* and *Jeanne d'Arc*. Two days advance notice would be given of movements of the converted merchant cruiser *Barfleur*. (3) The airplanes landed at Martinique from the *Béarn* would not be moved. (4) The gold would

---

*It is not clear whether Admiral Muselier's arrival in Ottawa two days earlier had anything to do with the haste with which Horne was sent to Martinique.

remain intact and not be moved. (5) The US consul would be informed immediately of any change in Admiral Robert's status.

In return, the American Government declared on December 23 that: (1) It did not anticipate any change in its relations with the French Antilles and French Guiana. [Still no mention of St. Pierre and Miquelon.] (2) Approval would be given for French merchant ships to operate between New York and Casablanca, and between Martinique and ports in the Western Hemisphere. (3) Monthly releases of frozen French funds would be increased to $1,000,000 beginning January 1, 1942.[81]

Although Cordell Hull appears to have considered the seizure of St. Pierre and Miquelon a flagrant breach of the Horne-Robert agreement, this was not strictly the case (though it did conflict with the Roosevelt-Pétain understanding). It is not even certain that the islands were covered by the agreement, though they may have been in a general sense. In any case, as the only French warship there had left more than a year earlier, the colony was not directly affected.* Moreover, when the Canadians anxiously inquired on December 19 whether the Horne-Robert accord would rule out their own plan to control the St. Pierre radio station, they were fully assured that "obviously" it would have "no effect" whatsoever.[82] St. Pierre and Miquelon entered the picture only incidentally in that Admiral Robert might have used the Free French action as a pretext to repudiate his obligations regarding the ships, planes, and gold in his possession. However, this was scarcely likely. Any unauthorized act would have been quickly detected and have invoked strong American retaliatory measures, including in all probability the overrunning of his little empire. Robert's pronouncements throughout the St. Pierre and Miquelon *affaire* were pretty violent, but his bark was really worse than his bite.†

Despite the tremendous fuss which the State Department made over the political and military implications of the Free French coup for the Western Hemisphere, its principal anxiety throughout the

*The omission of any specific mention of St. Pierre and Miquelon may also have been due to the fact that, at the time of the Robert-Greenslade agreement, Admiral Robert's jurisdiction as High Commissioner was limited to the Caribbean.

†Langer argues curiously that: "We were long-suffering with Admiral Robert at Martinique, but we could afford to be lenient, because in the case of a real threat we could have acted promptly and effectively."

crisis was over possible repercussions in Vichy-held territory in Europe and Africa. Its spokesmen repeatedly reiterated the theme that their great preoccupation was not to outrage Vichy. As Sumner Welles angrily reminded Lord Halifax, the United States had been "moving heaven and earth to keep on close terms with the Vichy Government." Two days later, Cordell Hull expounded at length to the same unfortunate British Ambassador on the "splendid results" of his efforts to cultivate close relations with Vichy. Hull then added: ". . . it is unthinkable to me and to my Government that all these benefits to the British and American Governments should be junked and thrown overboard in order to gratify the desire of the de Gaulle leaders, who, in open violation of their pledge to the contrary, suddenly seized and occupied St. Pierre and Miquelon by force, thereby inflicting on Great Britain and the United States unimaginable injury. . . ." Thus, Washington's reaction to the Free French coup is explicable only within the larger context of its Vichy policy as a whole.[33]

No detailed analysis of that policy is possible here, but a few general comments are pertinent. In the first place, the case for appeasement is not as weak as is sometimes suggested. "All the standard reasons advanced in defence of our Vichy policy," Eugene Rostow, a wartime adviser to the State Department, admits, "turned out to be wrong." Nonetheless, it "was and is defensible, not because . . . it worked perfectly and according to plan—it did not—but because at the time, and in the light of our terrible weakness, it reasonably seemed to be the least dangerous of alternatives." Moreover, the stakes were undeniably high: the French fleet, and French territory and bases particularly in North and West Africa. Appeasement was worth a price, and a fairly steep one at that.[34]

At the same time, it is important not to exaggerate the success of American efforts. Professor Langer does his best to prove to the public that "during most of 1941, American influence was real and effective." The Secretary of State himself asserts that, "throughout that time, our influence at Vichy was predominant over that of any other nation, with the possible—only the possible—exception of Germany." Yet it is doubtful if these claims can be sustained. Adrienne Hytier, who also felt this was "the logical policy for Washington to pursue," concludes that, "The so-called Vichy policy

. . . achieved little that was positive. The American influence in Vichy was, throughout, despite Hull's claims to the contrary, very slight and Washington hardly ever managed to modify the course of the French Government. . . . In the same breath Washington complained about the 'abject surrenders' of Vichy and boasted about having been able to prevent them."[35]

It should be remembered that the British were in full accord with Washington's policy of retaining a listening post in Vichy, though they were never as sanguine as the Americans about the prospects of exercising any real restraint on Pétain. At the same time, they felt that Washington was not exploiting its opportunities to the full. It seems altogether likely that, if the Department of State had not been so impressed with the weakness of its diplomatic bargaining position in Vichy and had been more aware of the importance which Vichy leaders attached to maintaining the American connection which, as Eden pointed out, was "their sole remaining link with respectability," it might have achieved more. Instead of forever worrying about being "booted out" of Vichy, Washington might well have made more effective use of the threat of a diplomatic break as a sanction to keep Vichy leaders in line. In other words, it was not so much the policy itself, but the timidity with which it was applied that can be questioned.[36]

It is also doubtful whether St. Pierre and Miquelon was ever as serious a threat to relations with Vichy as the Americans pretended. The Washington argument that to condone the action of the Free French would push Pétain into closer collaboration with the Germans seems quite fantastic. Surely, the degree of French collaboration was determined by more important considerations than the seizure of two insignificant islands in the Gulf of St. Lawrence.

This at least was the outlook of officials in the Canadian Department of External Affairs, though Mackenzie King personally appears to have shared many of Hull's illusions. King was an appeaser by habit and temperament and found it easy to let matters take their course. Moreover, he had Quebec to consider and there Vichy propaganda, with its appeal to religion and "Work, Family, Fatherland," had made considerable headway. General de Gaulle's broadcast to French-speaking Canadians on August 2, 1940, though a rather misguided attempt to appeal to their French patriotism, did help to counter the influence of the Vichy (and German) radio. Commandant d'Argenlieu's mission in March, 1941, was rather more successful, and culminated in a testimonial dinner in his honour in Quebec City attended by Premier Godbout and other French-Canadian leaders. D'Argenlieu was a Carmelite monk and therefore immune from the charge of anti-clericalism which was levelled at many Free French sympathizers in the province and which did so much damage. The connection with *Le Jour* was particularly embarrassing. One Free French leader from Quebec complained bitterly that: "*Le Jour* has in the past considerably hindered the development of Free France in Canada by its furious personal attacks on the Marshal. From the psychological and propaganda points of view, it is very stupid to link Free France with this group which exploits the movement for publicity purposes and not because it shares the same ideal." As a result, the Free French movement never won the allegiance of any significant number of the French-Canadian élite, and never penetrated to the masses. Most French-speaking Canadians, while regretting Marshal Pétain's concessions to the demands of the conqueror, applauded his efforts at national regeneration.[37]

The attitude of French Canada to Vichy was one factor in shaping Canadian policy towards St. Pierre and Miquelon. Yet the two issues were not quite the same. While a certain feeling existed in Quebec for the people of St. Pierre and Miquelon as members of another French-speaking community, there was little emotional or ideological interest in the islands. This was apparent in the response of the French-Canadian press to the Free French takeover. Apart from *Le Devoir* and *Le Droit*, the general reaction was surprisingly favourable. For this and other reasons, Mackenzie King felt able to oppose the use of force to expel Muselier, just as he had earlier resisted attempts to compel de Bournat by force to comply with Canadian demands.[38]

The real difference between Britain and the United States was over relations, not with Vichy, but with Free France and especially de Gaulle. Here we come up against the fundamental blind spot in American policy.

The Americans insisted that it was necessary to choose between the Marshal and the General: either you staked everything on Pétain, or you broke with Vichy and threw your whole weight behind the Free French. Faced with these stark alternatives, the decision was simple, for Pétain was thought to hold all the cards in his hand and de Gaulle none: the United States came down firmly on the side of Vichy. The British, on the other hand, insisted that it was both possible and highly desirable to keep a foot in each camp. As Churchill has explained: "This was not because I or my colleagues had any respect for Marshal Pétain, but only because no road that led to France should be incontinently barred. Our consistent policy was to make the Vichy Government and its members feel that, so far as we were concerned, it was never too late to mend." At the same time, however, he did his utmost to increase de Gaulle's influence, authority, and power.[39]

This contrast in approaches reflected differences in national interests and historical experiences. But it also stemmed from the nature of the contacts which the two countries had with France. The fact that United States embassy officials limited themselves pretty well to a narrow circle of officialdom centred on Vichy inevitably contributed to Washington's warped vision of the French scene. Raymond Bruyère, a former French minister to Canada who at this time was living in retirement in unoccupied France, has claimed that the American ambassador "understood nothing about the internal situation in France, except what he learned from Vichy propaganda. . . . Isolated in his embassy, confined by Vichy, Admiral Leahy had no time either to know us or to understand us. He spent his time among us without grasping anything of the popular outlook or the soul of the nation."* Nor were American career diplomats in Vichy any better informed.† The United Kingdom, on the other hand, with no direct diplomatic ties, was in much closer touch with the real French nation. This had three important consequences for the policies of the two countries.[40]

---

*Bruyère adds that Leahy was "without any doubt the man who contributed most to making [Roosevelt] sceptical of how much faith should be put in the Gaullist mystic." Sir Llewellyn Woodward writes that "The United States Government were not well informed about French opinion generally by Admiral Leahy during his time as Ambassador at Vichy, and the President paid too much attention to the Admiral's reports."

†Bruyère considered the fact that three so different people as Leahy, S. Pinkney Tuck (Counsellor) and H. Freeman Matthews (First Secretary) took "an identical position so contrary to reality can only occasion astonishment." Matthews was at first sympathetic to de Gaulle but, as a result of the St. Pierre and Miquelon incident, became bitterly opposed to him. He had left Vichy by this time, but continued to be influential in shaping US policy towards France.

In the first place, Washington was far too optimistic in its estimate of the willingness (as opposed to the ability) of anti-Nazi elements within the Vichy Government to resist German pressure. Admiral Leahy might describe Pétain as "a feeble, frightened old man, surrounded by self-seeking conspirators" and conclude that there was little prospect of giving any "semblance of backbone to a jellyfish."[41] Yet, the belief persisted that Pétain and the majority of Vichy leaders were sincere patriots serving the true interests of France and offering the best base on which to build a resistance movement. Hence, the perpetuation of the Vichy regime as such came to be regarded as almost an American national interest.

Secondly, the United States seriously underrated the military and political importance of the opposition to Vichy inside and outside France and, therefore, tended to overlook the depressing effect its collaboration with Vichy, and its spurning of de Gaulle had on the spirit of resistance of the French people. Indeed, the fact that the genuinely anti-Nazi elements were also anti-Vichy meant that they constituted an obstacle to the realization of American objectives. Leahy complained that "whenever [the Resistance] made trouble for the invader, the Germans passed it on to Pétain and it made trouble for the Marshal." He also wrote that, "I had not met [de Gaulle] personally, but from Vichy, his movement appeared to cause nothing but trouble for the Allies." This attitude was evident throughout the St. Pierre and Miquelon *affaire* in the way Washington arbitrarily assumed that de Gaulle could be safely ignored; the fate of the Free French was, as Pierrepont Moffat expressed it, an "entirely subsidiary" consideration. The British (and Canadians) on the other hand, considered it important for the Allied war effort not to undermine de Gaulle in any way.[42]

Finally, the Americans were reluctant to admit that de Gaulle had or was ever likely to have any substantial following in France. He was not only unreliable; he was unrepresentative. This wishful thinking in Washington was encouraged by the dissensions which periodically erupted within the ranks of the Free French movement, especially the rivalry between de Gaulle and Muselier which culminated in the Admiral's dramatic defection in March, 1942. When Churchill in Ottawa claimed that nine out of ten Frenchmen increasingly looked to de Gaulle for leadership, Hull countered the next day with the dogmatic assertion that less than 5 per cent supported the

Free French leader. "Our British friends," he wrote Roosevelt on December 31, 1941, "seem to believe that the body of the entire people of France is strongly behind de Gaulle, whereas according to all of my information and that of my associates, some 95 per cent of the entire French people are anti-Hitler whereas more than 95 per cent of this latter number are not de Gaullists and would not follow him."*43 The American attitude was best summarized by Sumner Welles two days after Christmas when Lord Halifax had the audacity to beg that the Free French Delegate in Washington be invited to a meeting with representatives of refugee governments at the White House that afternoon. To this outrageous suggestion, Welles replied that he was "unable . . . to see that the Free French movement at the present moment had anything very much to commend it from the practical point of view. . . . Unfortunately there were no outstanding men with qualities of leadership and of initiative directing the Free French movement and providing that kind of inspiration to free men, both in France and in other parts of the world, to join in a movement against their German oppressors." This consistent belittlement of de Gaulle led the State Department into a constant and futile search for an alternative leader—Weygand, Chautemps, Herriot, Giraud, almost anybody else—around whom Frenchmen could rally. However, its desperate manoeuvres only succeeded, as did its handling of the St. Pierre and Miquelon affair, in boosting de Gaulle's growing prestige.†44

As a result of these conflicting assessments of the strength and importance of the Free French movement, the British and American Governments established very different relations with it. As early as June 28, 1940, London recognized de Gaulle as "leader of all free

*Hull's figures agree with those of Otto Abetz, the German Ambassador in Paris. Langer, on the other hand, says the evidence concerning de Gaulle's popularity at this time among the French people was "utterly conflicting." "What percentage of them favoured de Gaulle we do not know."

†One American correspondent reported on December 30, 1941, that Hull's Christmas Day statement had caused enlistments of Free French volunteers from among French sailors, stranded in the United States, to dry up, and had also created consternation among Resistance leaders in France. "From within occupied and un-occupied France, de Gaulle agents have been sending frantic messages pleading for clarification of the State Department action. They report that droves of Free French members have begun to desert the movement and go straight into the arms of . . . the Communist Party." There is nothing to confirm these reports. Whatever effect Hull had in diminishing de Gaulle's popularity was purely temporary.

Frenchmen, wherever they may be," and this recognition was transferred to the Free French National Committee on its formation in
London in September, 1941. British political and financial support
for the Free French, however, did not imply diplomatic recognition
of de Gaulle as head of a provisional government, though in practice
it came very close to this. The Americans did not progress nearly this
far for three reasons: unlike the British, they still maintained official
relations with Vichy; then, up to Pearl Harbor they were formally
neutral (and even after that continued to act, in some ways, as if
they still were); most important of all, they entertained grave doubts
concerning de Gaulle and his movement. Nevertheless, during the
autumn of 1941, they braved Vichy's protests to the extent of develop-
ing certain tentative contacts. An observer group was sent to Equatorial Africa (though its head was recalled shortly after Pearl Harbor
for allegedly exceeding his instructions and treating the Free French
as allies), a Free French Delegate was accepted in Washington
(though Roosevelt and Hull refused to receive him), and Lend-Lease
assistance was extended indirectly through the British to Free French
forces, after Roosevelt had formally certified that "the defence of any
French territory under the control of the Free French is vital to the
defence of the United States," and the State Department was forced to
deal with de Gaulle directly over the acquisition of an American air
base in New Caledonia. On the eve of the takeover in St. Pierre and
Miquelon, therefore, the United States was beginning to recognize
that in its own interest it could not completely ignore the existence
of the Free French.[45]

While the storm which followed the seizure of St. Pierre and
Miquelon reflected conflicting conceptions of the common interest, it
was the personalities who participated in the drama who turned it
into an *affaire*. Two in particular stand out: General de Gaulle who
provided the initial spark and Cordell Hull who poured fuel on it.
In their different ways, both were proud, sensitive, stubborn, and self-
righteous, though de Gaulle's intransigence had a heroic quality to
it whereas Hull appeared petty and even childish. Both were men of
real ability, great personal integrity, and little tact. Both were moti-
vated by a sincere belief that their own interpretation of their
national interest coincided with the interests of all. Yet each was
shown at his worst in this incident. Each considered himself the

innocent victim of a diabolical plot instigated by the other. This was particularly true of Cordell Hull who wrote Roosevelt on December 31 that the St. Pierre and Miquelon situation was "a mess beyond question, and one for which this Government was in no remote sense responsible." Both made an early solution of the problem infinitely more difficult, though each assumed that the obstacle was the need to save the face of the other.[46] But for de Gaulle and Hull, the St. Pierre and Miquelon affair would have been the obscure footnote in history it surely deserved to be.*

*The comments of Sumner Welles (who had his own difficulties with Hull, though not over St. Pierre and Miquelon) on the role of personalities in foreign policies are perhaps relevant here: "The foreign policy of a government, like the relations between two or more governments, has from time immemorial been as much affected by the consequences of selfish rivalries and petty jealousies and vanities as by honest differences on major issues. And so it is today in the conduct of American foreign policy."[47]

7

SIGNIFICANCE

Did the St. Pierre and Miquelon affair have any long-term significance, or was it merely a curious episode which, as Churchill and
Hull suggest, was quickly forgotten?

According to Sumner Welles, "The most damaging feature of the
St. Pierre-Miquelon incident was that it greatly hampered the
American government in continuing its relations with Vichy and in
carrying out its policies in North Africa." This claim goes too far; at
most, the issue introduced a minor complication into relations with
Vichy. Certainly, none of the calamitous consequences which the
State Department had freely predicted came about. Hitler did not
seize the French Fleet or occupy North Africa, Admiral Leahy was
not sent packing from Vichy, and Admiral Robert did not scrap his
agreement on the neutralization of the French Antilles. Even the
Latin Americans refused to be affronted. Thus, after all the panic in
the State Department over the "real issues" at stake, its worst fears
did not materialize. No one in fact seems to have taken the *affaire*
quite as seriously as the prickly Secretary of State. All things considered, even Vichy, whom Hull was so fearful of offending, recon-
ciled itself remarkably easily to the loss of the islands.

Admittedly, Pétain and Darlan did drift steadily into ever closer
collaboration with the Germans, but this merely continued a trend of
events which had begun much earlier and had become more pronounced following the removal of Weygand from North Africa and
the Pétain-Goering meeting in the fall of 1941. There is no real
evidence to suggest that the rapid deterioration of American relations
with Vichy during the early months of 1942, culminating in the
return of Laval to power and the recall of Ambassador Leahy in

April, was in any significant way attributable to bitterness in Vichy over St. Pierre and Miquelon. Even the assertion of Conn and Fairchild that, "Unquestionably, this affair had an adverse effect on the chances of securing French connivance in an unopposed Anglo-American entry into North Africa," is difficult to substantiate.[*1]

While, therefore, the direct consequences were minimal, the incident did have a continuing influence on American policy and inter-Allied relations at least until the end of the war. Although it would be wrong to exaggerate its importance, "the extraordinary resentment that it caused," as Sherwood rightly points out, "remained to affect other and far more important developments during the war years." "This episode was, indeed, a fleabite but it developed into a persistent, festering sore" which was "a source of infection before Normandy and after it."[2] The results can be seen in three main spheres: Anglo-Canadian-American relations, the administration of American foreign policy and, above all, United States relations with de Gaulle.

One commentator has described the St. Pierre and Miquelon affair as "a microcosmic study of the vicissitudes of coalition warfare, with its frictions over primary objectives, its frustrations, its little 'treacheries' and conflicts of personalities—with the added difficulty in a democracy of necessary reliance on public opinion." Certainly the conviction in the Department of State that Britain and Canada had sadly betrayed the United States, strained relations within the North Atlantic triangle at a critical time when the Anglo-American partnership was in the process of being hardened into a coalition. Canada was thought in Washington to have been far too tolerant of Muselier's reckless behaviour, while Britain was accused of encouraging the Free French to defy the Americans and of whipping up anti-Vichy sentiment in the United States and elsewhere. Canada and Britain for their part were clearly out of sympathy with American policy and particularly with Hull's antics. The consequences might

---

[*]They also claim that: "If Mr. Hull on the one hand seemed to magnify the incident out of all proportion to its true dimensions, the President and Prime Minister on the other showed no real understanding of the underlying principles at stake or of the practical consequences of General de Gaulle's high handed action." Davis and Lindley also conclude that "there was no doubt that the Saint Pierre incident strengthened the hand of the pro-Axis elements in France."

well have been more serious but for the firm refusal of Churchill and Roosevelt to be distracted, by the petty squabbles of lesser men, from the primary task at hand.[3]

Canada's reluctance to become the chore-boy for the State Department also confirmed Washington's suspicions that she was unreliable, or at least too inclined to follow a British lead. As one American authority has commented,

The effect of the Canadian position [during the St. Pierre and Miquelon affair] on her relations with the United States was not beneficial. Canadian unwillingness to challenge the Free French action as detrimental to stability and order in the Western Hemisphere did not please the Department of State. Later, Canadian readiness to accept any solution agreeable to the United Kingdom was viewed by that department as evidence that Canada still tended to follow British guidance in foreign policy matters where vital Canadian interests were not affected.[4]

Actually, what Washington interpreted as Canadian subservience to Britain was merely a classic instance of Canadian foreign policy in operation. From the fall of France onwards, Ottawa attempted repeatedly to produce a policy for St. Pierre and Miquelon which met its essential security needs and yet commanded support in both Washington and London. Each in practice held a veto over Canadian decisions, and each exercised it on more than one occasion: the Americans to oppose a Free French take-over, and the British to block any alternative solution. As a result, no effective action was possible. Similarly, after the liberation, Canada refused to do anything to expel Muselier or normalize political relations with him without the agreement of both Britain and the United States. Some persons in the Department of External Affairs (such as King and Keenleyside) might incline to the American point of view, while others (Robertson, Pearson, and Stone, for example) were impressed with many of the same arguments as the British were. Yet all were agreed on the overriding importance of operating within a framework of Anglo-American harmony. Canada's fundamental objection to Hull's ultimatum was that it demanded that she deliberately disregard this time-tested traditional basis of Canadian policy.

There was also intense resentment at the way Cordell Hull presumed to order Canada about as if she were a banana republic. As one senior Canadian official said somewhat facetiously, if the British had behaved as abominably as the Americans did on this occasion, Mackenzie King would have "pulled Canada out of the war." Despite the immense respect in Ottawa for Hull, no Canadian leader could put up with this sort of treatment. Fortunately, the immediate crisis precipitated by the Christmas Day communiqué passed quickly. It is a striking testimony to the solid friendship existing between the countries that this nasty incident did not impair the underlying good relations or personal friendships.

St. Pierre and Miquelon did, however, serve to teach Ottawa a useful lesson. As a result of this and other developments at about the same time, notably Canadian exclusion from the Anglo-American Combined Boards and the Pan American Union, and the refusal to accept a Canadian Military Mission in Washington, the Canadian Government was shocked into the realization that the United States was not prepared to accord Canada the rights to which she felt entitled on the basis of her contribution to the war effort, and which she had come to expect from the United Kingdom. In particular, there was no assurance of full consultation in advance on all matters of direct concern to her. As Lester Pearson noted at the time, "We are finding out that our cherished status is more respected in Downing Street than in Washington, and there are very definite and discernible tendencies in the latter capital to consider us either as part of the British Empire to be dealt with through a British Empire spokesman from the United Kingdom or as a North American colony." This proved to be a continuing problem and gave birth to the Canadian concept of middle powers and the functional principle of representation enunciated by Mackenzie King in July, 1943.

Perhaps the major casualty of the St. Pierre and Miquelon affair was Secretary Hull himself. Although Roosevelt could not afford to let Hull resign, he could ignore him, and this very largely is what happened. Partly as a result of Hull's mishandling of the incident and his evident inability to get along with Churchill, the Secretary of State was quietly but effectively excluded from any real influence over the conduct of Washington's wartime foreign relations. While he lingered in office for another three years, he remained on the fringes of power. The President stopped inviting him to meetings of his War Council, rarely consulted him or kept him properly informed, excluded him from military discussions with Churchill in Washington, and left him behind when summit conferences were convened in Casablanca, Cairo, and Teheran, despite the enormous diplomatic repercussions of the decisions taken at these meetings. After Casablanca, Roosevelt even ordered Leahy not to divulge anything about the conference to Hull without his express permission.* Harry Hopkins rather than Cordell Hull became Roosevelt's chosen instrument—his "personal Foreign Office," as he was described by one British official.

This process of bypassing the Secretary of State was not an entirely new development. It had been going on ever since the outbreak of war in 1939, if not before. Persons like Robert Murphy, who later became the President's principal adviser on relations with France, had long had direct access to the White House. Although a comparatively junior official, he had been told by Roosevelt in the fall of 1940 to send anything of special interest straight to him: "Don't bother going through State Department channels." Pearl Harbor led to a further subordination of diplomacy to the needs of war. Yet, but for Hull's infantile behaviour over St. Pierre and Miquelon, his position would probably not have become quite so insecure. "The whole episode," Sumner Welles records, "accentuated the fundamentally dissimilar character of the two men . . . and sharply increased the President's disinclination to have more than official relations with his Secretary of State"—and with the Department of State generally.[5]

The reputation of the foreign service also suffered heavily in the eyes of the American people as a result of St. Pierre and Miquelon. Walter Lippman was not alone in wondering "whether the State Department is too bureaucratic . . . to adjust itself rapidly enough to the new and vaster responsibilities of war" with the United States no longer "a neutral, separate from our present allies and pursuing a course of its own."[6] The unpopularity of the Department's Vichy policy also had a good deal to do with its ugly public image.

The most damaging consequence of the St. Pierre and Miquelon affair was on American attitudes towards France. Prior to the seizure, policy towards Vichy had been largely an improvisation. But the explosion of public resentment over the State Department's handling

*Hull says rather pathetically that, "I learned from other sources than the President what had occurred at the Casablanca, Cairo and Teheran conferences. I had no special occasion to interrogate Mr. Roosevelt on developments at these conferences."

of the incident forced it on to the defensive. In the process of counter-ing the charges levelled at it, it became so convinced of the correctness of its policy that it was blinded to its limitations—at the very time when these were becoming increasingly apparent. On November 19, 1941, following Pétain's "unnecessary surrender" to Hitler's demand for the recall of Weygand from North Africa, Admiral Leahy advised that the time had come to consider a "complete revision" of American policy. Vichy, he concluded, was "responsive only to aggressive action." But, because of Pearl Harbor and St. Pierre and Miquelon, this radical reassessment did not take place. On the contrary, instead of being simply one possible means to an end, the State Department's Vichy policy became almost an end in itself—a sacred cow.* As Eugene Rostow has pointed out: "A genuine Vichy party emerged within the American Government which found endless excuses for Pétain, and endless objections to de Gaulle and other spokesmen of French resis-tance." The more violent the public outcry against "appeasement" of Vichy, the more tenaciously Hull and his advisers clung to their preconceptions. This set the stage both for the Darlan deal and the fresh wave of public criticism of the State Department which it pro-voked.† [7]

While the St. Pierre and Miquelon affair committed Washington more completely to a doctrinaire policy towards Vichy, its principal importance for the future conduct of the war was in widening the gap with General de Gaulle at a time when he was beginning to forge firm ties with the Resistance and to emerge as a really significant national leader. "Our relations with de Gaulle's movement," Cordell Hull writes, "were not helped by the incident. . . . The President and myself . . . regarded him as more ambitious for himself and less

---

*Langer argues that "the St. Pierre episode . . . had very little to do with our policy toward Pétain and the Vichy regime" as this had been formulated "long before and was adhered to unswervingly until the time of the invasion of North Africa. It never was and never became a policy that we thought we could rely on. On the contrary, it was a day-to-day, hand-to-mouth policy all the way through." Sherwood says that: "Before the St. Pierre and Miquelon episode, the Vichy policy had not been subjected to any widespread criticism, nor had it been considered a sacred cow in the State Department."

†When, on Darlan's recommendation, the Allies appointed the notorious Marcel Peyrouton Governor-General of Algeria, there was a tremendous public outcry in both the United States and Britain. As Sherwood says, "St. Pierre and Miquelon were alive again."

reliable than we had thought him before." Langer even suggests that, "This episode was of really crucial significance in determining our [the State Department's] future attitude toward both de Gaulle and the Free French. . . He had put the United States in a most embarrassing position and had thereby built up a resentment in official circles that it was almost impossible to overcome."* One reason after another was discovered for refusing to deal with de Gaulle. He was vain and arrogant, irresponsible and untrustworthy, autocratic and authoritarian. Above all, he was a disagreeable non-entity who had to be taught "the old diplomatic adage" that it was "dangerous to play little tricks on great powers."[8] Secretary of War Stimson might question whether it was "wise for the State Department to have so long a memory for such annoyances," but he had no influence on Cordell Hull who would neither forgive nor forget. "To Secretary Hull, whose sensitive pride had been deeply aroused by unjustified and violent attacks on American policy toward Vichy, the very mention of de Gaulle was enough to produce an outburst of skillful Tennessee denunciation."[9]

To make matters worse, the President quickly became if anything even more rabid in his antipathy to de Gaulle than was his Secretary of State—though St. Pierre and Miquelon was not the major factor accounting for his prejudice. A year after the liberation of the islands, Roosevelt confided in his son that, "I can't imagine a man I would distrust more" than de Gaulle. Admittedly, Churchill also became increasingly irritated at de Gaulle's "proud and haughty demeanour," even confessing on one occasion that the Cross of Lorraine was the heaviest cross he had to bear. Yet he continued to admire and respect the qualities of greatness of this *homme du destin*.†[10]

The inability or unwillingness of otherwise imaginative American statesmen to see in Charles de Gaulle the embodiment of the spirit

*Conn and Fairchild say the seizure "helped to make General de Gaulle *persona non grata* to the American Department of State for the remainder of the war."

†The British Foreign Office felt that the Prime Minister seemed at times to show "less than his usual generosity [to de Gaulle] and also to come near to risking British long-term interests in order to meet a certain prejudice on the part of President Roosevelt. . . . [Churchill] was for a long time very tolerant of the General's obstinacy . . . but he came understandably, though without full cause, to distrust and suspect his political aims, and not very willing to use his personal influence with Roosevelt to try to change the latter's attitude towards the Free French."

of the French nation—or to recognize Vichy as the shame it was—was as tragic as it was surprising.* For years, Washington stubbornly refused to face the facts concerning de Gaulle and deliberately went out of its way to slight him. As one American authority remarked, "American policy-makers did all they could to discourage the Gaullist movement and to produce rivals to it." So determined indeed was Washington to block de Gaulle's political advance that it appeared at times to be imposing its own nominee on the nation—all the while protesting that it was merely seeking (in Roosevelt's words) "to preserve for the people of France the right and opportunity to determine for themselves what government they will have."[11]

Although something of a *rapprochement* between the United States and Free France appeared in prospect in the fall of 1941, this hope was quickly shattered by the landing at St. Pierre. Only when the pressure from American military leaders was overwhelming, as in the demand for bases in French Equatorial Africa and New Caledonia, were the political objections to collaboration with the Free French waived.[12]

As an immediate result of the seizure of St. Pierre and Miquelon, the State Department emphatically rejected British pleas to include the Free French in a meeting which Roosevelt and Churchill had arranged with representatives of the refugee governments. Similarly, Free France was not invited to adhere to the United Nations Declaration on New Year's Day.†[13] Moreover, although de Gaulle managed to hold on to St. Pierre and Miquelon, it was the last overseas territory the Free French liberated. The Americans kept them out of the Caribbean and did their best to do the same elsewhere. The invasions of Madagascar in May, 1942, and North Africa in November of that

---

*At Admiral Stark's suggestion, de Gaulle attempted at Casablanca to interpret his attitude to Roosevelt in terms of French history, but the President would not listen. Later, the President poked fun at the General by recounting to various people that "the day [de Gaulle] arrived, he thought he was Joan of Arc and the following day he insisted that he was Georges Clemenceau." This was grossly unfair and bitterly resented.

†On December 27, 1941, and January 1, 1942, respectively. Roosevelt overruled Hull on the participation of Free France in the UN Declaration, but then could not get the approval of Moscow in time. When this was received, the United States announced on January 5 that it was prepared to receive statements of adherence (as opposed to signatures) from "appropriate authorities which are not governments." However, this was not good enough for de Gaulle who did not formally adhere until January 1, 1945, by which time his Provisional Government had been accorded recognition.

year, were planned without any advance notification to de Gaulle.*
Even in the case of the Normandy operation, the Free French leader
was informed only on the eve of the attack.[14] In fact, as late as
January, 1944, General Eisenhower was not permitted to discuss
with de Gaulle the question of co-operation with French resistance
movements, and no civil administration agreement was ready when
the Allies landed in France. Nevertheless, the Americans were compelled, much against their will, to deal with de Gaulle on a *de facto*
basis though Roosevelt, who still thought in terms of the situation in
1940, continued to believe de Gaulle would be repudiated by the
French people. Eventually, in October, 1944, *de jure* recognition was
accorded the Provisional Government, but only after the evidence of
de Gaulle's popularity had become overwhelming. When at Yalta
"Winston and Anthony," to quote Harry Hopkins, "fought like tigers
for France," they were trying to overcome the years of accumulated
hostility to de Gaulle which stemmed in part from the St. Pierre and
Miquelon affair.[15] Admittedly, this incident does not explain all the
blindness and stupidity which characterized much of American policy
towards the Free French, but it was a significant conditioning factor,
especially with Cordell Hull.

The St. Pierre and Miquelon incident undoubtedly strengthened
de Gaulle's conviction, which evidently he still holds, that a tough
line with the Americans was the only policy that paid dividends. Accordingly, the more hostile the reaction in Washington, the more
intransigent he became, a technique he once candidly explained to
Churchill. The way to be a world power, he felt, was to act like one.

De Gaulle paid a stiff price for his uncompromising defence of
every French sovereign right. Was it a price he could afford? "One
may put in question," one of his biographers has suggested,

de Gaulle's fundamental assumption that he must achieve the heights and
never descend from them—the basic conviction of the idealist that forever
stands in opposition to the pragmatist's concern for consequences. . . . A
more tolerant attitude in regard to Saint Pierre and Miquelon and the
Levant states would have been worth cultivating even at the expense of

*Apparently Hull had planned to exclude de Gaulle even before the St. Pierre
and Miquelon incident. In a letter to Roosevelt on December 31, 1941, he mentioned "our plans about North Africa and our omission of de Gaulle's cooperation
in that connection." St. Pierre and Miquelon made any reconsideration of this
decision impossible.

neglecting French "rights". . . . With Allied goodwill and co-operation de Gaulle might have achieved a position which would have enabled him to protect French interests far more successfully than he could do when he butted headlong against the stone wall of Allied indignation.[16]

General de Gaulle had much the same trouble with some of his subordinates as he had with his allies and benefactors, partly because he was at first compelled by circumstances to fashion an organization out of whatever bits and pieces happened to come his way. His most celebrated clash (prior to the encounter with Giraud) was with the redoubtable Admiral Muselier. As we have seen, these two great patriots had had a long history of friction and rivalry. Both were "difficult" men and the fact that Muselier was de Gaulle's senior in age and rank did not make relations any smoother. Moreover, their conflicting political philosophies reflected the basic schism in French politics between the Catholic authoritarian, liberal right and the secular republican left. Although, at the outset, the disputes betwen the General and the Admiral were normally over questions of internal administrative organization, these merely masked a bitter personal contest for power. In September, 1941, Muselier even seems to have attempted to displace de Gaulle as Free French leader. The decisive factor in their struggle was the St. Pierre and Miquelon affair. Muselier confided in the American Consul on December 26, 1941, that, while he had loyally obeyed de Gaulle's orders to liberate the islands and would defend them to the death, as soon as he returned to London, he intended to resign in protest against this flagrant breach of faith with the Allies. However, when he did defect in March, 1942, he did so on the grounds that de Gaulle had surrendered to Allied pressure over St. Pierre and Miquelon.[17]

The principal importance of this savage confrontation was in misleading the Americans further as to the true state of the Free French movement. Actually, the rupture indicated that de Gaulle now felt strong enough to dispense with his powerful rival. Far from the FNFL pulling out of the Free French movement as Muselier seems to have hoped, only three naval officers (including Captain de Villefosse) followed him into the political wilderness.* De Gaulle was left as unchallenged leader of the Free French organization. He could also

---

*Alain Savary, who was also ideologically on the political left, broke with de Gaulle sometime after the war.

by this time count increasingly on the support of the underground in France.

What of the brave people of St. Pierre and Miquelon? What has been the legacy of the events of Christmas, 1941, for them? Once the immediate crisis had passed, life in the islands returned remarkably quickly and smoothly to something approaching normality. Yet memories of the tragic and glorious events of 1940 and 1941 have not faded completely. Most people prefer not to talk much about these years for fear of reopening old wounds, but the cleavage between the followers of Marshal Pétain and the partisans of General de Gaulle has persisted, and remains a significant, if no longer dominant, factor underlying internal politics in the islands at all levels. Its influence is even felt at times in the functioning of the local administration. There still exists, on the one hand, a hard core of loyal Gaullists who rallied to Free France in June, 1940, and who continue to support the *Association Nationale pour le soutien de l'Action du Général de Gaulle* and, on the other hand, an aggressive group of unrepentant *Vichyards* led by Senator Claireaux. Moreover, sentiment in St. Pierre and Miquelon, at least as revealed by the results of successive referenda since 1958, is still overwhelmingly in favour of President de Gaulle. Even the despatch of French troops to the islands in April, 1965 did not seriously affect his personal popularity, as the voting in the presidential elections of December, 1965 shows:

	First Ballot: December 5		Second Ballot: December 19*	
	SPM	*France*	*SPM*	*France*
De Gaulle	68% (1510)	44%	83% (1496)	55%
Mitterand	2% (57)	32%	17% (313)	45%
Four other candidates	30% (669)	24%	————	————

On the other hand, many of de Gaulle's present supporters in the Territory are postwar converts.† Shifting party allegiances in metro-

---

*Cf. p. 12. Admittedly, the large number of abstentions—25% on the first ballot and 40% on the second—may indicate some increased dissatisfaction with de Gaulle's leadership.

†One St. Pierrais assesses current political allegiances of those who actively supported Free France or Vichy in 1941 approximately as follows:

	1964 *Opinions*			
1941 Active Supporters of:	*Active Gaullist*	*Inactive Gaullist*	*Neutral*	*Anti-Gaullist*
Free France	30%	10%	10%	30%
Vichy	30%	30%	30%	10%

According to this Free French source, de Gaulle has more support among former *Vichyards* than among former partisans of Free France.

politan France have contributed to changes in the social and ideological bases of political support in St. Pierre and Miquelon. New issues and ideas have arisen to blur the clear-cut division of opinion that split the islands so disastrously during the dark days of the Second World War. This is particularly apparent from the outcome of recent parliamentary elections. Henri Claireux, who has been Senator since 1947, and the present Deputy, Albert Briand, though political opponents, are both anti-Gaullists in different degrees.

The St. Pierre and Miquelon affair has been variously referred to as a "teapot tempest," as "a fleabite," and as "trivial to the point of ridiculousness." It was certainly all of these. Nevertheless, at a critical point in world affairs, this curious episode succeeded in engaging the attention of the leading statesmen of the Western alliance, and complicating their relations. That this should have happened is surely a sobering commentary on the role of the human personality in history.

APPENDIXES

APPENDIX A

ADMINISTRATOR DE BOURNAT'S PROCLAMATION OF NOVEMBER 12TH 1940[1]

THE FRENCH REPUBLIC

Liberty, Equality, and Fraternity

Territory of the Islands of St. Pierre and Miquelon

INHABITANTS OF THE TERRITORY

For some time the most extraordinary and often the most tendentious rumours have been circulating in St. Pierre. These rumours are derived from various sources: newspapers, radio transmissions and even just from the over-fertile imagination of certain residents. They are raising doubts in people's minds and giving rise to partisan quarrels even in family circles. Do not therefore be misled by all these rumours. Have the patience and good sense to wait until they are verified.

You must also know what to say in reply to those who are spreading false rumours and who are, in particular, stating verbally or in writing that the French soldiers did not have the courage of their forebears, that French sailors were not present at Dunkirk, that French airmen had received orders not to fly, that it was in France's interest not to suspend hostilities, that Marshal Pétain is not the great figure respected by the whole world, that a modification of the political status of the Territory would be more profitable to the inhabitants than the maintenance of the position taken since last June, that the maintenance of the Archipelago's supply line is conditioned upon a change in that position, that the dollars which are at present being used in connection with our supplies do not belong to France, etc. . . . .

To the questions raised by these wild rumour mongers, I suggest you give the following replies which are based on the most simple reasoning and which you can quite easily verify for yourselves:

THE FRENCH SOLDIERS:

R: Their bravery was highly commended in particularly moving and convincing terms by Mr. Bullitt, United States Ambassador to France, during the course of several *broadcast talks* given on his return to America.

DID THE FRENCH NAVY TAKE NO PART IN THE DUNKIRK OPERATION?

R: In the Dunkirk operation, the French Navy lost six destroyers (including the renowned *Sirocco*) and it was the French Navy which, in collaboration with British warships and troops of the *French* army, provided at Dunkirk itself the cover for the retreat of our British friends— who were naturally evacuated first, it being French territory—and then for the remainder of the French troops.

HAD THE FRENCH AIRMEN RECEIVED ORDERS NOT TO FLY DURING THE GERMAN OFFENSIVE?

R: All the Allied broadcasting services announced that from the 10th May to the 10th June the allied air forces had shot down 2,000 German planes; now, it has been possible to announce *officially* both verbally and in writing without anyone—not even the Germans—denying it, that the French airmen could pride themselves on having shot down, on their own, almost half this figure, i.e. nearly 1,000!

WAS IT IN FRANCE'S INTEREST NOT TO SUSPEND HOSTILITIES?

R: Again, it was Mr. Bullitt who replied to this question by affirming in the same *broadcast talks* that at the time of the suspension of hostilities, the French no longer had in the country enough aeroplanes, tanks, guns and ammunition to continue the struggle and that the French colonies could no longer be counted on for any substantial contribution except for the physical courage of our soldiers. . . .

MARSHAL PÉTAIN?

R: Marshal Pétain, the victor of Verdun, is the head of the French State, a man to whom King George VI and President Roosevelt have recently addressed expressions of their admiration. His praises were also sung by the President of the St. Pierre war veterans at their meeting on October 24th, 1940. Marshal Pétain is still Head of the *Legion française des anciens combattants* which 99 per cent of the War Veterans Associations of the French Empire have joined.

THE MINISTER FOR THE COLONIES?

R: The Minister for the Colonies is Rear Admiral Platon, one of the heroes of Dunkirk.

WHAT IS THE PRESENT POSITION OF THE ISLANDS OF ST. PIERRE AND MIQUELON?

R: It is still as defined in the telegram which we sent on June 23rd to the head of the French State. This telegram has been posted up in the Territory and broadcast throughout the world.

IS IT IN OUR INTEREST TO CHANGE THIS POSITION AT THE PRESENT TIME?

R: Our position is plain and clearly defined. To change it at the present time would result in raising doubts in people's minds, would cause embarrassment to our great neighbours and friends, would be a disservice to France and would place the Territory in a very difficult financial situation.

CAN THE TERRITORY HELP IN THE LIBERATION OF FRANCE AT THE PRESENT TIME?

R: The French have no armaments and in such conditions anything they might do at the present time would only be harmful to France. We can, however, be quite sure that the day is not far off when it will be possible for us to take part in that great task. When that day comes, we shall be better informed than we are at present and we shall all know therefore *exactly* what steps we should take.

WHAT ARE OUR RELATIONS WITH OUR NEIGHBOURS?

R: Our present relations with Newfoundland, Canada, and the United States are most friendly and, moreover, such as they should be between countries which have the same moral aspirations.

IS IT TRUE THAT FRENCH WARSHIPS AND OUR OVERSEAS NAVAL BASES HAVE BEEN LENT TO GERMANY TO HELP HER IN HER FIGHT AGAINST ENGLAND?

R: No, it is not true.

IS IT POSSIBLE, IN THE NAME OF LIBERTY, TO FORCE ONE'S FELLOW CITIZENS TO ADOPT AN ATITUDE OF WHICH THEY DO NOT APPROVE?

R: Mere common sense dictates the answer: "No."

IS IT POSSIBLE TO CONSIDER SERIOUSLY AND SINCERELY RALLYING TO A COMMANDER OF AN EXPEDITIONARY FORCE WITHOUT BEING COMMITTED TO GO AND FIGHT IN HIS RANKS IF HE SO REQUESTS?

R: No, for otherwise this support would only be a worthless platonic gesture the only result of which would be to disappoint deeply the Commander in question on the day when he might deem it necessary to call up a fighting force.

HAVE FATHERS, MOTHERS, WIVES, SISTERS, YOUNG WOMEN, MEN OVER 40 AND UNDER 20 (WHO ARE VERY WELL AWARE THAT IF TROOPS WERE CONSCRIPTED THEY WOULD NOT BE CALLED UP THEMSELVES) AND THOSE WHO HAVE NO SONS ELIGIBLE FOR CALL-UP, THE RIGHT TO OBLIGE THEIR SONS, HUSBANDS, BROTHERS, FIANCÉS, OR OTHER PEOPLE'S CHILDREN TO SACRIFICE THEIR LIVES?

R: No. This right belongs only to the persons concerned or to a *regular* Government of France.

IS THE MAINTENANCE OF THE ARCHIPELAGO'S SUPPLY LINE CONDI-
TIONAL UPON A CHANGE IN OUR ATTITUDES?
R: Our supply line is at present assured *by France* in friendly collaboration with our neighbours. What better can one therefore hope for under
these conditions?

WHO IS AT PRESENT PAYING THE SALARIES OF OFFICIALS AND ASSIS-
TANTS, PENSIONS, UNEMPLOYMENT ASSISTANCE, FAMILY ALLOWANCES?
R: The Territory, *with French money.*

TO WHOM DO THE DOLLARS BELONG WHICH ARE AT PRESENT BEING
USED FOR THE MAINTENANCE OF OUR SUPPLY LINE?
R: *To France.* France in fact possesses on this side of the Atlantic considerable sums in gold which have been put in safe-keeping in different
places, American dollars deposited in New York with the French-American
Banking Corporation and Canadian dollars deposited in Montreal with
the Bank of Montreal. It is these American and Canadian dollars (which, I
repeat, belong *to France*) which are being used for the maintenance of our
supply line.

WHAT CAN BE DEDUCED FROM THE ABOVE?
R: Notably this: that one must not believe all that is said and also that
before taking a major decision one must think carefully, weigh up the
pros and cons well and above all wait for *reliable* and *complete* information which is at the moment still rather difficult to obtain here.

FRENCHMEN OF SAINT-PIERRE AND MIQUELON, HAVE YOU ALL HEARD
OF GOOD OLD FRENCH REALISM? . . . WELL THEN, IN ALL CIRCUMSTANCES,
THINK AND ACT JUST LIKE—FRENCHMEN.

ST. PIERRE, NOVEMBER 12, 1940
The Administrator,
G. DE BOURNAT

APPENDIX B

PROPOSALS FOR SETTLEMENT OF ST. PIERRE AND MIQUELON QUESTION DECEMBER, 1941–JANUARY, 1942

1. State Department Communiqué (December 25)[2]

Our preliminary reports show that the action taken by three so-called Free French ships at St. Pierre-Miquelon was an arbitrary action contrary to the agreement of all parties concerned and certainly without the prior knowledge or consent in any sense of the US Government.

This Government has inquired of the Canadian Government as to the steps that Government is prepared to take to restore the *status quo* of these islands.

2. Vichy Government Note to US Government (December 27)[3]

The French Government has noted with satisfaction the declaration whereby the American Government disapproved the action undertaken against St. Pierre and Miquelon.

But it deems that the condition of political and pecuniary dependence in which the Gaullist leaders find themselves with respect to the Imperial authorities and the support which ex-Admiral Muselier must have received in English or Canadian territory impose upon it the obligation to request of the Governments concerned the immediate re-establishment of the *status quo ante.*

Such re-establishment would involve in the first place the evacuation of the territory by the Gaullist mercenaries and the reinstallation of the Governor in his functions.

The French Government would attach the greatest value to obtaining at this time precise indications as to the measures taken to this end by the Governments concerned.

3. Hull Proposal to French Ambassador (December 27)[4]

I then said to him that my own country, along with Canada and Great

Britain, has become increasingly concerned for some time about the possibilities of the use of the wireless station on these two islands to the detri-
ment of our and their shipping. . . . I emphasized that it is very important
that the French officials clear up this matter against any possibility of
injury by signals to enemy vessels on the high seas; that the French
Government on the islands should be only too glad to take the necessary
steps to do so either by closing down this wireless station during the war,
with some Canadians there as observers, or, if it desired to operate the
station, to agree to two or three Canadians and an American to be attached
to our Consulate, who would exercise the necessary authority over the
operation of the station to assure Great Britain, Canada and the United
States against any possible injury. I said that this would not interfere at
all with the sovereignty of the Government [of St. Pierre and Miquelon],
whose sovereignty only extends to internal affairs, but would relate to the
international phase of the operations of the wireless station. . . .

I then said to the Ambassador that the Governor of these islands has
made himself personally offensive to Canada and to some of the people
of the islands and that it would be desired that he be transferred to some
other island and that another governor be assigned to take his place.

4. Churchill-Halifax Proposal (January 1)[5]

. . . Mr. Churchill and Lord Halifax had talked of a formula which
would set forth the circumstances of seizure, protect the collateral position
of the Havana Act, and then leave the Free French in occupation.

5. Hull Proposals

(a) as worked out with Ambassador Henry-Haye (January 2)[6]
. . . we reached the conclusion that his Government could well afford at
once to propose on its part that it would select a governor whose conduct
and attitude would be broad enough and impersonal enough to be free
from reasonable objections on the part of the United States, the Canadians
and the British and any considerable number of people on the islands, and,
second, to shut down each of the radio or wireless stations on these islands
and agree for the Canadians to observe these stations sufficiently to see that
they are not reopened and used at any time and for any purpose. We
further reached the conclusion that this Government could well attach one
or two naval observers to the American Consulate at St. Pierre just as we
have done at Martinique. The Canadians could do likewise with the
further understanding that their newly established naval attachés were to
observe the radio situation at all times to the extent of seeing to it that
none of the stations is used.

(b) as transmitted to Vichy (January 3)[7]
Simultaneous action in regard to

1. Withdrawal of the Free French forces.

2. Admiral Robert will call the present Administrator to Fort-de-France for extended consultation and will name as temporary Administrator a local inhabitant of the Islands whose appointment would be agreeable to the population of the Islands.

3. The American and Canadian Governments to name observers attached to their Consulates at the Islands to supervise the closing and continued cessation of all wireless operation.

6. HULL DRAFT DECLARATION (January 2)[8]

The proposed statement . . . said that the President and the Prime Minister were in entire agreement that an arrangement satisfactory to all concerned should not be difficult. It added that the matter was receiving further attention in the light of the United States' commitments under the 1940 Havana Treaty and other international policies and agreements of great importance to the conduct of the war. This referred to our policy of continuing diplomatic relations with Vichy. The statement finished with the thought that "there should be no occasion for confusion or misunderstanding since there is complete cooperation and understanding between the United States, Great Britain and Canada in this as in other matters."

7. ROOSEVELT-CHURCHILL DRAFT DECLARATION (January 3)[9]

The United States, British and Canadian Governments view this incident as on a very small scale compared to what is going on all over the world. The problems involved relate to the safeguarding of British, Canadian and American shipping in the North Atlantic and existing international commitments. Nevertheless it must be made clear that the Free French action was taken not only without their assent, but in the face of the declared wishes of the British Government.

Accordingly, the three Governments have agreed that the principle that these islands are to be regarded in the present phase as demilitarized and out of the war shall be maintained. All armed forces will be withdrawn, it being understood that at the same time adequate steps shall be taken to assure that no radio station situated on the islands shall be used contrary to the interests of the United Nations.

The local inhabitants will be left in full exercise of their rights of domestic self-government, arrangements being made both to continue the supplies from the United States and Canada on which they are dependent, and also to provide for the seasonal supply of fish to the French inhabitants of Martinique.

Meanwhile, in the light of the relevant facts there should be no occasion for confusion or misunderstanding since there is no divergence of policy and there is complete cooperation and understanding between the United States, Great Britain, and Canada in this as in other matters.

8. Admiral Robert's Reply to Hull Proposals (January 6)[10]

The French Government, after considering Mr. Hull's proposals [*see* no. 5] authorizes me to reply through you.

Referring to President Roosevelt's communication of December 13 to Marshal Pétain regarding French possessions in this hemisphere, confirmed by yours [American Consul in Martinique] to me of December 23, I regard the American Government as obligated to obtain the reestablishment of French sovereignty over St. Pierre-Miquelon.

The French Government, which has never deviated from its policy of strict neutrality and desires like myself to facilitate the American Government's task under the circumstances, is prepared in this case to give further proof thereof satisfactory to all interested parties.

It requests in exchange that the Canadian Government on this occasion give assurances to respect French sovereignty over these territories similar to those received from the American Government.

It accepts the principle of the presence at Saint Pierre of American and Canadian observers, three at most, attached to their respective Consulates, charged with watching over the strict neutrality of the territory, without interfering with the administration proper except as concerns the radio station for which the French Government consents to a control permitting verification that there is no transmission *en clair* susceptible of being used by the belligerents and that there is no transmission in code other than official telegrams sent under the administrator's responsibility. It is understood that no meteorological bulletins will be sent.

The Administrator of the islands, M. de Bournat, retains the French Government's confidence and mine. I desire that he be reinstated in authority, it being understood that no reprisal will be exercised. It is indispensable that he come to Martinique, as much to receive my instructions conforming to the new agreement, as to report on the situation to me. I request that his journey be facilitated and that he may immediately enter into telegraphic communication with me for choosing a substitute to administer the territories during his absence.

Finally, I request that his return from Fort-de-France to St. Pierre Miquelon by the *Barfleur* be recognized in order to confirm the restoration of French sovereignty in these islands. The *Barfleur* would return to Fort-de-France immediately after this peaceful mission.

9. Hull Draft Agreement (January 8)[11]

(1) The islands are French and will remain French.

(2) To avoid any potential threat to the shipping of the governments concerned, the use of the wireless stations on the islands will be subject to the supervision and control by observers appointed by the American and Canadian Governments and attached to their respective consulates.

(3) The islands shall be neutralized and demilitarized and shall be considered out of the war.

(4) The present Administrator shall be withdrawn for the period of the war; the appointment of an Administrator shall be withheld for the same period, and the administration of the islands shall be left in the hands of the Consultative Council.

(5) All armed forces will be withdrawn.

(6) The Canadian and American Governments agree and undertake to continue economic assistance to the inhabitants of the islands, and the respective consuls of those countries will confer with the local authorities as to the nature of the assistance to be given. Arrangements are being made both to continue the supplies from the United States and Canada on which the islands are dependent, and to provide the seasonal supply of fish to the French inhabitants of Martinique.

10. DE GAULLE RESERVATIONS (January 14)[12]

[General de Gaulle] was willing to go along with a modified draft [of 9 above] excluding [the third] sentence subject to three secret reservations. These reservations were:

1. that the Free French Administrator remains on the island, though he might be assimilated into the new elective Consultative Council;

2. that the French Marines remain on the island in order to protect it from attack;

3. that the Canadian-American observers do not control the wireless but co-operate with the authorities.

General de Gaulle would issue a statement that it had never been his intention to keep ships stationed at the islands.

11. EDEN DRAFT DECLARATION (January 15?)[13]

(a) The islands are French and will remain French.

(b) The Vichy administrator will be withdrawn. The administration will be carried out by the Consultative Council.

(c) The Consultative Council will accept the appointment of Canadian and American officials to assist it in the exploitation of the wireless station in the common interest of the Allies.

(d) The French National Committee has informed His Majesty's Government in the United Kingdom that it had no intention of keeping its ships at Saint Pierre and Miquelon and that these ships would shortly resume their normal function, which is to attack the enemy wherever he is to be found.

(e) The Canadian and American Governments have agreed to

undertake to continue giving economic assistance to the islands and the respective Consuls of these two countries will confer with the local authorities as to the nature of the assistance which should be given. Arrangements are being made both to continue the supplies from the United States and Canada on which the islands are dependent, and to provide the seasonal supply of fish to the French inhabitants of Martinique.

DRAMATIS PERSONAE

AMERICAN

RAY ATHERTON (1883–1960). Career diplomat, 1917–48. Acting Chief, European Division, Department of State, 1940–43. Minister (later Ambassador) to Canada, 1943–48.

GEORGE BRITT (1895–   ). Newspaperman since 1916. Editorial writer, *New York Post*, 1941–42. Visited St. Pierre, January 7–14, 1942. Organized mission of St. Pierrais spokesmen to Washington, January–February, 1942. Managing Editor of *The Survey Graphic*, 1947–50.

JAMES CLEMENT DUNN (1890–   ). Career diplomat, 1920–56. Advisor on Political Relations, State Department, 1937–44. Assistant Secretary of State, 1944–46. Ambassador to Italy, France, Spain, Brazil, 1946–56.

JOHN D. HICKERSON (1898–1964), Career Foreign Service Office, 1920–61. Assistant Chief, Division of European Affairs, Department of State, 1930–44 (in charge of Canadian desk). Member of Permanent Joint Board on Defence, 1940–46. Assistant Under-Secretary of State, 1949–53. Ambassador to Finland, 1955–59 and to the Philippines, 1960–61.

CORDELL HULL (1871–1955), Secretary of State, 1933–44. Awarded Nobel Peace Prize, 1944. Author of *Memoirs*.

ADMIRAL WILLIAM D. LEAHY (1875–1959), Chief of Naval Operations, 1937–39. Ambassador to Vichy, 1940–42. Chief of Staff to Presidents Roosevelt and Truman, 1942–49. Author of *I Was There*.

H. FREEMAN MATTHEWS (1899–   ), Career diplomat, 1924–62. Served in France, 1939–41 and 1946. *Chargé d'affaires*, Vichy, July–December 1940. Political advisor to Eisenhower, 1942. Ambassador to Sweden, Netherlands and Austria.

JAY PIERREPONT MOFFAT (1896–1943), Career diplomat, 1917–1943. Chief of Division of European Affairs, Department of State, 1937–40. Minister to Canada, June, 1940, until his untimely death in January, 1943.

MAURICE PASQUET (1902–   ), Career consular officer, 1926–55. Consul in St. Pierre, 1940–43, and subsequently in Rabat, Sydney, Tananarive and Valencia. Ardently pro-Free French.

SAMUEL REBER (1903–   ), Career diplomat, 1925–53. Assistant in charge of the French desk, Department of State, 1939–42. Deputy High Commisioner for Germany, 1952–53.

FRANKLIN DELANO ROOSEVELT (1882–1945), President, 1933–45.

SUMNER WELLES (1892–1961), Career diplomat, 1915–43. Under Secretary of State, 1937–43.

IRA WOLFERT (1908–1964), Journalist with North American Newspaper Alliance, 1929–45. Accompanied expedition to St. Pierre and Miquelon, 1941. Ardently pro-Free French. Received Pulitzer Award, 1943. Staff writer for *Reader's Digest*, 1956–64.

BRITISH (and NEWFOUNDLAND)

ARCHIBALD BARTLETT (1887–1948), Born in St. Pierre. Joined Western Union Telegraph Company in St. Pierre, 1908. Superintendent, 1941–48. British Vice-Consul, St. Pierre, 1937–41, 1943–48. Appointed an OBE in New Year's Honours List, 1942, for service to the Resistance.

WINSTON S. CHURCHILL (1874–1965), Prime Minister, 1940–45, 1951–55.

ANTHONY EDEN (1897–   ), Foreign Secretary, 1935–38, 1940–45, 1951–55. Prime Minister, 1955–57.

L. EDWARD EMERSON (1890–1949), Newfoundland's Commissioner for Justice, 1937–44, and for Defence, 1940–44. Knighted, 1944. Chief Justice, Supreme Court of Newfoundland, 1944–49.

RAYMOND GUSHUE (1900–   ), Chairman, Newfoundland Fisheries Board, 1936–49. Acted as virtually a one-man Department of External Affairs for Newfoundland during the war. Visited St. Pierre about a dozen times on special missions, 1940–44. President of Memorial University of Newfoundland 1952–65. Member of Royal Commission on Canada's Economic Prospects, 1955–57.

F. A. JAMES LAWS (1910–   ), Newfoundland businessman. Engaged in fishing trade along South Coast and in St. John's since emigrating from England in 1934. General Manager, Newfoundland Associated Fish Exporters Ltd. On mission to St. Pierre, September 13–19, 1940.

J. HUBERT PENSON (1893–   ), Commissioner of Finance, Newfoundland, 1937–41. Sent on mission to St. Pierre, July 17–20, 1940. British Embassy, Washington, 1942–53.

CANADIAN

JEAN O. CALLÈDE (1885–   ), President and founder of the Manitoba Free French Committee, 1940, and National President of Free French Federation of Canada, 1945. Emigrated from France to Canada, 1903 (with assistance from the father of Monseigneur Poisson). Served in French army, 1907–8, 1914–19. Naturalized Canadian citizen.

SQUADRON LEADER H. M. CARSCALLEN (1908–   ), Career air force officer, 1933–63. Anti-submarine patrols, East Coast, 1939–42. Commanded detachment of No. 10 Squadron, Gander, June to October, 1940. Bomber Command, UK, 1942–44. Chief of Staff, 4th Allied Tactical Air Force, Germany, 1956–60. Air Vice Marshal and AOC, Air Transport Command, 1960–63.

LIEUT.-COL. HERBERT COOK (1893–1961), Commanding Officer of Lake Superior Regiment, 1938–43. Military Commander for proposed Operation "Q", 1941. Joined a Fort William, Ontario, contracting firm in 1912, later becoming its President.

MAJOR-GENERAL H. D. G. CRERAR (1888–1965), Career army officer, 1910–46. Chief of the General Staff, 1940–41. Promoted General, 1944. General Officer Commanding-in-Chief, First Canadian Army in Northwest Europe, 1944–45.

CHRISTOPHER EBERTS (1913–   ), Career diplomat since 1940. Vice-Consul, St. Pierre, with local rank of Acting Consul, September 1941 to October 1942. Ardently pro-Free French. High Commisioner to Pakistan, 1960–62. Chief of Protocol since 1964.

MAJOR-GENERAL W. H. P. ELKINS (1883–1964), Career army officer, 1905–44. General Officer Commanding-in-Chief, Atlantic Command, Halifax, 1940–43.

HENRI GAUTHIER (1898–   ), Civil servant, Ottawa, 1914–60. Emigrated to Canada from France, 1909. Naturalized 1915. Volunteer in French Army, 1915–18. Member of Free French Committee, Ottawa, 1940–45. Visited St. Pierre, March, 1942, to investigate alleged stamp racket. Currently Director of Sales, Royal Philatelic Society of Canada.

COLONEL LESLIE C. GOODEVE (1889–1955), Career army officer, 1914–47. Colonel (later Brigadier), General Staff, Atlantic Command and Secretary of Joint Services Committee, Halifax, 1940–45.

EMILE-CHARLES HAMEL (1914–1963), Editor of Montreal Le Jour, 1938–46. Head of Polish Section, CBC International Service, 1955–63.

JEAN-CHARLES HARVEY (1891–   ), Editor and Director of Montreal Le Jour, 1937–46. Assistant publisher of Le Petit Journal (Montreal) since 1953.

FLYING OFFICER JOHN HOWELL (1903–1951), Served in fishing boats and home trade vessels off East Coast, 1919–40. Never caught by RCMP. RCAF Marine Section, Dartmouth, 1940–46, retiring as Squadron Leader. Operated fishing vessel out of Yarmouth, Nova Scotia, 1946–51.

COMMODORE GEORGE C. JONES (1895–1945), Carrer naval officer, 1911–45. Commanding Officer Atlantic Coast (Halifax), 1941–42. Vice-Admiral and Chief of the Naval Staff, 1944–45.

HUGH L. KEENLEYSIDE (1898–   ), Career diplomat, 1928–47. Assistant Under-Secretary of State for External Affairs (responsible for American and Far Eastern relations), 1941–44. Secretary, Permanent Joint

Board on Defence, Canada-United States, 1940–45. Director-General, UN Technical Assistance Administration, 1950–58. Chairman, British Columbia Power Commission since 1959.

WILLIAM LYON MACKENZIE KING (1874–1950), Prime Minister and (except for the final two years) Secretary of State for External Affairs, 1921–30, 1935–48.

OSCAR LARIVIÈRE (1900–   ), RCMP Officer. Inspector, "C" Division, Montreal, 1940–42. Sent on mission to St. Pierre, May 26–June 11, 1941. Retired as Assistant Commissioner, 1957. Head of security for Banque Canadienne Nationale, Montreal.

ANGUS L. MACDONALD (1890–1954), Minister of National Defence for Naval Service, 1940–45. Premier of Nova Scotia, 1933–40, 1945–54.

MAJOR D. MILLER MARSHALL (1893–   ), Retired automobile dealer, Vancouver. Served overseas, 1916–19. Wounded twice. MC and Bar. Company Commander, Lake Superior Regiment, 1940–46. Commanded "Q" Force, 1941–42.

REAR-ADMIRAL LEONARD W. MURRAY (1896–   ), Career naval officer, 1911–1946. Flag Officer, Newfoundland, 1941–42. C-in-C, Canadian North West Atlantic, 1943–45. Barrister-at-Law in England since 1949.

VICE-ADMIRAL PERCY W. NELLES (1892–1951), Career naval officer, 1908–45. Chief of Naval Staff, 1933–44. Admiral, 1945.

LESTER B. PEARSON (1897–   ), Career diplomat, 1928–48. Assistant Under-Secretary of State for External Affairs (responsible for British Commonwealth and European relations), 1941–42. Secretary of State for External Affairs, 1948–57. Prime Minister since 1963.

C. G. POWER (1888–   ), Member of Parliament for Quebec South, 1917–55 and Senator since 1955. Minister of National Defence for Air, 1940–44.

JAMES L. RALSTON (1881–1948), Minister of National Defence, 1926–30, 1940–44.

NORMAN A. ROBERTSON (1904–   ), Career diplomat since 1929. Under-Secretary of State for External Affairs, 1941–46, 1959–64. High Commissioner to London, 1946–49, 1952–57. Secretary of the Cabinet, 1949–52. Ambassador to Washington, 1957–59.

COMMANDER J. W. R. ROY (1901–1940), Career naval officer, 1919–40. Senior Naval Officer, Gaspé, July-August 1940. Sent on mission to St. Pierre, July 17–20, 1940. Commanded destroyer HMCS *Margaree* and went down with her when sunk in collision with merchantman in North Atlantic on her maiden voyage, October, 1940.

THOMAS A. STONE (1900–1965), Career diplomat, 1927–35, 1939–59. First Secretary, Department of External Affairs, Ottawa, 1939–44. responsible *inter alia* for relations with France and for economic warfare. Ardently pro-Free French. Ambassador to the Netherlands, 1952–58. Special Assistant to the President, International Nickel Company of Canada, New York City, 1959–65.

BRIGADIER GEORGES P. VANIER (1888–   ), Minister to France, 1939–42, and Ambassador, 1943–52. Member of Permanent Joint Board on Defence, Canada-United States, 1940–42. Officer Commanding Military District No. 5, Quebec City, 1941–43. Governor-General since 1959.

HUME WRONG (1894–1954), Career diplomat, 1927–54. Minister-Counsellor, 1941–42 and Ambassador, 1946–53 in Washington.

FREE FRENCH

CAPTAIN GEORGES THIERRY D'ARGENLIEU (1889–   ), Naval officer, 1902–20, 1939–47. Entered Carmelite Order, 1920, as "Père Louis de la Trinité." Rallied to Free France, 1940, and wounded at Dakar. Sent on mission to Canada, March, 1941. Promoted Rear Admiral in December 1941 despite Muselier's protests. Admiral High Commissioner for French Indo-China, 1945–47. Retired to a monastery, 1947.

CAPTAIN PHILIPPE AUBOYNEAU (1899–1961), Career naval officer, 1917–60. Commanding Officer of destroyer *Triomphant*, 1940–42. Succeeded Muselier as C-in-C of FNFL, 1942–43. C-in-C Mediterranean Fleet and NATO Commander, Western Mediterranean, 1955–60.

MARCEL ESTIENNE BENDA (1895–   ), Former French intelligence officer. Escaped from occupied France and arrived in Canada, July, 1941. Journalist with *Le Jour* and sent to St. Pierre. In charge of surcharging St. Pierre and Miquelon stamps. Subsequently served a two-year prison term in Montreal. Ordered deported and left for France, 1947.

COMMANDER C. F. BIROT (190?–42), Commanded *Mimosa*, and Free French corvettes in North Atlantic, 1941–42. Participated in liberation of St. Pierre and Miquelon. Went down with his ship, June 9, 1942.

COMMANDER GEORGES BLAISON (1906–42), Career submarine officer, 1929–42. Rallied to Free France, August, 1940. Commanded *Surcouf*, the largest submarine in the world. Participated in liberation of St. Pierre and Miquelon. Rammed by American freighter near Panama Canal and lost with all hands, February 18, 1942.

GENERAL CHARLES DE GAULLE (1890–   ), Career army officer and protégé of Pétain, 1913–40. Under-Secretary of State for War, June, 1940. Leader of the Free French, June, 1940. Sentenced to death *in absentia* for treason, July, 1940. President of French National Committee, 1941–43, French Committee of National Liberation, 1943–44, and Provisional Government of France, 1944–46. President of the Republic of France since 1958. Author of *War Memoirs* and several books on military affairs.

EMILE-JEAN GUILLOT (1903–   ), Chief of the Judicial Service, St. Pierre, 1938–40, and Acting Administrator in the absence of de Bournat. Also served as chief censor and code officer. Transferred to

Martinique, December, 1940, for political reasons. Defected in
Halifax and joined Free France. Awarded *Médaille de la Résistance
française*. Served in various judicial posts in Indo-China, 1933–37,
and Tahiti, French Somaliland, Madagascar and Mali, 1941–64.
Counsel to Court of Cassation, Paris, since 1964.

JEAN LeBRET (1889–1961), Journalist, adventurer, and humanist. Emi-
grated to Canada from France, 1925. Foreign news editor of Montreal
Le Jour, 1937–41. Rallied to Free France, June 1940. Gunnery officer
in FNFL 1941–42. Accompanied expedition to St. Pierre. Chief of
Press and Information Service, St. Pierre and Miquelon, 1941–42.
Married in St. Pierre to Paulette L'Espérance, a Free French volun-
teer from Montreal. Administrator of Radio Brazzaville, 1943–47.
Editorial Division, United Nations, 1947–52. Manager of St. Siméon
Uranium Corp., St. Siméon, P.Q., 1952–56. His full name was
Count Jean Marcel Antoine LeBret de Vankalque.

LIEUT.-CDR. J. PÉPIN LEHALLEUR (1911–   ), Career naval officer,
1933–65. Commanded corvette *Alysse*, 1941–42. Participated in the
liberation of St. Pierre and Miquelon. Torpedoed in North Atlantic,
February 8, 1942, and mined in English Channel, February 24, 1945.
Retired as Rear-Admiral, 1965. Deputy counsellor, Court of State
Security, Paris.

LIEUT.-CDR. L. V. LEVASSEUR (191?–47), As Commander of the corvette
Aconit, 1941–42, participated in liberation of St. Pierre and Miquelon
and sank U432 and U444, April, 1943. Killed in a shell-firing
accident, 1947.

VICE-ADMIRAL EMILE HENRI MUSELIER (1882–1965), Career naval
officer, 1899–1946. His energy, courage and personality brought him
into conflict with Darlan and later de Gaulle. Navy commander,
Marseilles, at outbreak of war, 1939. Promoted Vice-Admiral and
compulsorily retired, October, 1939. Rallied to Free France, June,
1940, the only admiral to do so. Stripped of his rank and sentenced
to death *in absentia* for desertion, October, 1940. Proposed Cross of
Lorraine as Free French emblem. C-in-C, Free French Naval Forces,
1940–42. Member of French National Committee and National
Commissioner for the Navy and Merchant Navy, 1941–42. Visited
Ottawa, December 15–17, 1941. Liberated and defended St. Pierre,
December 24, 1941 to February 13, 1942. Broke with de Gaulle,
March, 1942. Rallied to General Giraud and appointed Civil and
Military Commander of Algiers, May–June, 1943. Head of Naval
Delegation to Military Mission on German Affairs, Ministry of
Defence, Paris, 1944–45. As President of the *Union pour la Défense
de la République*, he sought election to the National Assembly
unsuccessfully, November, 1946. Honorary President of the Franco-
British Group, London. Active in extreme leftwing veterans' organi-
zations. Outspoken opponent of colonial war in Indo-China. Grand
Officer of the *Légion d'honneur*, 1946. Knight Commander of the

Order of the Bath. Decorated by Imperial Russia and honoured at his funeral by two Communist former ministers. Author of *Marine et Résistance* and *De Gaulle contre la Gaullisme*.

LIEUT.-COL. PHILIPPE HENRI PIERRENÉ (1892–1952), Career army officer, 1914–52. Tank expert in Department of Munitions and Supply, Ottawa, 1940–41. Free French Representative in Ottawa, 1941–42. Promoted a General and appointed Chief Inspector of Armaments, 1947.

RENÉ PLEVEN (1901–   ), Deputy Head of French Air Mission, Washington, 1939–40. Rallied to de Gaulle, 1940. Member of French National Committee and Commissioner for the Colonies, Finance and Foreign Affairs, 1941–43. Emissary in Washington, June–October, 1941. Prime Minister, 1950–51, 1951–52. Author of Pleven Plan for a European Defence Community.

COMMANDANT MAURICE QUÉDRUE (1883–1957), Ran away to sea at age 15. Captain in French merchant marine until 1919. Came to Canada, 1921. Founded the *Compagnie aérienne franco-canadienne*, 1925. President of the *Chambre de commerce française*, Montreal. Rallied to de Gaulle, 1940. Head of Free French Military and Naval Office and Information Service, Montreal, 1941–43. Active in planning liberation of St. Pierre and Miquelon. Served as Commander with French navy in England, 1943–46. Officer of the *Légion d'honneur*, 1946.

LIEUTENANT ALAIN SAVARY (1918–   ), Officer in FNFL. Aide-de-Camp to Thierry d'Argenlieu and Muselier on missions to Canada, 1941. Administrator of St. Pierre and Miquelon, 1941–43. Resigned to fight with French Marines in Italy, 1943–44. Councillor of the French Union, 1948–51. Socialist Deputy representing St. Pierre and Miquelon in National Assembly, 1951–58. Defeated candidate, 1947. Secretary of State for Moroccan and Tunisian Affairs, 1956. Deputy Secretary-General and later member of the National Bureau of the opposition *Parti Socialist Unifié*. Author of *Nationalisme algérien et grandeur française* (1960).

SUB-LIEUTENANT PAUL VIAUD (1914–1953), Naval cypher officer, 1940–44, and major in Marines, 1944–45. Served in *Mimosa*, 1941. Visited Montreal in August, 1941, to plan liberation of St. Pierre and Miquelon. Stationed in St. Pierre, 1941–43. Chinese language specialist. Served in French army in China, 1936–38, and in French Consulate in Canton, 1945–51.

COMMANDER LOUIS HÉRON DE VILLEFOSSE (1900–   ), Career naval officer, 1918–49. Served on *Ville d'Ys* off St. Pierre and Miquelon, 1924–25. Rallied to Free France and appointed Deputy Chief of Staff to Muselier, May, 1941. Accompanied him to Ottawa and to St. Pierre, December, 1941. Military commander after departure of Muselier. Faithful disciple of Muselier. Broke with de Gaulle, April, 1942. Joined Giraud and Muselier in Algiers, May, 1943. Fellow traveller, 1949–56. Broke with Communists over Hungary. Author of numerous books including *Souvenirs d'un Marin de la France Libre* (1951) and *Abraham Lincoln* (1956).

VICHY FRENCH

EDGAR AUBERT DE LA RÜE (1901–   ), Swiss geological engineer who had led scientific expeditions to many parts of the world including St. Pierre and Miquelon (1933, 1941, 1948) and Quebec, 1943–45. Author of 15 books and 250 articles, including many on St. Pierre and Miquelon. Under house arrest in Langlade, 1942–43, before being deported to Canada. Pro-Vichy.

COUNT GILBERT DE BOURNAT (1896–   ), An able Colonial official who had served in the Chad, the Congo, Morocco, and Gabon before going to St. Pierre and Miquelon as Administrator, 1937–41. Promoted Officer of the *Légion d'honneur* and awarded personal *Francisque* medal by Pétain, December 29, 1941. Repatriated to Vichy, April, 1942. Delegate of the Ministry of Colonies in Occupied France, 1942–44. Unsuccessful candidate for election as St. Pierre and Miquelon's deputy in National Assembly, 1945. Served in Madagascar for some years after the war as Government Representative and General Manager of a large-scale building project. Served in artillery and air force during World War I. Wounded and decorated with the *Croix de Guerre* with 5 citations and the *Médaille Militaire* for his exploits at Verdun and elsewhere. His Alsatian wife, Suzanne, was French by citizenship but German in origin and, so it was widely believed, in her sympathies too.

ADMIRAL JEAN FRANÇOIS DARLAN (1881–1942), Commander-in-Chief of French Naval Forces, 1939–42. Minister of the Navy and Marine, 1940. Vice-Premier, Minister of National Defence, Foreign Affairs and Information Services, 1941–42. Named by Pétain as his successor. High Commissioner for French North Africa following Allied landings, 1942. Assassinated, December, 1942.

RENÉ DELORT (   ), Chief of Radiotelegraphic Services, St. Pierre, 1940–41. Leading *Vichyard*. Refused to serve under Muselier and arrested, December, 1941. Residing in United States.

GASTON HENRY-HAYE (1889–   ), Deputy and Senator, 1928–40. Advocate of rapprochement with Germany and organizer of *Comité Franco-Allemand*, 1935. Ambassador to Washington, 1940–42. Mayor of Versailles, 1935–44. Condemned to death for collaboration, 1947, but escaped to Angola where he operates an agricultural business.

JEAN CHARLES LIOREL (   ), *Vichyard* Chief of Public Works in St. Pierre and Miquelon until dismissed, January, 1942. Later served in Free French offices in Washington and Montreal. Proprietor of hotel-restaurant, *Auberge de la Chaumière*, Ste. Adèle, Quebec.

EMILE-RAOUL MACÉ (1911–   ), Judge in St. Pierre, 1940–41. Replaced Guillot as Chief of the Judicial Service in St. Pierre and Miquelon, April, 1941. Arrested by Muselier, December, 1941. Since 1942 has served in various judicial offices in Senegal, French Sudan, Dahomey, Ivory Coast and French Somaliland.

MARSHAL HENRI PHILIPPE PÉTAIN (1856–1951), Marshal of France, 1918. Head of State, 1940–44. Sentenced to death for treason, 1945 (commuted to life imprisonment).

MONSEIGNEUR ADOLPHE POISSON (1887–   ), Ordained Holy Ghost Father, 1914. *Chevalier de la Légion d'honneur* for service in First World War. Director of Collège St. Christophe, St. Pierre, 1924–33. Apostolic Prefect in St. Pierre, 1933–45. Passionately pro-Vichy. Parish priest, St. Scolastique, Quebec, since 1945.

PIERRE RAYMOND (1888–   ), Chief of Police in St. Pierre and Miquelon. Courageous and tactful in difficult circumstances. (Two of his gendarmes, including Sgt.-Maj. Roger Potier, were Free French sympathizers.) Rallied to Free France after Liberation and given accelerated promotion to rank of sub-lieutenant.

RENÉ RISTELHUEBER (1881–1960), Career diplomat, 1905–42. Served in China, Lebanon, Greece, Switzerland, Turkey, Tunisia, Lithuania, Norway, and Bulgaria before coming to Canada as Minister, May, 1940, to November, 1942. Recalled to Vichy, but stayed in Canada as Professor of Diplomatic History, University of Montreal, 1943–48. Author of numerous books, mainly on diplomatic history.

ADMIRAL GEORGES ROBERT (1875–   ), Career naval officer, 1893–1937. Recalled to active service, 1939, and appointed C-in-C French Naval Forces in the Western Atlantic and High Commissioner in the French West Indies, 1939–43. Supreme Commander of French Islands in the Western Hemisphere, 1940–43. Repatriated to France, 1943. Sentenced to 10 years' hard labour for withholding aid from the Allies, 1947. Author of *La France aux Antilles, de 1939 à 1943*.

ST. PIERRAIS

FERNAND APESTÉGUY (1918–   ), Labourer and young *résistant*. Arrested for "incidents" on May 27 and July 14, 1941.

JEAN BOUDREAU (1923–42), Young *résistant*. Lost with *Alysse*, February, 1942, at age 18.

EMMANUEL CAZIER-RUAULT (1896–   ), Public Works employee. Had left-wing tendencies. Supported Giraud rather than de Gaulle, 1943–44. Served overseas in both wars. Proprietor of a cinema theatre and dance-hall since 1947.

HENRI CLAIREAUX (1911–   ), Educated in Paris and at Laval University. Teacher in Roman Catholic Collège St. Christophe, St. Pierre, 1936–45. *Conseiller d'administration*, 1939–41; resigned after liberation. A leading *Vichyard*. Arrested for his opposition to conscription,

January, 1944. President of *Conseil Général*, 1947–64, and Senator since 1947. Senator of the French Community, 1959–60. Member of *Mouvement Républicain Populaire* (MRP). The leading *notable* of St. Pierre.

ANDRÉ CLÉMENT (1916–1942), Office boy in Treasury Department, 1937–42. Resistance leader, 1940–41. Enlisted in FNFL and went down with *Mimosa*, June, 1942. Awarded *Médaille de la Résistance française avec Rosette*, 1946.

LÉONCE DUPONT (1879–1946), Merchant. *Conseiller d'administration*, 1914–45 (except for 1920–21), and official local leader, 1934–40. President of the semi-governmental Chamber of Commerce, 1914–46 (apart from two brief periods). *Chevalier de la Légion d'honneur*. Free French.

ALBERT FLAHAUT (1894–1961), Captain in French merchant marine. Born in France but married to a St. Pierrais. Active in Resistance.

EDOUARD FLOQUET (1895–1963), A leading Vichyard. Member of Conseil Général. Canadian Press correspondent in St. Pierre, 1949–63.

EMILE GLOANEC (1860–1946), Merchant, Mayor of St. Pierre from 1924 until 1936 (when the commune was abolished). *Conseiller d'administration*, 1910–13, 1920–21, 1923–24, 1936–46. *Chevalier de la Légion d'honneur*. Ardent Free French partisan.

AUGUST GOUPILLIÈRE (1895–   ), Postman. "Dismissed" by Vichy, October, 1942. Awarded *Chevalier de la Légion d'honneur*, 1946, for his devoted service to the administration, in the Resistance, and as Treasurer of the *Association des Anciens Combattants*. President of the *Anciens Combattants* since 1956.

JOSEPH GROSVALET (1896–   ), Tinsmith. On Executive of the *Association des Anciens Combattants*. Active in Resistance. Fined 50 francs for calling Christian Morazé *"un bochephile et un cou"*, April, 1941. Served in Free French forces in St. Pierre and in London.

HENRY HUMBERT (1893–1948), Insurance agent, 1939–41. Prisoner of war in Germany, 1915–18. Secretary of the *Association des Anciens Combattants*, 1921–42. Leader of the Resistance, 1940–41. Taught English at public school and served as court interpreter until dismissed for political reasons, September, 1941. Reinstated, January, 1942. Visited Washington, February, 1942, to plead with State Department. Cypher officer, 1942–44. Awarded *Médaille de la Résistance française avec Rosette* and *Chevalier de la Légion d'honneur*, 1946.

FRANÇOIS LEROUX (1908–   ), Merchant. Leading *Vichyard*. Served in French Army in Tunisia, 1944–45. President of Tourist Bureau and of the *Association des Commerçants*. Past President of the Lions Club.

HENRI MORAZÉ (1899–   ), Wealthy merchant and dynamic personality. Arrested for his pro-Vichy sympathies, December, 1941.

Vice-President of the *Conseil Général* since 1947. His younger brother, Christian (1911–   ) was also a leading *Vichyard* and *matelot de port auxiliaire* until dismissed by Free French, January, 1942.

FRANK PATUREL (1899–   ), Businessman. Member of *Conseil d'administration*, 1938–40. Dismissed for opposing the Administrator, June, 1940. Joined Free French in Montreal in May, 1941. Active in plotting liberation of St. Pierre and Miquelon. Accompanied Muselier to St. Pierre as a Sub-Lieutenant, FNFL. (It was intended that he should become Administrator, but the local Free French objected.) Free French Delegate in Halifax, 1942–44. Resident of Halifax, 1942–48 and since 1952. A brother, Henri Paturel, who succeeded him as *conseiller*, was active in the Resistance.

LOUIS PLANTEGENEST (1897–1949), Chief Clerk of the court, 1938–49. Justice of the peace, 1942–49. Veteran and Resistance leader. Supplied identity cards to young men escaping to Newfoundland to join Free French. Member of mission to Washington, January–February, 1942. Free French delegate, 1945–46.

PIERRE M. RENOU (1915–   ), Resistance leader and Public Works foreman. Transferred and later dismissed for his activities, 1940. Went overseas with first group of volunteers, December 27, 1941. Flying Officer in Royal Air Force, 1942–45. Undertook two secret missions to Occupied France, 1943–44. Awarded the DSM, DFC, the Belgian *Croix de Guerre* and the French *Croix de Guerre* (with four citations) and *Médaille Militaire*, the latter for service both in the war and in the Resistance. Customs officer, St. Pierre since 1946. Delegate for St. Pierre and Miquelon of the *Association Nationale pour le soutien de l'Action du Général de Gaulle* (Paris) since September, 1958. Brother of William Renou who served in the Free French navy, and of Joseph Renou who served overseas as a military policeman in the marines (under Savary) and won the *Médaille de la Résistance française* and the *Médaille Militaire*. Their father, Joseph Renou, piloted Admiral Muselier's ship into harbour on the morning of December 24, 1941.

ARMAND SLANEY (1903–1942), Office boy in the American consulate, 1940–42. Resistance leader. Enlisted in FNFL and went down with *Mimosa*, June, 1942. Awarded *Médaille de la Résistance française avec Rosette*, 1946.

JOSEPH VIGNEAU (1913–1942), Brickyard worker. Dismissed from government service for resistance activities, 1940. Enlisted in FNFL and went down with corvette *Alysse*, February, 1942.

SELECT BIBLIOGRAPHY

ST. PIERRE AND MIQUELON

Annuaire des îles Saint-Pierre et Miquelon. St. Pierre: Imprimerie du Gouvernement.

ARNOLD, FREDERIC K. "Islands Adrift: St. Pierre and Miquelon," *National Geographic Magazine,* LXXX (1941), 743–68.

AUBERT DE LA RÜE, EDGAR. *Saint-Pierre et Miquelon.* Montreal: Editions de l'Arbre, 1944.

—— "Le territoire de Saint-Pierre et Miquelon (étude de géographie physique et humain)," *Journal de la Société des Américanistes,* XXIX (N.S.) (1937), 239–372.

—— "Aspects du territoire de Saint-Pierre et Miquelon," *Bulletin des Sociétés de Géographie de Québec et de Montréal,* I (N.S.) (1942), 49–69.

BOURDE DE LA ROGERIE, HENRI. "Saint-Pierre et Miquelon des origines à 1778," *Le Pays de Granville,* 2ᵉ série (1937), pp. 57–84, 133–55, 197–221.

CURTON, EMILE DE. *Les îles Saint-Pierre et Miquelon.* Algiers: Imprimerie Nord-Africaine, 1944.

GAUVIN, DANIEL (comp.) *Almanach du centenaire, 1816–1916.* Paris: Charles Renaudie, [1916].

GREENAWAY, C. R. "Rum Heaven," *Canadian Geographical Journal,* XI (1935), 219–27.

HANNA, WILLIAM. "La prise de Saint-Pierre-et-Miquelon par les forces de la France Libre: Noël 1941," *Revue de l'histoire de l'Amérique française,* XVI (1962), 369–87.

HITSMAN, J. MACKAY. "Capture of Saint-Pierre-et-Miquelon, 1793," *Canadian Army Journal,* XIII (1959), 77–81.

Journal officiel du Territoire des îles Saint-Pierre and Miquelon. St. Pierre: Imprimerie du Gouvernement, annually.

La Liberté de Saint-Pierre et Miquelon: Hebdomadaire indépendant. St. Pierre: Imprimerie du Gouvernement, 1942–45.

LAUVRIÈRE, EMILE. "A Saint-Pierre et Miquelon," in *La tragédie d'un peuple. Histoire du peuple acadien de ses origines à nos jours.* Rev. Ed. 2 vols. Paris: Plon, 1924, II, 206–26.

Le Foyer paroissial. Bulletin mensuel. Iles Saint-Pierre et Miquelon. St. Pierre: Imprimerie du "Foyer paroissial," 1924–52.

LEITCH, ADELAIDE. "The Poker-Faced Islands of France," *Canadian Geographical Journal,* XXXXI (1950), 104–19.

"Le territoire des îles Saint-Pierre et Miquelon," *Notes et études documentaires.* Paris: La Documentation française, no. 1.308, 6 avril 1950.

LOUIS-LEGASSE, FERDINAND. *Evolution économique des îles Saint-Pierre et Miquelon.* Paris: Librairie du Recueil Sirey, 1935.

MARTINEAU, ALFRED. "L'archipel de Saint-Pierre et Miquelon," in Gabriel Hanotaux and Alfred Martineau. *Histoire des colonies françaises.* 6 vols. Paris: Plon, 1929–33, I, 243–59.

——— "Esquisse d'une histoire de Saint-Pierre et Miquelon," *Revue de l'histoire des colonies françaises,* XXI (1928), 677–700.

PICK, ALFRED J. "St. Pierre and Miquelon under the Fighting French." Unpublished paper presented to the Newfoundland Branch of the Royal Institute of International Affairs, St. John's, February 25, 1943.

PROWSE, D. W. "St. Pierre and Miquelon, The French Colony," in *A History of Newfoundland.* 2 vols. London: Macmillan, 1895, pp. 564–86.

RANNIE, WILLIAM F. *Saint Pierre and Miquelon.* Beamsville: Rannie Publications, 1963.

RAWLINGS, CHARLES. "Dilemma on St. Pierre," *Maclean's,* January 1, 1941, pp. 10–11, 25–6.

REVERT, EUGÈNE. *La France d'Amérique: Martinique, Guadeloupe, Guyane, Saint-Pierre et Miquelon.* 2e éd. Paris: Editions maritimes et coloniales, 1955.

RIBAULT, JEAN-YVES. *Les îles Saint-Pierre et Miquelon (des origines à 1814).* St. Pierre: Imprimerie du Gouvernement, [1963].

ROBEQUAIN, CHARLES. *Madagascar et les bases dispersée de l'Union française.* Paris: Presses universitaires de France, 1958.

ROUSSIER, PAUL. "Les îles Saint-Pierre et Miquelon," in *Martinique, Guadeloupe, Guyane, St. Pierre-Miquelon.* Paris: Société d'éditions géographiques, maritimes et coloniales, 1931, 1pp. 1–35.

ROY, CARMEN. *Saint-Pierre et Miquelon: une mission folklorique aux îles.* Ottawa: Queen's Printer, 1962.

SASCO, EMILE. "Un peu de notre histoire," *Le Foyer paroissial* (St. Pierre), 1924–42.

Saint-Pierre et Miquelon. Paris: Agence de la France d'Outre-Mer, 1950.

Tracts clandestins qui circulaient à St.-Pierre et Miquelon, avant l'occupation des îles par les forces navales françaises libres du général de Gaulle, le jour de Noël 1941. Ottawa: Service de l'information, France Libre, [1942]. Brochures No. 1 and 2.

MEMOIRS AND BIOGRAPHIES

CHURCHILL, SIR WINSTON S. *The Second World War.* 6 vols. Boston: Houghton Mifflin, 1948–1953.

GAULLE, CHARLES DE. *War Memoirs.* Vol. I. *The Call to Honour, 1940–1942.* 2 parts. London: Collins, 1955.

HARVARD UNIVERSITY LIBRARY. Jay Pierrepont Moffat Papers.

HOOKER, NANCY H. (ed.). *The Moffat Papers: Selections from the Diplomatic Journals of Jay Pierrepont Moffat, 1919–1943.* Cambridge: Harvard University Press, 1956.

HULL, CORDELL. *The Memoirs of Cordell Hull.* 2 vols. New York: Macmillan, 1948.

LEAHY, WILLIAM D. *I Was There: The Personal Story of the Chief of Staff to Presidents Roosevelt and Truman.* London: Gollancz, 1950.

MUSELIER, EMILE. *De Gaulle contre le Gaullisme.* Paris: Editions du Chêne, 1946.

——— *Marine et Resistance.* Paris: Flammarion, 1945.

PICKERSGILL, J. W. *The Mackenzie King Record.* I: *1939–1944.* Toronto: University of Toronto Press, 1960.

RISTELHUEBER, RENÉ. "Le coup de main de la France Libre sur Saint-Pierre-et-Miquelon," *Ecrits de Paris,* July–August, 1954, pp. 64–70.

ROBERT, GEORGES. *La France aux Antilles de 1939 à 1943.* Paris: Plon, 1950.

SHERWOOD, ROBERT E. *Roosevelt and Hopkins: An Intimate History.* New York: Harper, 1948.

VILLEFOSSE, LOUIS DE. *Souvenirs d'un marin de la France Libre.* Paris: Les Editeurs français réunis, 1951.

——— "Les petites îles de la liberté," *Les Temps modernes,* V (1949), 868–95.

SECOND WORLD WAR

"Concern of the United States over the control of the wireless radio station at St. Pierre and the seizure of St. Pierre and Miquelon by the Free French forces," *Foreign Relations of the United States, 1941.* Vol. II. *Europe.* Washington: Government Printing Office, 1959.

"Concern of the United States over the seizure of St. Pierre-Miquelon Islands by Free French Forces," *Foreign Relations of the United States, 1942.* Vol. II. *Europe.* Washington: Government Printing Office, 1962.

CONN, STETSON, and BYRON FAIRCHILD. *The Framework of Hemispheric Defense.* Washington: Government Printing Office, 1960.

DZIUBAN, STANLEY W. *Military Relations between the United States and Canada, 1939–1945.* Washington: Government Printing Office, 1959.

HYTIER, ADRIENNE DORIS. *Two Years of French Foreign Policy: Vichy 1940–1942.* Paris: Librairie Minard, 1958.

LANGER, WILLIAM L. *Our Vichy Gamble.* New York: Knopf, 1947.

——— and S. Everett Gleason. *The Undeclared War, 1940–41.* New York: Harper, 1953.

LOGAN, JOHN A. *No Transfer: An American Security Principle.* New Haven: Yale University Press, 1961.

McKAY, DONALD C. *The United States and France.* Cambridge: Harvard University Press, 1951.

MARTIN DU GARD, MAURICE. "Un corsaire: Muselier prend Saint-Pierre-et-Miquelon," in his *La Carte Impériale.* Paris: Bone, 1949, pp. 223–37.

MORTON, SIR DESMOND. "The Free French Movement, 1940–42," in Arnold and Veronica M. Toynbee, eds. *Hitler's Europe: Survey of International Affairs, 1939–1946.* London: Oxford University Press, 1954, pp. 434–74.

STANLEY, GEORGE F. G. *In the Face of Danger: The History of the Lake Superior Regiment.* Port Arthur: The Lake Superior Scottish Regiment, 1960.

WHITE, DOROTHY SHIPLEY. *Seeds of Discord: De Gaulle, Free France and the Allies.* Syracuse: Syracuse University Press, 1964.

WOODWARD, SIR LLEWELLYN. *British Foreign Policy in the Second World War.* London: H. M. Stationery Office, 1962.

NOTES

It is not possible to refer here to all the sources consulted or quoted. This is regrettable, particularly as many of the omissions are important, but in the circumstances it is unavoidable. The following abbreviations are used:

FRUS; Foreign Relations of the United States: Diplomatic Papers (Washington, various dates).
De Gaulle, I; Charles de Gaulle, *War Memoirs*, Vol. I, *The Call to Honour, 1940–1942* (London, 1955).
De Gaulle, Doc, I; Charles de Gaulle, *War Memoirs*, Vol. I, *The Call to Honour, 1940–1942: Documents* (London, 1955).
De Villefosse; Louis de Villefosse, *Souvenirs d'un marin de la France Libre* (Paris, 1951).
Hull; Cordell Hull, *The Memoirs of Cordell Hull* (2 vols., New York, 1948).
JO; Journal officiel du Territoire des îles Saint-Pierre-et-Miquelon (St. Pierre, annually).
Moffat Papers; Nancy H. Hooker, ed., *The Moffat Papers: Selections from the Diplomatic Journals of Jay Pierrepont Moffat, 1919–1943* (Cambridge, 1956).
Moffat Papers; Harvard University Library, Jay Pierrepont Moffat Papers.
Muselier; Émile Muselier, *De Gaulle contre le Gaullisme* (Paris, 1946).
NYT; New York Times.
Sherwood; Robert Sherwood, *Roosevelt and Hopkins: An Intimate History* (New York, 1948).

I. REMNANTS OF EMPIRE

1. Pierre Demartres, *Les Terre-Neuvas* (Paris, 1930), pp. 92, 93.

2. A. J. Pick, "St. Pierre and Miquelon under the Fighting French" (Feb. 25, 1943), typed. Pick papers.

3. Arthur G. Doughty and Adam Shortt, *Canada and Its Provinces* (23 vols., Toronto, 1914–17), I, 21.

4. Emile de Curton, *Les îles Saint-Pierre et Miquelon* (Algiers, 1944), p. 36.

5. Public Archives of Canada, M.G. 11 (Colonial Office Records, C.O. 217), Nova Scotia A, 118, p. 144; A, 119, p. 230 (1793). See also J. Mackay Hitsman, "Capture of Saint-Pierre-et-Miquelon, 1793," *Canadian Army Journal*, XIII (1959), 77–81.

6. Un missionnaire, *Les îles Saint-Pierre-et-Miquelon* (Paris, n.d. [1939]), p. 35.

7. PAC, Minto Papers, XXII, 165–6, 194–7.

8. P. T. McGrath, "The Second St. Pierre," *New England Magazine*, XXVIII (N.S.) (1903), 285–7, which confuses Admirals Camara and Cervera; Walter Millis, *The Martial Spirit* (Boston, 1931), pp. 201–7.

9. PAC, Minto Papers, II, 56–7, 61; *Canadian Annual Review*, 1903, pp. 389, 426.

10. American Consulate, St. Pierre, Despatch No. 7, Nov. 19, 1908; Stetson Conn and Byron Fairchild, *The Framework of Hemispheric Defense* (Washington, 1960), pp. 11, 47; NYT, Sept. 3, 1938, p. 3.

11. JO, 1959, pp. 162–5.

12. American Consulate, St. Pierre, Despatch No. 7, Nov. 19, 1908.

13. William F. Rannie, *Saint Pierre and Miquelon* (Beamsville, 1963), p. 80; Jacques Soustelle, *Envers et Contre Tout* (2 vols., Paris, 1947, 1950), I, 271.

14. Daniel Gauvin, *Saint-Pierre-et-Miquelon* (Paris, 1916), pp. 35–36; Muselier, p. 279; NYT, Aug. 13, 1961, p. 3; Toronto *Globe and Mail*, Nov. 21, 1961, p. 3.

15. JO, 1954, pp. 1180, 1182, 1185; 1960, pp. 194–5; Winnipeg *Tribune*, Sept. 22, 1954, p. 7; NYT, Jan. 4, 1960, p. 5; Rannie, *Saint Pierre and Miquelon*, p. 42.

16. Walter Stewart, "Trouble in Paradise", *The Star Weekly* (Toronto), June 5, 1965, pp. 5–11.

17. *Allocutions prononcées le 30 novembre 1959 pour l'ouverture de la deuxième Session ordinaire du Conseil Général* (St. Pierre: Imprimerie du Gouvernement, n.d.), p. 13.

2. RESISTANCE

1. NYT, Jan. 6, 1942, p. 8 (this article contains extensive extracts from de Bournat's confidential despatches to the Vichy Minister of the Colonies); JO, 1940, p. 588; St. John's *Evening Telegram*, July 9, 1940, p. 5.

2. Moffat Papers, memo/conv with Robertson, Nov. 13, 1941; Charles Rawlings, "Dilemma on St. Pierre," *Maclean's*, Jan. 1, 1941, pp. 11, 26; S. S. Jones and D. P. Myers, eds., *Documents on American Foreign Relations*, Vol. III, *July 1940–June 1941* (Boston, 1941), p. 96.

3. JO, 1941, pp. 205–6, 338–40.

4. St. Pierre *Le Foyer paroissial*, XVII (1939–40), 128; Muselier, p. 247.

5. Montreal *Star*, Apr. 10, 1942, p. 25.

6. St. Pierre *La Liberté*, I (11) (Apr. 14, 1942), p. 6.

7. *NYT*, Jan. 6, 1942, p. 8.

8. De Bournat, CBC interview. This and other interviews in connection with the St. Pierre and Miquelon *affaire* were filmed Aug. 29 to Sept. 4, 1961. Extracts appeared on the Canadian Broadcasting Corporation television documentary "Close Up," Dec. 17, 1961.

9. *NYT*, Jan. 6, 1942, p. 8; Rawlings, "Dilemma on St. Pierre," p. 26; *Repertoire des jugements rendus en matière correctionelle en l'année 1940* (St. Pierre: Tribunal de la Justice de paix, unpublished), Minutes nos. 21, 22, 26; *JO*, 1940, pp. 618, 628; 1942, p. 18.

10. De Gaulle, I, 36–7.

11. "The Future of St. Pierre," St. John's *Daily News*, Aug. 26, 1940, p. 4.

12. The following account is based mainly in minutes written at the time by Henry Humbert, but also on de Bournat's own report, see *NYT*, Jan. 6, 1942, p. 8, and recollections of others present at the meeting.

13. *Tracts clandestins qui circulaient à St.-Pierre et Miquelon, avant l'occupation des îles par les forces navales françaises libres du général de Gaulle, le jour de Noël 1941* (Ottawa, [1942]), Brochure no. 1, pp. 5, 11–12, no. 2, pp. 26–28.

14. *Ibid.*, no. 2, p. 10; de Bournat, CBC interview.

15. Letter: LeBuf to de Bournat, Nov. 12, 1940, and reply, same date.

16. *NYT*, Jan. 6, 1942, p. 8; Rawlings, "Dilemma on St. Pierre," pp. 10, 26.

17. *Le Foyer paroissial*, XVII (1940–1), 223, 256.

18. Muselier, pp. 268, 290; Vancouver *Province*, Feb. 21, 1942, p. 6.

19. *JO*, 1941, p. 579; *NYT*, Jan. 6, 1942, p. 8; "Pour nos glorieux morts," *Le Foyer paroissial*, XVII (1940–1), 188–92 (Armistice Day address, Nov. 2, 1940).

20. *JO*, 1940, pp. 662–6, 692–5, 787, 793–4; 1941, pp. 145–8, 286–99, 359–60, 407–8, 469–74; St. Pierre and Miquelon, *Arrêté*, nos. 393 (Oct. 27) and 398 (Oct. 31), 1941, typed; *NYT*, Dec. 26, 1941, p. 11.

21. *JO*, 1941, pp. 180–2, 448–9, 535–8, 554–5, 574–5; William D. Leahy, *I Was There* (New York, 1950), pp. 469–70; Montreal *Le Jour*, Aug. 9, 1941, p. 4; *NYT*, Dec. 26, 1941, p. 11; *Tracts clandestins*, no. 1, pp. 9, 10, no. 2, p. 29; LeBuf, CBC interview.

22. *NYT*, Sept. 9, p. 4, Sept. 26, p. 4, Nov. 5, p. 5, Dec. 25, 1941, p. 11; *Le Jour*, Apr. 26, p. 5, Aug. 30, p. 2, Oct. 4, p. 5, Oct. 18, 1941, p. 4; Jan. 17, 1942, pp. 1, 2; New York *Post*, Feb. 3, 1942, p. 5; *JO*, 1941, *Avis*, p. 57; *The Times* (London), Dec. 29, 1941, p. 3; *Tracts clandestins*, no. 1, pp. 12–14, no. 2, p. 6; Raoul Aghion, *The Fighting French* (New York, 1943), p. 118.

23. *The Times*, Dec. 29, 1941, p. 3; *NYT*, Dec. 28, 1941, p. 21; de Bournat, CBC interview; *Post*, Jan. 10, 1942, p. 11. Italics in original.

24. Rawlings, "Dilemma on St. Pierre," p. 25; *JO*, 1940, p. 768; *NYT*, Jan. 6, 1942, p. 8; *La Liberté*, II (36) (Oct. 7, 1943), p. 4.

25. *Arrêté*, nos. 114 (April 14) and 333–4 (Sept. 16), 1941; *La Liberté*, I (13) (Apr. 28, 1942), p. 4; *NYT*, Jan. 6, 1942, p. 8.

26. Montreal *Gazette*, Feb. 26, 1942, p. 11; *NYT*, Dec. 26, 1941, p. 11; *Tracts clandestins*, no. 1, p. 8.

27. *Journal officiel de l'Etat français* (Vichy), Oct. 28, 1942, p. 359; *Post*, Jan. 3, 1942, p. 2.

28. *JO*, 1946, p. 1353.

29. *Le Jour*, Mar. 22, 1941, p. 5.

30. *Tracts clandestins, passim; NYT*, Apr. 12, 1941, p. 6; *La Liberté*, III (1) (Mar. 9, 1944), p. 4.

31. *Le Jour*, Aug. 30, p. 2, Oct. 18, 1941, p. 4; Toronto *Globe and Mail*, Aug. 24, 1941, p. 17; Aghion, *Fighting French*, p. 118; *Répertoire*, 1941, Minute no. 15 (Oct. 13, 1941); Montreal *La Presse*, Feb. 13, 1942, p. 11.

32. *Tracts clandestins*, no. 1, p. 16, no. 2, p. 13; *Evening Telegram*, Dec. 27, 1941, p. 6; LeBuf, CBC interview.

33. *JO*, 1940, pp. 707–8; 1941, p. 510; *NYT*, Dec. 26, 1941, p. 11; *Post*, Feb. 3, 1942, p. 5; *Globe and Mail*, May 24, 1941, p. 17.

34. *Globe and Mail*, Jan. 12, 1942, p. 9; *Répertoire*, 1941, Minute no. 12 (July 21, 1941).

35. *NYT*, Dec. 26, 1941, pp. 1, 11; Louis de Villefosse, "Les petites îles de la liberté," *Les Temps modernes*, V (1949), 876; *Le Jour*, Oct. 18, 1941, p. 4; *Post*, Feb. 3, 1942, p. 5; *La Liberté*, I (10) (Apr. 7, 1942), p. 6.

36. *NYT*, Dec. 28, 1941, p. 21; de Bournat, CBC interview; *JO*, 1940, pp. 689–91; Aghion, *Fighting French*, p. 118.

37. *Tracts clandestins*, no. 1, pp. 6, 9; *Le Jour*, Aug. 30, 1941, p. 2; Muselier, p. 260.

38. *FRUS*, 1941, II, 197–201; Stetson Conn and Byron Fairchild, *The Framework of Hemispheric Defense* (Washington, 1960), p. 162.

3. INTERVENTION

1. Muselier, pp. 247–8; Georges Robert, *La France aux Antilles de 1939 à 1943* (Paris, 1950), p. 100; de Villefosse, p. 143; St. John's *Daily News*, Aug. 25, 1940, p. 4.

2. *Ibid.*, pp. 315, 321.

3. *Moffat Papers*, p. 322.

4. *FRUS*, 1940, II, pp. 357–8, 743–5.

5. Canada, House of Commons, *Debates*, Sept. 8, 1939, p. 35, June 18, 1940, p. 854.

6. Department of External Affairs, press release, July 19, 1940; de Gaulle, *Doc*, I, 38–9.

7. J. W. Pickersgill, *The Mackenzie King Record*. I: *1939–1944* (Toronto, 1960), 98–9, 112.

8. Order in Council, P.C. 2833, June 27, 1940; St. John's *Evening Telegram*, July 20, 1940, p. 4; *NYT*, July 8, 1940, p. 9, Jan. 6, 1942, p. 8.

9. External Affairs, press release, July 19, 1940; *NYT*, Jan. 6, 1942, p. 8; *Moffat Papers*, pp. 322–3.

10. Toronto *Globe and Mail*, July 20, 1940, p. 8; External Affairs, press release, July 19, 1940; *Evening Telegram*, July 20, 1940, p. 4.

11. J. H. Penson, "Recollections of Visit to Saint Pierre in July 1940," 14 April, 1962, personal memo to author.

12. *Evening Telegram*, July 20, 1940, p. 4.

13. External Affairs, press release, July 19, 1940; de Gaulle, *Doc*, I, 38–9.

14. CBC interview, Dec. 17, 1961.

15. Montreal *Le Jour*, Jan. 25, 1941, p. 4; also Aug. 30, 1941, p. 2.

16. *Moffat Papers*, p. 322.

17. Stetson Conn and Byron Fairchild, *The Framework of Hemispheric Defense* (Washington, 1960), pp. 35, 38, 367.

18. Hull, I, 820; *Documents on German Foreign Policy, 1918–1945*, Series D, X (Washington, 1957), 480–1; FDR Memorial Library, Franklin Delano Roosevelt Papers, File OF 67, letters, Welles to Roosevelt, Nov. 16, 1939.

19. Muselier, pp. 97, 248–9, 269; *Evening Telegram*, Sept. 27, 1940, p. 4.

20. De Gaulle, *Doc*, I, 38; Muselier, pp. 249–50; Sir Llewellyn Woodward, *British Foreign Policy in the Second World War* (London, 1962), p. 94; Margaret Carlyle, ed., *Documents on International Affairs, 1939–1946*, Vol. II *Hitler's Europe* (London, 1954), p. 124.

21. De Gaulle, *Doc*, I, 39–45, 49–50; Woodward, *British Foreign Policy*, pp. 94–102; A. D. Hytier, *Two Years of French Foreign Policy: Vichy, 1940–42* (Paris, 1958), Ch. III.

22. *The Times* (London), Sept. 16, 1940, p. 3.

23. Muselier, p. 250; St. Pierre and Miquelon, *Arrêté*, No. 480, Dec. 31, 1940; Rawlings, "Dilemma on St. Pierre," p. 26; *NYT*, Jan. 6, 1942, p. 8.

24. *Documents on International Affairs*, II, 125–6.

25. Pickersgill, *King Record*, I, 147; Muselier, p. 259.

26. G. A. J. P. Auphan, *La Marine au service des Français* (Paris, 1947), p. 131; Robert, *La France aux Antilles*, p. 100; *Le Foyer paroissial*, XVII (1939–40), 144.

27. René Ristelhueber, "Le coup de main de la France Libre sur Saint-Pierre-et-Miquelon," *Ecrits de Paris*, July–August 1954, pp. 65–6; External Affairs, press release, July 19, 1940; Moffat Papers, memo/conv with Robertson, Jan. 2, 1942; *NYT*, Jan. 6, 1942, p. 8.

28. S. W. Roskill, *The War at Sea, 1939–45* (3 vols., London, 1955–61), I, 369 chart, 375–6; Sir Winston S. Churchill, *The Second*

World War (6 vols., Boston, 1948–53), III, 144; Friedrick Ruge, *Der Seekrieg* (Annapolis, 1957), 164–70. 215–19; St. Pierre *La Liberté*, II (40) (Nov. 4, 1943), p. 1.

29. May 4, 1941. Quoted in George Kirk, *The Middle East in the War* (London, 1952), p. 93.

30. René Ristelhueber, "Mackenzie King et la France," *Revue des deux mondes*, Mar. 15, 1954, p. 295; *NYT*, May 17, 1941, p. 3; *Le Jour*, Jan. 25, p. 4, Apr. 19, pp. 1, 2, May 31, p. 5, Aug. 30, 1941, p. 2; André Chéradame, *Defence of the Americas* (New York, 1941), p. 218.

31. Moffat Papers, memo/conv with Robertson, May 12, 28, July 8, 1941; Roosevelt Papers, President's Secretary's File, Box 22, Roosevelt Memorandum for Secretary of War and of the Navy, Apr. 26, 1941.

32. Canada, H. of C. *Debates*, May 19, p. 2913, May 27, 1941, p. 3165.

33. Moffat Papers, memo/conv with Robertson, May 17, 1941.

34. Montreal *La Presse*, May 27, 1941, p. 8.

35. *JO*, "Avis," Apr. 30, 1941, p. 24.

36. *NYT*, May 25, 1941, p. 30.

37. *Ibid.*

38. Moffat Papers, memo/conv with Robertson, May 12, 17, 28, July 8, 15, 1941.

39. Pickersgill, *King Record*, I, 212; Moffat Papers, memo/conv with Robertson, June 3, Stone, June 13, and Welles dated July 14, 1941.

40. Letters: Callède to Brig. H. J. Riley, May 19, 1941, and Lt. Col. H. Desrosiers to Callède, May 30, 1941.

41. Muselier, pp. 186, 250–1.

42. See also, De Gaulle, *Doc*, I, 161; *FRUS*, 1941, II, 176, 355–9.

43. Muselier, pp. 177, 251; Moffat Papers, memo/conv with Roberts, July 15, 31, 1941.

44. *NYT*, Aug. 14, 1941, p. 6; Vancouver *Province*, Aug. 13, 1941, p. 9; Ristelhueber, "Le coup de main," p. 66.

45. Moffat Papers, memo/conv with Robertson, Nov. 3, 1941.

46. Moffat Papers, memo/conv with Robertson, May 12, July 15, 1941; Order in Council, P.C. 6439, Aug. 13, 1941; Ristelhueber, "Le coup de main," p. 66; *The Times*, Aug. 26, 1941, p. 4. On the technicalities of the appointment, see *Report of the Secretary of State for External Affairs, 1941* (Ottawa, 1942), p. 12; Moffat Papers, memo/conv with Robertson, Aug. 26, 1941.

47. Based in part on G. F. G. Stanley, *In the Face of Danger* (Port Arthur, 1960), pp. 72–6; D. Miller Marshall, "The Saga of St. Pierre Miquelon", unpublished manuscript, June 1965, author's files.

48. *The Times*, Aug. 26, 1941, p. 4.

49. Pickersgill, *King Record*, I, 98–9, 145, 147.

50. *Montreal Matin*, Dec. 26, 1941, p. 2; *NYT*, Jan. 18, 1942, p. 31; *Le Jour*, Jan. 3, p. 1, Jan. 25, p. 1, Feb. 25, 1942, p. 1; Montreal *Le Petit Journal*, Aug. 21, 1961, p. A6.

51. "L'opinion de la presse canadienne française devant l'occupation des îles St.-Pierre et Miquelon," pp. 2–3, 14, manuscript in French Embassy, Ottawa; *Le Foyer paroissial*, XIX (1942), 187; Elizabeth Armstrong, "French Canadian Opinion on the War," *Contemporary Affairs*, no. 12 (Toronto, 1942), p. 30.

52. De Gaulle, I, 217; *Doc*, I, 230–1; Muselier, pp. 252–3.

53. Moffat Papers, memo, Dec. 19, 1941.

54. Moffat Papers, memo/conv with Welles, dated July 14, and Robertson, July 15, 1941; *FRUS*, 1941, II, 385, 524; Sumner Welles, *Seven Major Decisions* (New York, 1951), p. 62.

55. *The Times*, Aug. 26, 1941, p. 4; Montreal *Gazette*, Aug. 26, 1941, p. 20; *Le Foyer paroissial*, XVIII (1941), 384.

56. Moffat Papers, memo/conv with Robertson, Nov. 3, 13 and Keenleyside, Nov. 14, 1941; *FRUS*, 1941, II, 540–2.

57. Moffat Papers, memo/conv with Robertson, Nov. 3, 13, 1941; *FRUS*, 1941, II, 540–1.

58. *Ibid.*, pp. 542–4; W. L. Langer, *Our Vichy Gamble* (New York, 1947), p. 213.

59. Moffat Papers, memo/conv with Robertson, Nov. 3, and Keenleyside, Nov. 14, 1941; *FRUS*, 1941, II, 540.

60. Moffat Papers, memo/conv with Robertson, Nov. 22, 1941.

61. Moffat Papers, memo/conv with King, Feb. 12, 1941.

62. Pickersgill, *King Record*, I, 319; Moffat Papers, memo/conv with Robertson, Nov. 3, 1941.

63. *Moffat Papers*, pp. 372–3; Pickersgill, *King Record*, I, 319.

64. *FRUS*, 1941, II, 542–4.

65. *Ibid.*, pp. 543–7.

66. Moffat Papers, memo/conv with Robertson, Dec. 16, 1941; *FRUS*, 1941, II, 547–8.

67. Moffat Papers, memo/conv with Robertson, Nov. 13, 1941.

68. Moffat Papers, memo/conv with Robertson, Dec. 8, 15, 1941; W. M. Medlicott, *The Economic Blockade* (2 vols., London, 1952–59), II, 362.

69. Moffat Papers, memo/conv with Robertson, Dec. 15, 16, 1941; *FRUS*, 1941, II, 542, 548, 569.

70. Muselier, pp. 256–7; de Gaulle, *Doc*. I, 234; de Villefosse, pp. 151–3.

71. De Gaulle, I, 217; *Doc*, I, 235; Colonel Passy, *Souvenirs* (3 vols., Monte Carlo, 1947–51), II, 204–5; Daniel Barlone, *La Route des sommets* (Monte Carlo, 1953), p. 47.

72. Moffat Papers, memo/conv with Robertson, Dec. 16, 1941; *FRUS*, 1941, II, 548; Churchill, *Second World War*, III, 666; Robert Sherwood, p. 480.

73. Muselier, pp. 259, 262, 302; de Villefosse, p. 154; Hull, II, 1129; Moffat Papers, memo/conv with Robertson, Dec. 15, 16, and King, Dec. 17, 1941.

74. Letter: Murray to author, Mar. 22, 1965; Muselier, p. 256; *La Presse*, Dec. 27, 1941, p. 45; Savary, CBC interview, Dec. 17, 1961.

75. *La Presse*, Dec. 15, 1941, p. 3; Ottawa *Journal*, Dec. 17, 1941, p. 10; Canada H. of C. *Debates*, July 8, 1942, p. 4021; Muselier, pp. 259–60.

76. Moffat Papers, memo/conv with Robertson, Dec. 15, 1941, memo of Dec. 19, 1941.

77. Moffat Papers, memo/conv with Keenleyside, Dec. 15, Robertson, Dec. 16, and King, Dec. 17, 1941.

78. *Moffat Papers*, p. 360; Hull, II, 1128–9; Moffat Papers, memo/conv with Robertson, Dec. 16, 1941.

79. Muselier, p. 262; de Gaulle, I, 217; *Doc*, I, 246, 254; *Moffat Papers*, p. 361; Sherwood, pp. 480, 482; Churchill, *Second World War*, III, 666; *FRUS*, 1941, II, 542.

80. De Gaulle, *Doc*, I, 239, 246; Muselier, pp. 263–5.

81. *FRUS*, 1941, II, 552, 556–7; Muselier, pp. 265, 277–8, 300; de Villefosse, p. 157; Moffat Papers, memo/conv with Robertson, Jan. 2, 1942; *NYT*, Dec. 26, 1941, p. 10.

82. De Gaulle, I, 218; *Doc*, I, 239–54; *NYT*, Jan. 11, 1942, Sec. IV, p. 3.

83. De Gaulle, I, 218; *Doc*, I, 239; *FRUS*, 1941, II, 550, 556; Muselier, p. 262.

84. Moffat Papers, memo Dec. 19, 1941; memo/conv with Stone, Dec. 20, and Robertson, Dec. 22, 1941; *FRUS*, 1941, II, 550–1, 556; Hull, II, 1129; Muselier, pp. 262, 304.

85. Robert, *La France aux Antilles*, pp. 110–15; de Gaulle, I, 217; *Doc*, I, 239–54.

86. *FRUS*, 1940, II, 504.

87. De Gaulle, I, 216–7; *Doc*, I, 235, 238; Muselier, p. 283.

88. Quoted in Hytier, *Vichy, 1940–42*, pp. 78–9.

89. Barlone, *La Route des sommets*, p. 47.

90. De Gaulle, I, 95, 151–3; *Doc*, I, 75–8; Passy, *Souvenirs*, I, 202; Muselier, pp. 78, 93–5, 251–2, 263–4, and Ch. XVI, XX; David Thomson, *Two Frenchmen* (London, 1951), pp. 184–5.

91. De Gaulle, I, 218; Muselier, p. 282; Henri de Kerillis, *I Accuse de Gaulle* (New York, 1946), pp. 26–7, 69, 120.

4. LIBERATION

1. Muselier, p. 265; de Villefosse, p. 158; René Ristelhueber, "Le coup de main de la France Libre sur Saint-Pierre-et-Miquelon," *Ecrits de Paris*, July–August, 1954, pp. 67, 68.

2. Muselier, pp. 266–7, 277–8; de Villefosse, p. 160.

3. Muselier, p. 266; de Villefosse, pp. 158–60; Vancouver *Province*,

Feb. 21, 1942, p. 6; Sherwood, p. 949; Wolfert, CBC interview, Dec. 17, 1961; *Newsweek*, Jan. 5, 1942, pp. 49–50.

4. Ristelhueber, "Le coup de main," pp. 66–8; *Moffat Papers*, pp. 363–4; J. W. Pickersgill, *The Mackenzie King Record*. I: *1939–1944* (Toronto, 1960), 319.

5. Muselier, pp. 266, 268; de Villefosse, p. 158.

6. Muselier, p. 268; de Villefosse, pp. 160–3; *NYT*, Dec. 25, 1941, pp. 1, 7; Maurice Martin Du Gard, *La Carte impériale* (Paris, 1949), pp. 230–1.

7. CBC interview, Dec. 17, 1961.

8. *FRUS*, 1941, II, 197–201; Stetson Conn and Byron Fairchild, *The Framework of Hemispheric Defense* (Washington, 1960), p. 162.

9. Ristelhueber, "Le coup de main," pp. 68, 70; *Winnipeg Tribune*, Dec. 27, 1941, p. 28; *NYT*, Dec. 25, p. 1, Dec. 26, p. 1, Dec. 27, p. 8, Dec. 29, 1941, p. 5; *FRUS*, 1941, II, 555, 561; Muselier, pp. 279, 288, 298; de Villefosse, p. 164. Figures quoted by various sources vary; Ristelhueber's are the most complete.

10. *NYT*, Apr. 9, 1942, p. 4.

11. Muselier, pp. 288–9; de Villefosse, p. 164; *NYT*, Dec. 26, 1941, pp. 1, 11; Georges Robert, *La France aux Antilles de 1939 à 1943* (Paris, 1950), p. 107.

12. Muselier, pp. 288–9, 298; de Villefosse, pp. 163–4, 166; *NYT*, Dec. 26, 1941, p. 1.

13. CBC interview, Dec. 17, 1961.

14. *JO*, 1939, p. 724.

15. *FRUS*, 1941, II, 555.

16. Muselier, pp. 278–92, 297, 314–5; de Villefosse, pp. 163, 165–8, 187–92, 195, 215; Martin Du Gard, *La Carte impériale*, pp. 233–4; *NYT*, Dec. 27, p. 8, Dec. 28, p. 21, Dec. 30, 1941, p. 4; Jan. 3, 1942, p. 7; New York *Post*, Jan. 9, p. 2, Jan. 13, 1942, p. 8; *Répertoire des jugements rendus en matière correctionelle en l'année 1942* (St. Pierre: Tribunal de la Justice de paix, unpublished), minutes nos. 1, 3, 5.

17. Sumner Welles, *Seven Major Decisions* (New York, 1951), p. 62; *JO*, 1945, p. 782.

18. *JO*, 1941, pp. 647; 1942, pp. 51–2, 62–3, 181, 204.

19. Muselier, p. 278; *Tracts clandestins* (Ottawa, [1942]), no. 1, p. 19; *JO*, 1942, p. 198; letter, Aubert de la Rüe to author, Sept. 11, 1961.

20. Muselier, pp. 280, 292; de Villefosse, pp. 168, 188.

21. De Bournat, CBC interview, Dec. 17, 1961; de Villefosse, pp. 167, 192–3; *NYT*, Mar. 29, p. 30, Apr. 9, 1942, p. 4.

22. Muselier, pp. 280, 284–5; de Villefosse, pp. 165–6, 188–92; St. Pierre and Miquelon, *Décision*, No. 8, Dec. 27, 1941, typed.

23. Muselier, p. 291; *Post*, Jan. 13, 1942, p. 8; Muselier, CBC interview, Dec. 17, 1961; St. Pierre and Miquelon, *Arrêté*, No. 66, Feb. 3, 1942, typed.

24. Muselier, pp. 284, 297; *Post*, Jan. 3, 1942, p. 2; *NYT*, Dec. 27, 1941, p. 8; de Villefosse, p. 168; de Gaulle, *Doc*, I, 260.

25. *FRUS*, 1941, II, 563; Muselier, pp. 289–90, 294; *The Times* (London), Jan. 1, 1942, p. 3.

26. De Villefosse, pp. 170–1; Martin Du Gard, *La carte impériale*, pp. 234–5; Ira Wolfert: letter to author, Nov. 3, 1961; *FRUS*, 1941, II, 556.

27. *NYT*, Jan. 5, p. 2, Jan. 12, 1942, p. 4; Montreal *Le Jour*, Jan. 3, 1942, p. 2; *Nation*, Jan. 3, 1942, p. 2; Muselier, pp. 300, 302–3, 311, 315; de Villefosse, pp. 170, 180; Moffat Papers, memo/conv with Robertson, Jan. 2, 1942.

28. Muselier, pp. 283, 289–91, 296; de Villefosse, pp. 168–71, 182–5; *NYT*, Dec. 29, 1941, p. 5; *JO*, 1942, p. 25; St. John's *Evening Telegram*, Dec. 29, 1941, p. 1.

29. Muselier, pp. 283, 289.

30. Muselier, pp. 289–90, 294, 308; de Villefosse, pp. 177–8, 182, 205–7.

31. Muselier, p. 267; de Villefosse, pp. 185–8; *Répertoire des jugements*, *1942*, minutes, nos. 9–12; A. J. Pick, "St. Pierre and Miquelon under the Fighting French" (1943); St. Pierre *La Liberté*, I, (22) (June 30, 1942), p. 5, (23) (July 7, 1942), p. 5.

32. Muselier, pp. 279–83, 286–7, 296, 309; de Villefosse, pp. 171–3.

33. Muselier, p. 287; de Villefosse, pp. 173, 215; *JO*, 1942, pp. 114, 126, 160; *Stamps*, XLIII (1943), 164–6.

34. Moffat Papers, memo/conv with Robertson, Jan. 29. Feb. 9, 13, and 25, 1942; Muselier, pp. 281, 289, 295, 307–9; de Villefosse, pp. 177–8; *Montreal Star*, Mar. 6, 1942, p. 25.

35. *Post*, Feb. 3, pp. 1, 5, Feb. 5, p. 18, Feb. 6, 1942, p. 22.

36. *JO*, 1942, pp. 58, 69–70; Muselier, pp. 281, 288; de Villefosse, p. 173; Montreal *Le Canada*, Feb. 13, 1942, p. 3.

37. *JO*, 1942, pp. 27, 29–30, 69–70; de Villefosse, pp. 172–3.

5. ANGER

1. *NYT*, Dec. 26, 1941, p. 12.

2. De Gaulle, *Doc*, I, 250, 283.

3. J. W. Pickersgill, *The Mackenzie King Record*. I: *1939–1944* (Toronto, 1960), 319, 321; *Moffat Papers*, p. 363; Stanley W. Dziuban, *Military relations between the United States and Canada, 1939–1945* (Washington, 1959), p. 159; Montreal *La Presse*, Dec. 27, 1941, p. 45. See also *NYT*, Dec. 26, p. 10, Dec. 27, 1941, p. 8.

4. Department of State *Bulletin*, V (1941), 580.

5. Hull, II, 1130; Sumner Welles, *Seven Major Decisions*, (New York,

1951), p. 72 and *The Time for Decision* (New York, 1944), p. 162; *Moffat Papers*, p. 379; Robert Bendiner, *The Riddle of the State Department* (New York, 1942), p. 181; Vincent Massey, *What's Past Is Prologue* (Toronto, 1963), p. 351.

6. Hull, II, 1130–1; de Gaulle, *Doc*, I, 264; *FRUS*, 1941, II, 551–2, 565, 586; Muselier, p. 303; Sherwood, p. 482; de Villefosse, p. 169; *NYT*, Dec. 25, 1941, p. 1; Jan. 13, 1942, p. 4; Bendiner, *Riddle of the State Department*, p. 94; F. Davis and E. K. Lindley, *How War Came* (New York, 1942), p. 325; Roosevelt Papers, Official File 20 (Misc.); New York *Post*, Jan. 2, 1942, p. 4; New York *Herald Tribune*, Jan. 14, 1942, p. 14.

7. *Moffat Papers*, pp. 364–5; *NYT*, Dec. 26, 1941, p. 9; Hull, II, 1130; Montreal *Gazette*, Dec. 26, 1941, p. 10.

8. *FRUS*, 1941, II, 564.

9. *Moffat Papers*, pp. 364–5.

10. Davis and Lindley, *How War Came*, p. 326; *Nation*, Jan. 3, 1942, p. 6; Jan. 17, 1942, p. 58; Pickersgill, *King Record*, I, 321.

11. *Moffat Papers*, pp. 362–4; Moffat Papers, memo/conv with Atherton, Mar. 3, 1942. René Ristelhueber, "Mackenzie King et la France," *La Revue des deux mondes*, Mar. 15, 1945, pp. 295–6; Savary, CBC interview, Dec. 17, 1961.

12. Massey, *What's Past Is Prologue*, p. 351; *Moffat Papers*, pp. 368–9.

13. *Moffat Papers*, pp. 365–7; Dziuban, *Military Relations*, p. 160.

14. Massey, *What's Past Is Prologue*, p. 350; D. G. Anglin, "United States Opposition to Canadian Membership in the Pan American Union," *International Organization*, XV (1961), 8–10.

15. *Moffat Papers*, pp. 367–70; Pickersgill, *King Record*, I, 320; Moffat Papers, memo/conv with Dunn, Dec. 25, 1941; Pearson, letter to V. Massey, Jan. 9, 1942.

16. *NYT*, Dec. 26, p. 10, Dec. 27, 1941, p. 8; *Post*, Dec. 26, 1941, p. 3; *Gazette*, Dec. 26, 1941, p. 1; Toronto *Globe and Mail*, Dec. 26, 1941, p. 2.

17. "L'opinion de la presse canadienne française devant l'occupation des îles St. Pierre et Miquelon," manuscript in French Embassy, Ottawa.

18. "Reaction of English Language Press in Canada on Seizure of St. Pierre-Miquelon on Dec. 24 by Free French Forces," manuscript in French Embassy, Ottawa; *Ottawa Citizen*, Dec. 27, 1941, p. 16; C. C. Lingard and R. F. Trotter, *Canada in World Affairs, September 1941 to May 1944* (Toronto, 1950), pp. 126–8; *FRUS*, 1942, II, 654–5.

19. Pickersgill, *King Record*, I, 321–4; *FRUS*, 1941, II, 557–61; Sherwood, p. 485; Hull, II, 1131; *Moffat Papers*, p. 372.

20. *Moffat Papers*, pp. 371–2; *FRUS*, 1941, II, 561, 569; Pickersgill, *King Record*, I, 323, 432.

21. *FRUS*, 1941, II, 558; Hull, II, 1131, 1132; William L. Langer,

Our Vichy Gamble (New York, 1947), *Moffat Papers*, p. 366; Pickersgill, *King Record*, I, 321.

22. Hull, II, 1132–3; *Moffat Papers*, pp. 371–2; Pickersgill, *King Record*, I, 321,322.

23. Sir Winston S. Churchill, *The Second World War* (6 vols., Boston, 1948–53), III, 666–7; *FRUS*, 1941, II, 562, 567–70; 1942, II, 662–3; Sherwood, p. 483; Langer, *Vichy Gamble*, p. 222; Hull, II, 1136.

24. Canada, House of Commons, *Debates*, Jan. 21, 1942, p. 4481; *Moffat Papers*, p. 371.

25. Hull II, 1133; Sherwood, pp. 483–6; Langer, *Vichy Gamble*, pp. 217–8; Elliott Roosevelt, *F.D.R.: His Personal Letters, 1928–1945* (2 vols., New York, 1950), II, 1268–9; *NYT*, Jan. 2, 1942, p. 3.

26. *Moffat Papers*, p. 371; Pearson, letter to Massey, Jan. 9, 1942.

27. *Post*, Jan. 3, 1942, p. 9; New York *PM*, Jan. 6, 1942, p. 23.

28. *Herald Tribune*, Dec. 28, p. 6, Dec. 30, p. 20, Dec. 31, 1941, p. 14, Jan. 6, 1942, p. 21; *Post*, Dec. 26, 1941, p. 1; *Washington Post*, Dec. 27, 1941, p. 10; *NYT*, Jan. 7, 1942, p. 18; *Christian Science Monitor*, Dec. 31, 1941, p. 20.

29. Hull, II, 1130, 1132–4, 1137–8; Sherwood, pp. 482–3, 486, 488; Welles, *Seven Major Decisions*, p. 73; Churchill, *Second World War*, III, 666–7; *Moffat Papers*, pp. 378–9.

30. *FRUS*, 1941, II, 503, 543, 553, 556; Sherwood, p. 482; William D. Leahy, *I Was There* (New York, 1950), p. 75; Moffat Papers, memo/ conv with Robertson, Jan. 3, 1942; *NYT*, Dec. 27, p. 8, Dec. 28, p. 15, Dec. 29, 1941, p. 5; *The Times*, (London), Jan. 1, p. 3, Jan. 7, 1942, p. 5; A. D. Hytier, *Two Years of French Foreign Policy: Vichy, 1940–1942* (Paris, 1958), p. 324; Langer, *Vichy Gamble*, p. 218; Alain Darlan, *L'amiral Darlan parle . . .* (Paris, 1952), p. 125.

31. Sir Llewellyn Woodward, *British Foreign Policy in The Second World War* (London, 1962), p. 111; *FRUS*, 1942, II, 674.

32. Hull, II, 1130, 1132; *FRUS*, 1941, II, 558, 560–2, 565–8; 1942, II, 655; Moffat Papers, memo/conv with Robertson, Jan. 2, 1942; *NYT*, Dec. 30, 1941, p. 1; *Gazette*, Dec. 26, 1941, p. 10; *The Times*, Dec. 30, 1941, p. 3.

33. Sherwood, p. 484.

34. Hull, II, 1133–4; *Herald Tribune*, Dec. 31, 1941, p. 8; *Post*, Dec. 29, 1941, p. 3, Jan. 3, p. 9, Jan. 12, 1942, p. 6.

35. *FRUS*, 1942, II, 655–61.

36. Hull, II, 1134–5.

37. *FRUS*, 1942, II, 656–7; Woodward, *British Foreign Policy*, p. 111; Moffat Papers, memo, Jan. 5, 1942; *Moffat Papers*, p. 371; Hull, II, 1135.

38. Moffat Papers, memos, Dec. 31, 1941, Jan. 5, 1942.

39. Letter to Massey, Jan. 9, 1942.

40. Moffat Papers, memo, Jan. 5, 1942; *Herald Tribune*, Jan. 6, 1942,

p. 8; Muselier, p. 302; *FRUS*, 1942, II, 657, 662–3; Hull, II, 1136.

41. *FRUS*, 1942, II, 663; Moffat Papers, memo, Jan. 5, 1942.

42. Pickersgill, *King Record*, I, 321; *FRUS*, 1941, II, 558–60, 567; 1942, II, 656, 658, 660–1; Moffat Papers, memo/conv with Ristelhueber, Feb. 4, 1942; de Gaulle, *Doc*, I, 258, 260.

43. *La Presse*, Dec. 30, 1941, p. 13; *NYT*, Dec. 30, 1941, p. 4; *FRUS*, 1941, II, 567.

44. Pickersgill, *King Record*, I, 321–3; *FRUS*, 1941, II, 560, 562, 565; 1942, II, 656–8, 660–1; Moffat Papers, memo/conv with Robertson, Jan. 5, and Ristelhueber, Feb. 4, 1942.

45. *Moffat Papers*, p. 371; *FRUS*, 1942, II, 657, 659, 663–4; Moffat Papers, memo, Jan. 5, 1942.

46. *FRUS*, 1942, II, 667, Langer, *Vichy Gamble*, p. 220; Hull, II, 1135; Moffat Papers, memo/conv with King, Jan. 9, 1942.

47. *NYT*, Jan. 16, 1942, p. 1; *Post*, Jan. 16, p. 11, Jan. 27, 1942, p. 1; *Time*, Jan. 26, 1942, p. 14; *Globe and Mail*, Feb. 27, 1942, p. 1.

48. *JO*, 1939, pp. 722–4, 764–5; 1942, pp. 15, 17–18, 50; Muselier, pp. 278, 314; *Post*, Jan. 13, p. 8, Feb. 4, 1942, p. 12.

49. *FRUS*, 1942, II, 667; de Gaulle, *Doc*, I, 258, 265; *NYT*, Jan. 27, 1942, p. 13; Muselier, pp. 289, 312.

50. *FRUS*, 1941, II, 558, 569–70; 1942, II, 664, 669; Pickersgill, *King Record*, I, 321–4; Moffat Papers, memo/conv with Robertson, Jan. 3, 5, 1942; Muselier, p. 300.

51. *FRUS*, 1942, II, 665–7; Woodward, *British Foreign Policy*, p. 111; de Gaulle, I, 219; *Doc*, I, 258; Carlyle, *Documents on International Affairs, 1939–1946*, II, 124.

52. *FRUS*, 1942, II, 665–6; Roosevelt, *F.D.R.*, II, 1268; Sherwood, pp. 488–9; Langer, *Vichy Gamble*, p. 220.

53. De Gaulle, I, 219; *Doc*, I, 257–9; *FRUS*, 1942, II, 666–7.

54. Muselier, pp. 313–4, 323–7.

55. De Gaulle, I, 220; *Doc*, I, 258–9, 265–7; *FRUS*, 1942, II, 667–9; Moffat Papers, memo/conv with Dill, Jan. 20, and Robertson, Jan. 29, Feb. 13, 1942; Muselier, pp. 311–5, 322–7.

56. *Moffat Papers*, pp. 374–5; Moffat Papers, memo/conv with Robertson, Feb. 9, 13, 1942; Langer, *Vichy Gamble*, pp. 220, 233–7; *FRUS*, 1942, II, 611, 669–70; Hull, II, 1136–7.

57. Moffat Papers, memo/conv with Ristelhueber, Feb. 4, 1942; René Ristelhueber, "Le coup de main de la France libre sur Saint-Pierre-et-Miquelon," *Ecrits de Paris*, July–August, 1954, p. 70; Pickersgill, *King Record*, I, 423.

58. Moffat Papers, Notes on visit to Washington, Mar. 2–4, 1942; memo/conv with Hickerson, June 25, 1942; *FRUS*, 1942, II, 670–1.

59. Sherwood, p. 489; A. and V. Toynbee, eds., *Hitler's Europe* (London, 1954), p. 363.

6. ISSUES

1. Stetson Conn and Byron Fairchild, *The Framework of Hemispheric Defense* (Washington, 1960), pp. 11, 45.

2. *Report of the Secretary of State for External Affairs, 1942* (Ottawa, 1943), p. 12.

3. *Documents on German Foreign Policy, 1918–1945*, Series D, XI (Washington, 1960), 484; Conn and Fairchild, *Hemispheric Defense*, pp. 35, 38, 47.

4. Wallace B. Alig, "Down East to France," *Americas*, Nov. 1940, p. 35; "St. Pierre and Miquelon," *National Review*, Feb. 1942, p. 121; Canada, *House of Commons Debates*, May 13, pp. 2390–1, May 14, 1942, p. 2416; Robert Bendiner, *The Riddle of the State Department* (New York, 1942), p. 93; de Gaulle, *Doc*, I, 244; Toronto *Globe and Mail*, Dec. 26, 1941, p. 2; A. J. Pick, "St. Pierre and Miquelon under the Fighting French," (1943).

5. *Ibid.*, pp. 372, 417.

6. *FRUS*, 1942, II, 611–20.

7. "Fuehrer Conferences on Naval Affairs" in *Brassey's Naval Annual, 1948*, pp. 81, 183–4, 192–3, 218, 222, 232–3; F. H. Hinsley, *Hitler's Strategy* (London, 1951), pp. 58–9, 169–75; H. L. Trefousse, *Germany and American Neutrality, 1939–1941* (New York, 1951), esp. pp. 41, 85–9, 115–22; *Documents on German Foreign Policy, 1918–1945*, Series D, XI, 505–6, 514.

8. S. W. Roskill, *The War at Sea, 1939–1945* (3 vols., London, 1955–61), I, 375–6, 472; S. E. Morison, *History of United States Naval Operations in World War II* (15 vols., Boston, 1947–60), I, 59, 95; Sir Winston S. Churchill, *The Second World War* (6 vols., Boston, 1948–53), III, 144; Conn and Fairchild, *Hemispheric Defense*, p. 387; H. A. Halliday, "War on the Front Doorstep," *Roundel* (Mar. 1965), pp. 10–11.

9. G. N. Tucker, *The Naval Service of Canada* (2 vols., Ottawa, 1952), II, 390–2; Morison, *U.S. Naval Operations*, I, 413; S. W. Dziuban, *Military Relations between the United States and Canada, 1939–1945* (Washington, 1959), p. 174; Jack McNaught, "The Battle of the St. Lawrence," *Maclean's*, Oct. 15, pp. 7, 68–70, Nov. 17, 1949, pp. 22, 27–9; C. P. Stacey, *Six Years of War* (Ottawa, 1955), p. 176; Friedrick Ruge, *De Seekrieg* (Annapolis, 1957), p. 253.

10. J. H. Penson, "Recollections of Visit to Saint Pierre in July, 1940," 14 April 1962, personal memo to author; *Tracts clandestins* (Ottawa, 1942), no. 1, p. 7, no. 2, pp. 23–5.

11. New York *Herald Tribune*, Jan. 26, 1942, p. 10; Charles Graves, *The Thin Red Lines* (London, n.d.), p. 88.

12. Penson, "Recollections"; Moffat Papers, memo/conv with Robertson, June 3, and Stone, June 13, 1941.

13. Dziuban, *Military Relations*, pp. 158–9; *FRUS*, 1941, II, 541, 544: Moffat Papers, memo/conv with Robertson, Nov. 13, 1941.

14. Hull, II, 1128; Sumner Welles, *Seven Major Decisions* (New York, 1951), p. 62; *FRUS*, 1941, II, 540–1, 560, 566–7, 1942, II, 659; Canada *House of Commons Debates*, May 19, 1942, p. 2913; Moffat Papers, memo/conv with Robertson, July 8, 1941.

15. Churchill, *Second World War*, III, 666; New York *Post*, Dec. 30, 1941, pp. 1, 5; *Herald Tribune*, Dec. 27, 1941, p. 6; Bendiner, *State Department*, pp. 92–3.

16. Churchill, *Second World War*, III, 666; Georges Robert, *La France aux Antilles de 1939 à 1943* (Paris, 1950), p. 109; *Post*, Dec. 29, 1941, p. 6; "Fuehrer Conferences on Naval Affairs," pp. 246, 249–51; Galeazzo Ciano, *Ciano's Diplomatic Papers* (London, 1948), pp. 469–71; *NYT*, Dec. 26, 1941, p. 10; Jan. 5, 1942, p. 2; *FRUS*, 1941, II, 544.

17. *NYT*, Jan. 8, 1942, p. 2; Moffat Papers, memo/conv with Robertson, July 8 and Nov. 3, 1941.

18. Churchill, *Second World War*, III, 666; A. & V. Toynbee, eds., *Hitler's Europe* (London, 1954), p. 463; Sherwood, p. 480.

19. *Herald Tribune*, Sept. 1, pp. 1, 3, Dec. 27, 1941, p. 1; *Post*, Dec. 30, 1941, p. 1, Jan. 2, 1942, p. 5; *NYT*, Dec. 31, 1941, p. 8; Moffat Papers, memo/conv with Robertson, May 28, 1941.

20. Pan American Union, *Report on the Second Meeting of the Ministers of Foreign Affairs of the American Republics* (Washington, 1940), pp. 23–4, 38. My italics.

21. *NYT*, July 9, 1940, p. 6.

22. *FRUS*, 1940, II, 499–500, 504–5. See also Robert, *La France aux Antilles*, pp. 90–1; de Gaulle *Doc*, I, 249–50.

23. S. S. Jones and D. P. Myers, eds., *Documents on American Foreign Relations*, Vol. III, *July 1940–June 1941*, p. 233.

24. *FRUS*, 1941, II, 355, 540, 562; Hull, II, 1130, 1135; William L. Langer, *Our Vichy Gamble* (New York, 1947), p. 217; Sherwood, p. 485; John A. Logan, *No Transfer* (New Haven, 1961), pp. 253, 380; *NYT*, Dec. 26, p. 10, Dec. 31, 1941, p. 1, Jan. 2, p. 22, Feb. 14, pp. 1, 8, Feb. 15, 1942, p. 19; St. John's *Evening Telegram*, July 31, 1940, p. 4.

25. *FRUS*, 1941, II, 562–3; *NYT*, Jan. 13, p. 4, Jan. 16, 1942, p. 6.

26. *Post*, Dec. 30, 1941, p. 5.

27. *FRUS*, 1940, II, 502–4; Muselier, pp. 260–1, 292–4, 316; de Villefosse, p. 174.

28. Moffat Papers, memo/conv with Welles, dated July 14 and Robertson, Nov. 3, 1941; *FRUS*, 1941, II, 563.

29. *NYT*, Jan. 10, p. 7, Jan. 16, 1942, p. 6; Elliott Roosevelt, ed., *F. D. R: His Personal Letters, 1928–1945* (2 vols., New York, 1950), II, 1268; Bendiner, *State Department* p. 95; Sherwood, p. 485; J. W. Pickersgill, *The Mackenzie King Record. I: 1939–1944* (Toronto, 1960), 321; Muselier, p. 302.

30. Sumner Welles, *The Time for Decision* (New York, 1944), p. 162; *FRUS*, 1941, II, 197–8, 200, 499; William D. Leahy, *I Was There* (New York, 1950), p. 67.

31. *FRUS*, 1941, II, 199–202; Conn and Fairchild, *Hemispheric Defense*, pp. 86, 162–3; Robert, *La France aux Antilles*, pp. 109–15; W. N. Medlicott, *Economic Blockade* (2 vols., London, 1952–59), II, 358; Leahy, *I Was There*, pp. 65–7.

32. Hull, II, 1128, 1130; Sherwood, p. 485; Montreal *Gazette*, Dec. 26, 1941, p. 10; *NYT*, Dec. 27, 1941, pp. 1, 8; *FRUS*, 1942, II, 661; Moffat Papers, memo/conv with Robertson, Dec. 19, 1941; *Moffat Papers*, p. 365.

33. Hull, II, 1130, 1132, 1137; Langer, *Vichy Gamble*, pp. 221–6, 389; *FRUS*, 1941, II, 204, 558, 563.

34. Eugene Rostow, "Wartime Policies towards Vichy and France," *World Politics*, I (1949), 390–1. Cf. Langer, *Vichy Gamble*, pp. 387–96; William L. Langer and S. Everett Gleason, *The Undeclared War, 1940–1941* (New York, 1953), pp. 785–6.

35. Langer, *Vichy Gamble*, p. 392; Hull, II, 966, 1045; A. D. Hytier, *Two Years of French Foreign Policy* (Paris, 1958), p. 320; *FRUS*, 1941, II, 558.

36. Churchill, *Second World War*, II, 508, III, 837; Hytier, *French Foreign Policy*, pp. 267–70; *FRUS*, 1941, II, 455, 563; Sir Llewellyn Woodward, *British Foreign Policy in The Second World War* (London, 1962), p. 111; Sherwood, pp. 487–8; Moffat Papers, memo/conv with King, Sept. 18, 1941.

37. Mason Wade, *The French Canadians, 1760–1945* (Toronto, 1955), pp. 936–8, 945–7, 952; R. M. Dawson, *Canada in World Affairs, 1939–1941* (Toronto, 1943), pp. 261–2, 264; Henry Torrés, *Campaign of Treachery* (New York, 1942), pp. 229–37; Elizabeth Armstrong, "French Canadian Opinion on the War," *Contemporary Affairs*, no. 12 (1942), pp. 10–15, 30; *Moffat Papers*, pp. 323–41; Vincent Massey, *The Past Is Prologue* (Toronto, 1963), p. 337.

38. "L'opinion de la presse Canadienne française devant l'occupation des îles St.-Pierre et Miquelon," manuscript in French Embassy, Ottawa; Moffat Papers, memo/conv with Robertson, Jan. 15, 1942.

39. Langer and Gleason, *Undeclared War*, p. 785; Churchill, *Second World War*, II, 509.

40. Raymond Bruyère, *Veni, Vidi, Vichy . . . et la suite: Témoignages, 1940–1945* (Paris, 1953), pp. 91–6; Woodward, *British Foreign Policy*, p. xlv; Hytier, *French Foreign Policy*, p. 320.

41. Leahy, *I Was There*, pp. 469–70.

42. *FRUS*, 1941, II, 204, 562, 570; Leahy, *I Was There*, pp. 43, 75; *Moffat Papers*, p. 366, 368–9; Langer, *Vichy Gamble*, p. 225; de Gaulle, *Doc* I, 264.

43. Canada, *House of Commons Debates*, Jan. 21, p. 4481, May 19, 1942, p. 2543; *FRUS*, 1941, II, 205; Sherwood, pp. 485–6; Leahy, *I Was*

There, pp. 42–3, 75, 462; Langer, *Vichy Gamble*, pp. 77, 165–7, 212, 217–20, 225, 291–304; Langer and Gleason, *Undeclared War*, pp. 582, 772–4; *Moffat Papers*, p. 362; "Fuehrer Conferences on Naval Affairs," p. 274. See also Kenneth Pendar, *Adventure in Diplomacy* (New York, 1945), pp. 87–8; D. S. White, *Seeds of Discord: De Gaulle, Free France and the Allies* (Syracuse, 1964), pp. 316–23.

44. *FRUS*, 1941, II, 180, 204–5; Langer *Vichy Gamble*, p. 212; White, *Seeds of Discord*, pp. 320–1; *Post*, Dec. 30, 1941, p. 5.

45. A. & V. Toynbee, *Hitler's Europe*, pp. 460–3; *FRUS*, 1941, II, 180, 502–3, 578–86; Langer, *Vichy Gamble*, pp. 186, 293–5; Langer and Gleason, *Undeclared War*, p. 582; Department of State *Bulletin*, V (1941), 589; de Gaulle, I, 99–100, 214–17, 220–7; *Doc*, I, 19, 22–7, 215–87; L. M. Goodrich, ed., *Documents on American Foreign Policy*, Vol. IV, *July 1941–June 1942* (Boston, 1942), p. 178.

46. De Gaulle, I, 266; Hull, II, 1131.

47. Welles, *Seven Major Decisions*, p. xvi.

7. SIGNIFICANCE

1. Sumner Welles, *The Time for Decision*, (New York, 1944), p. 163; *FRUS*, 1941, II, 558, 563; Stetson Conn and Byron Fairchild, *The Framework of Hemispheric Defense* (Washington, 1960), p. 163; F. Davis and E. K. Lindley, *How War Came* (New York, 1942), p. 326.

2. Sherwood, p. 489.

3. John A. Logan, *No Transfer* (New Haven, 1961), p. 378; Sir Winston Churchill, *The Second World War* (6 vols., Boston, 1948–53), III, 144; Sherwood, pp. 486, 488.

4. *Moffat Papers*, pp. 369, 373–4; Moffat Papers, memo/conv with King, Dec. 16, 1941, and Jan. 9, 1942, Keenleyside, Dec. 22, 1941, and Mar. 22, 1942, Milo Perkins, Jan. 26, 1942; Vincent Massey, *The Past Is Prologue* (Toronto, 1963), p. 350.

5. Sherwood, pp. 202, 211–2; W. H. McNeill, *America, Britain and Russia* (London, 1953), pp. 96, 118; Sir Llewellyn Woodward, *British Foreign Policy in the Second World War* (London, 1962), p. xxxvi; Hull, II, 1109–10; William D. Leahy, *I Was There* (New York, 1950), p. 173; Robert Murphy, *Diplomat Among Warriors* (New York, 1964), p. 70; Norman A. Graebner, *An Uncertain Tradition* (New York, 1961), pp. 201–2; Arthur L. Funk, *Charles de Gaulle* (Norman, Okla., 1959), pp. 18–19; Sumner Welles, *Seven Major Decisions* (New York, 1951), p. 73; D. S. White, *Seeds of Discord* (Syracuse, 1964), pp. 14, 316–7.

6. New York *Herald Tribune*, Jan. 6, 1942, pp. 486, 488.

7. William Langer, *Our Vichy Gamble* (New York, 1947), p. 225; *FRUS*, 1941, II, 465; Sherwood, pp. 486, 676; Eugene V. Rostow, "Wartime Policies towards Vichy and France," *World Politics*, I (1949), 389.

8. Hull, II, 1137; Langer, *Vichy Gamble*, pp. 212, 221; Conn and Fairchild, *Hemispheric Defense*, p. 163; Leahy, *I Was There*, pp. 136, 145–6, 167–9; Donald C. McKay, *The United States and France* (Cambridge, 1951), pp. 124, 132–4.

9. Henry L. Stimson and McGeorge Bundy, *Our Active Service in Peace and War* (New York, 1948), pp. 546, 552.

10. Elliott Roosevelt, *As He Saw It* (New York, 1946), p. 73; Churchill, *Second World War* II, 182, 509; Woodward, *British Foreign Policy*, p. xlv.

11. Woodward, *British Foreign Policy*, p. xlv–lvi; Sherwood, pp. 679–81, 955–6; Hull, II, 1160, 1429; McKay, *U.S. and France*, p. 134; James Roosevelt and Sidney Shalett, *Affectionately F.D.R.* (New York, 1959), p. 343.

12. Department of State *Bulletin*, VI (1942), 208, 273, 613; *NYT*, Mar. 3, 1942, p. 7. See also *FRUS*, 1942, II, 502–96.

13. *FRUS*, 1941, II, 204; Sherwood, pp. 448–53, 483; Churchill, *Second World War*, III, 665–6; de Gaulle, *Doc*, I, 251; *Bulletin*, VI (1942), 44; Hull, II, 1125–6, 1243; Jacques Soustelle, *Envers et contre tout* (2 vols., Paris, 1947–50), I, 273. See also Montreal *Star*, Mar. 28, 1942, p. 2.

14. Leahy, *I Was There*, pp. 133, 146; de Gaulle, *Doc*, I, 344–5; Churchill, *Second World War*, IV, 224, 604–6, 801, V, 628–30; Langer, *Vichy Gamble*, pp. 289–90, 368–9; Hull, II, 1133–4; A. & V. Toynbee, eds., *Hitler's Europe* (London, 1954), pp. 466–9; Georges Catroux, *Dans la Bataille de la Meditérranée* (Paris, 1949), p. 21.

15. Stimson and Bundy, *Active Service*, pp. 545–52; Churchill, *Second World War*, V, 90; Sherwood, p. 858.

16. Funk, *De Gaulle*, pp. 316, 317.

17. Sherwood, p. 956; Muselier, Ch. XX, XXV; de Gaulle, I, 258–61; *Doc*, I, 256; de Villefosse, pp. 112, 115, 197–205, 213–24; *FRUS*, 1941, II, 556–7; *NYT*, Jan. 8, 1942, p. 2; Colonel Passy, *Souvenirs* (3 vols., Monte Carlo, 1947–51), pp. 206–8; A. & V. Toynbee, *Hitler's Europe*, pp. 465–8; Henri de Kerillis, *I Accuse de Gaulle* (New York, 1946), pp. 69–70; Daniel Barlone, *La Route des sommets* (Monte Carlo, 1953), pp. 53–8.

APPENDIXES

1. Charles Rawlings, "Dilemma on St. Pierre," *Maclean's*, Jan. 1, 1941, p. 26.

2. Dept. of State *Bulletin*, V (1941), 580.

3. *FRUS*, 1941, II, 565.

4. *Ibid.*, p. 560.

5. Moffat Papers, memo, Jan. 5, 1942.

6. *FRUS*, 1942, II, 655–6.

7. *Ibid.*, pp. 657–8.

8. Hull, II, 1135.

9. *FRUS*, 1942, II, 656–7.

10. *Ibid.*, p. 661.

11. *Ibid.*, p. 663.

12. Moffat Papers, memo/conv with Robertson, Jan. 19, 1942.

13. De Gaulle, I, *Doc.*, p. 265; Muselier, p. 311. Retranslation of a translation into French.

INDEX